Praise for *There's No Business That's Not Show Business*

"*There's No Business That's Not Show Business* candidly looks at the realities of business. It offers great business tools not just for trendy consumer products, but for B2B companies as well. This immensely practical book shows marketing directors how to differentiate their brand, attract and retain loyal customers, and make a real impact on their bottom line."

—MARTIN HOMLISH
Executive Vice President
and Global Chief Marketing Officer, SAP

"If you're looking for ideas to differentiate your offering, you'll find over a hundred in this delightful new book by Bernd Schmitt, David Rogers, and Karen Vrotsos."

—PHILIP KOTLER
Northwestern Kellogg School of Business
and author of *Marketing Management*, 11th edition

"This is the book that every CEO will be forcing their marketing department to read. Don't get caught with your pants down."

—DAVID ADLER
CEO, BiZBash.com
Co-Chair, Event Marketing Council

"This book cleverly and insightfully makes explicit a clear (if upsetting to some) trend, i.e., 'all the world's a stage.' ... Using a variety of well-known (e.g. Victoria's Secret, Intel) and less obvious (e.g. the Guggenheim) examples, the book explores the implications of a focus on the show/experience... [T]he book also provides an eight-step procedure for moving from identification of a desired image to the quantitative measurement of performance. This raises the book above the level of identifying a phenomenon to the position of suggesting something useful to do about it."

—DON LEHMANN
George E. Warren Professor of Business
Columbia University Graduate School of Business

"Bernd Schmitt is unquestionably one of the most creative and original minds in marketing. Well worth the price of admission, his new book with David Rogers and Karen Vrotsos provides sharp, witty insights and engaging case studies that brilliantly illuminate how entertaining experiences can build strong brands."

—KEVIN LANE KELLER
E.B. Osborn Professor of Marketing
Amos Tuck School of Business, Dartmouth College

"This will be one of the most important business books you'll ever read! It will convince you you're really in show business and that if you're not, you'd better be. Implement the star-studded findings [the authors] reveal, and you'll have a huge competitive advantage over your competition. Let the show begin."

—JASON JENNINGS
worldwide bestselling author of *It's Not the Big That Eat the Small—It's the Fast That Eat the Slow* and *Less Is More*

"The authors practice what they preach by presenting a book that is both entertaining and thought-provoking. This book is an important contribution to our deeper understanding of the complex experiences surrounding the consumption of goods and services."

—GERALD ZALTMAN
Professor, Harvard Business School
and author of *How Customers Think*

"*There's No Business That's Not Show Business* raises the curtain higher on understanding the role that show business holds in creating distinctive experiences.

This book is a significant tool in the new arena of leveraging the value of experience."

—LOU CARBONE
President and Chief Experience Officer
ExperienceEngineering®, Inc.
Minneapolis, MN.

There's No Business That's Not Show Business

Marketing in an Experience Culture

FINANCIAL TIMES

Prentice Hall

In an increasingly competitive world, it is quality
of thinking that gives an edge—an idea that opens new
doors, a technique that solves a problem, or an insight
that simply helps make sense of it all.

We work with leading authors in the various arenas
of business and finance to bring cutting-edge thinking
and best learning practice to a global market.

It is our goal to create world-class print publications
and electronic products that give readers
knowledge and understanding which can then be
applied, whether studying or at work.

To find out more about our business
products, you can visit us at www.ft-ph.com

Pearson
Education

There's No Business That's Not Show Business

Marketing in an Experience Culture

Bernd H. Schmitt
David L. Rogers
Karen Vrotsos

 Prentice Hall
FINANCIAL TIMES

An Imprint of PEARSON EDUCATION
Upper Saddle River, NJ • New York • London • San Francisco • Toronto • Sydney
Tokyo • Singapore • Hong Kong • Cape Town • Madrid
Paris • Milan • Munich • Amsterdam

www.ft-ph.com

Library of Congress Cataloging-in-Publication Data

Schmitt, Bernd.
    There's no business that's not show business: marketing in an experience culture /
Bernd H. Schmitt, David L. Rogers, and Karen Vrotsos.
        p. cm. -- (Financial Times Prentice Hall books)
    Includes index.
    ISBN 0-13-047119-4
        1. Brand name products--Marketing. 2. Corporate image. 3. Customer relations.
    I. Rogers, David L. II. Vrotsos, Karen. III. Title. IV. Series.

HF5415.13.S344 2003
659.1'52--dc21

                                        2003050877

Editorial/Production Supervision: *Techne Group*
VP, Editor-in-Chief: *Tim Moore*
Editorial Assistant: *Rick Winkler*
Marketing Manager: *John Pierce*
Manufacturing Manager: *Alexis Heydt-Long*
Manufacturing Buyer: *Maura Zaldivar*
Cover Design: *Anthony Gemmellaro*
Cover Design Director: *Jerry Votta*
Series Design: *Gail Cocker-Bogusz*
Full-Service Project Manager: *Anne Garcia*

 © 2004 Pearson Education, Inc.
Publishing as Financial Times Prentice Hall
Upper Saddle River, New Jersey 07458

Prentice Hall books are widely used by corporations and government agencies for
training, marketing, and resale.

**Prentice Hall PTR offers excellent discounts on this book when ordered in quantity
for bulk purchases or special sales. For more information, please contact:
U.S. Corporate and Government Sales, 1-800-382-3419,
corpsales@pearsontechgroup.com. For sales outside of the U.S., please contact:
International Sales, 1-317-581-3793, international@pearsontechgroup.com.**

Company and product names mentioned herein are the trademarks or registered
trademarks of their respective owners.

Printed in the United States of America

First Printing

ISBN 0-13-047119-4

Pearson Education Ltd.
Pearson Education Australia PTY, Limited
Pearson Education Singapore, Pte. Ltd.
Pearson Education North Asia Ltd.
Pearson Education Canada, Ltd.
Pearson Educación de Mexico, S.A. de C.V.
Pearson Education—Japan
Pearson Education Malaysia, Pte. Ltd.

Contents

FOREWORD

Smart companies today realize that traditional forms of marketing and communications don't cut it any more. Customers want more than a smiling face accompanied by a catchy slogan and jingle aired on prime-time TV. Instead, customers judge products, brands, and entire organizations based on the experiences that they offer. Companies therefore need to provide experiences, and these experiences must be entertaining, engaging, boundary breaking, and at the same time value creating. Show business delivers such experiences, and in a more cost-effective way than any other form of marketing. As a result, there is no business that can't benefit from show business.

But what is the right type of show for your brand? How do you stage and manage a show? How do you instill show business into the organization as a whole?

This book shows you how by providing numerous examples of successful show business practices in today's organizations. As you will see, we found most cases outside the frame of traditional marketing and traditional media. Customers are getting quite skeptical and cynical about advertising and other traditional media. In response, many of the newest forms of marketing that we have found echo traditions that predate television. These new forms offer experiences instead of cut-and-dried messages: road shows, jamborees, product play shops, street theater, fairs, and other face-to-face encounters. That's why the old-fashioned term *show business* makes sense. The old razzle-dazzle experience mixed with up-to-the-minute technology is bringing marketing into the future.

By now, the uses of experience by businesses have multiplied beyond theater-like performances at theme parks and restaurants to include buzz marketing, product launches, customer retention, internal communications, and nontraditional advertising. We view these show business experiences as a branding tool and a part of your increasingly diversified marketing mix. These experiences are valuable because they are face-to-face, interactive, help you reach and focus on your most valuable customers, and are capable of creating real loyalty and genuine relationships. They are not just razzle-dazzle, Las Vegas style. They are strategic and value-creating.

Our take on the experience aspect of show business is related to two other books (as well as a series of articles) authored by one of us, Bernd Schmitt. *Experiential Marketing*, published in 1999, provided an integrated marketing approach that moves beyond the functional features and benefits of a product to differentiate a brand. *Customer Experience Management*, published in 2003, provided a five-step process for connecting with customers through unique brand experiences, customer interfaces, and innovations.

As a consultant and CEO of The EX Group, Schmitt has used these frameworks and tools with companies in consumer packaged goods, automobile, electronics, software, financial services, pharmaceuticals, beauty and cosmetics, hospitality, and media industries. In working with these clients and with David L. Rogers and Karen Vrotsos, it became clear that many companies needed not only long-term strategic initiatives to manage customer experiences, but also concepts and tools for how to use creative, fun experiences to engage their customers and their own employees. In this book you find such concepts and tools as well as numerous cases of successful show business projects.

In many successful companies show business is alive and kicking, a well-kept secret behind the corporate curtain. This book will open the curtain and let you see the value that show business can offer to your business.

Ladies a-a-a-n-n-n-d Gentlemen in Business! Let the show begin!

Bernd H. Schmitt, David L. Rogers, Karen Vrotsos
The EX Group, LLC <showbiz@exgroup.com>
New York City, May 2003

ACKNOWLEDGMENTS

Every show has a large cast behind the curtains. We would like to thank the many people who helped to make this book a reality.

First, many thanks to our publisher, Tim Moore, for believing in the book and in show business every step of the way; his irrepressible enthusiasm was a boon to the project. Thanks also to Russ Hall, Anne Garcia, Dmitri Korzh, and everyone at Prentice Hall who helped carry the manuscript through to completion. Thank you to our panel of anonymous reviewers who provided critical feedback during the writing process. Thanks also to Sandra Lee for her edits, Sam Schindler for his diagrams, and Nick Peterson for his original photography.

We would like to thank our colleagues at The EX Group for their input and ideas. For their crucial research assistance at various stages of the book's development, we would particularly like to thank Claudia Laviada, Nutan Prabhu, Stephen Nasi, and Joseph Timmons.

We'd also like to thank all of the many people who shared with us their experience of show business in their own companies and work, most especially: Eddie Bamonte, Liz Bigham, Anthony Bucci, Bill Cahan, Nicole Cardillo, Becky Chambers, Kelly Cullen, Nancy DeBellis, Marc Gobé, Jud Heflin, Lois Jacobs, Chris Katsuleres, Jackson Kelly, George Kurkowski, David Laks, Claudine Mangano, Maggie McDonnell, Steve Mochel, Phil Mooney, Theresa Nasi, Drew Neisser, Grace Nichols, Bill Perrino, Mike Rubin, Costantino Sambuy, Tom

Shepansky, Richard Sherwin, Carol Simantz, Craig Singer, Kerry Smith, Ken Stansbury, Eric Steidinger, Katherine Stone, Michelle Torio, Michael Trovalli, Rona Tuccillo, Erik Ulfers, Adrian van Hooydonk, Laura Venna, Carsten Wierwille, Jay Wilson, Rena Wong, and Ann Woolman.

Special writers' thanks go to Nick Peterson for keeping everything going when we disappeared for days or weeks on end, and to Susie and George Vrotsos for providing an idyllic writers' retreat.

INTRODUCTION: ALL BUSINESS IS SHOW BUSINESS

There's no bus'ness like show bus'ness,
Like no bus'ness I know.
Ev'rything about it is appealing,
Ev'rything that traffic will allow;
Nowhere could you get that happy feeling
When you are stealing that extra bow.

IRVING BERLIN[1]

Show business is everywhere—in business.

Every industry—automotive, retail, technology, packaged goods, high art, and professional sports—has started to realize that business as usual won't do anymore. From peppermints to computers, from lingerie to skyscrapers, companies have discovered that they need to move beyond business as usual to reach out and engage their customers.

Creativity, humor, and play are showing up among cutting-edge companies in every corner. These companies are breaking through the boredom of one-way communications and using great experiences to surprise their audiences and get them involved with their brands.

---

1. "There's No Business Like Show Business" by Irving Berlin. © Copyright 1946 by Irving Berlin. © Copyright Renewed. International Copyright Secured. All Rights Reserved. Reprinted by permission.

Show business is used to dazzle customers, to communicate internally, to launch new products, and to attract business partners. Show business is extremely effective. It helps to differentiate products and brands. It creates powerful connections with customers. It attracts media coverage. Show business can be a surprising new weapon to use against competition and to attract talent and motivate employees. At its best, show business can transform a business, or even an entire industry.

WHAT IS SHOW BUSINESS?

Company initiatives that we call show business have the following key characteristics:

- **Entertaining.** Show business begins with entertainment. It is no news today that customers want to be entertained. Every part of our culture—the news, education, sports, food—increasingly targets this desire. When times are tough, the appeal of experiences that are entertaining and positive is even greater. Show business creates experiences that are fun. It does so by appealing to fantasy, humor, or drama. Show business can use high technology or old-style razzle-dazzle to create an experience that can be surprising, playful, thrilling, or sexy.

- **Engaging.** Show business is engaging. Media-savvy customers are looking for a different relationship with companies. Rather than being *talked* at, *branded* to, and inundated with top-down advertising messages, they want experiences that engage them directly and reward or invite their participation. Show business provides customers with an experience that is face-to-face or interactive. It often invites them to learn, explore, offer their own views, and even take a role in the show themselves. At its best, show business provides an experience that allows customers to form communities and connect with each other.

■ **Boundary-Breaking.** Show business is boundary-breaking. For their true loyalty and sustained attention, customers demand an experience that goes beyond the expected. Show business creates experiences that are innovative, sometimes even outrageous, and that reach customers in new and unexpected ways. Show business can even redefine the way a product or category is perceived. It creates the kinds of experiences that dissolve boundaries and distinctions between company and customer—creating excitement or buzz and turning customers into evangelists for a brand.

■ **Value Creating.** Show business also delivers real value to a business. The experiences it creates are aligned with the company's brand, linked to strategic goals, and integrated with other marketing communications. They produce real and measurable returns on investment. They target, understand, and build relationships with valued customers. They also create value for the customer, often in the form of learning, pleasure, stimulation, or lasting lifestyle value. Show business experiences use an understanding of the changing role of entertainment and experience in our popular culture to connect brands and customers to important trends and exciting cultural developments.

When companies create an experience for customers that does all of this, we call it *show business*.

WHY BUSINESS NEEDS SHOW BUSINESS

Many marketing books have argued that three trends are transforming business: the declining power of traditional advertising, the rise of the informed and independent consumer, and the emergence of an experience culture. Each of these trends provides a reason for why show business is essential for companies.

Media fragmentation has reduced the customer mind share of any single advertising channel because television channels have proliferated, and the Internet offers a medium with theoretically infinite channels of communication. At the same time, media saturation has led to a widespread feeling of information overload for consumers, who seem increasingly numbed by the thousands of advertising messages that are directed at each of them every day. With each new generation weaned on mass media, consumers also seem to be growing increasingly skeptical of the didactic advertising tools of the last half of the twentieth century. Most recently, new technologies like TiVo raise the prospect of consumers empowered to edit out commercials between TV programs.

All of these factors have led to a widespread decline of confidence in traditional advertising's ability to sway customers and deliver compelling arguments about products, services, and brands. A recent *Intellitrends* study of companies in automotive, IT, media, electronics, and healthcare found that 47 percent chose event marketing as their communications tool with the greatest return on investment, versus only 32 percent for advertising.[1] Traditional mass-communications advertising is not going to disappear any time soon, but it is clearly no longer enough. Companies of all kinds are realizing the need for something more local and targeted that provides communication with customers that is more interactive and high-touch. These are exactly the kinds of communication that show business creates between companies and customers.

On the other side of the equation, consumers themselves are being seen as increasingly tough to reach. They are increasingly fragmented themselves—no longer bowing to the single master brands that until recently dominated the market (the soft drink market share of Coca-Cola Classic fell from 33 percent to 20 percent, and Pepsi-Cola from 23 percent to 13 percent, between 1998 and 2001).[2] Part of this may be a proliferation of competing products, but customers are also becoming more savvy, more interconnected, and more likely to make their choices based on consultation and informed opinions. The Internet, in particular, has given a dynamic new medium for customer-to-customer communication that companies are striving to reckon with.

Just one example of growing consumer power can be found at the web site televisionwithoutpity.com. On this consumer-run message board, viewers post comments immediately after hit shows like *Alias*, *The Sopranos*, and *Charmed*—and the leading networks are paying close attention. TV producers have found out which of their plot lines viewers felt were unrealistic, which costumes were better or worse, and which supporting character was too lust-worthy to cut from the following season. After years of talk about the future of interactive TV, television has, in fact, finally become responsive to immediate customer feedback. More and more companies are waking up to the same realization. Today's consumers expect companies to listen to what they have to say, and they plan to listen more to each other than to Madison Avenue in deciding what to buy. Show business encourages customers to talk to each other and relate through a company's brands. By providing a role for customers to play in creating its experiences, show business welcomes them into the show.

The third trend is the rise of experience and entertainment within all aspects of our culture. *The Experience Economy*, published in 1999 by B. Joseph Pine II and James H. Gilmore, argued that economic value had progressed from producing commodities, to goods, to services, and, finally, to experiences. Consumers no longer expect to find experiences and entertainment just at the movie theater. They expect it in their nightly news, in their classrooms, in their retail environments, on web sites, and when they go out to eat in a restaurant. Experiences that entertain—through humor, drama, surprise, or sexiness—are becoming a mainstay in such realms as politics, art museums, and even in the law courts. This is not about shallowness—entertainment can be part of an experience that is also informed, complex, or very personal. But the culture at large expects even serious parts of their life to include a dimension of fun; and companies who are trying to understand their customers have to understand the challenge this poses to them. Consumers' need for entertainment is even greater in a difficult economic climate.

Show business offers customers an entertaining experience that can be "a smile when you are down." It is upbeat, often a bit offbeat, offering an uplifting new experience that connects customers to a brand.

MAKING SHOW BUSINESS DELIVER

The response to these trends has been a groundswell of new approaches to communicating with customers that has been growing across all industries. Many companies are turning to creative events and mobile marketing campaigns in order to target specific customer demographics and meet them face-to-face, in hopes of adding value and becoming a part of their customer's lifestyle. Experiential customer environments have moved out of the realm of theme restaurants and flagship stores and into new ideas for interactive retail, customer product-testing labs, and branded destinations. Companies are constantly trying new ways to reach the hard-to-reach consumer with guerilla marketing, new types of product placements, and interactive web experiences. Recruited street teams of customer evangelists are being sent out to spread buzz and word of mouth on behalf of products and brands. At times, customers are taking the reins themselves and creating shows about the brands they care about, and the companies are trying to catch up and find ways to participate.

These fun, innovative approaches to reaching customers reflect enormous creativity and interest in delivering an entertaining, engaging, and boundary-breaking experience. But that alone is not enough. If they are to work, and to truly be show business, all of these shows need to fulfill critical strategic goals as well:

- Integration with brand identity throughout implementation
- Strategic objectives that are clearly identified
- Useful metrics to measure return on investment in terms of brand-building, customer retention, sales generation, and market research

- Meaningful targeting of high-value customers and use of interaction and dialogue to gain insight and build customer relationships
- Real value provided to customers through a great experience that builds trust in and affiliation with a brand
- In-depth understanding of current trends in customer culture, entertainment, and lifestyle

To make show business deliver value, companies also need to realize how broad their audience can be. Entertaining, engaging, and boundary-breaking experiences are not just useful for reaching your average consumer audiences. Of course show business is "in" for things like consumer packaged goods and electronics—with clothing, beverage, and electronics brands devoting increasingly more of their budgets to show business. But show business is also extremely effective for business consumers. The old story that B2B consumers don't respond to branding or experience is pure myth. As we will see, even purchasers of enterprise software solutions appreciate a great experience that educates them in an exciting and interactive way.

But external customers are not the only audience for show business either. Companies know that to succeed, they need to communicate effectively with internal audiences as well: employees at every level and business partners such as sales channels and vendors. Show business is an important tool for all kinds of internal communication, whether it is for education, motivation, or brand alignment within a company. As the importance of internal branding becomes apparent to more and more companies, they are realizing that the show they put on about their brand on the inside needs to be just as engaging as the one they put on for the outside.

Figure I-1 shows a model for how show business builds brand relationships for both external customers and a company's own employees. Show business puts customers and a company's personnel in parallel relationships with the brand: both can relate to the brand when they experience the show, help to develop the brand by their participation in the show, and help to build the brand when they create a show. Shows provide customers and

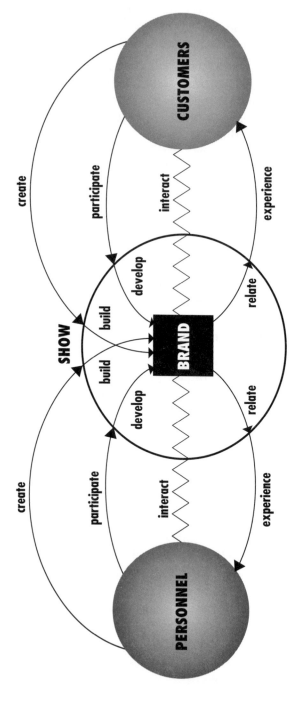

FIGURE I-1 The Show Business Brand Relationship model.

personnel with a chance to interact with each other and themselves. Shows facilitate feedback with a brand, and they help to create community among customers and personnel alike.

Now that we have a sense of what show business is and how it works, let's take a look at some successful recent cases of show business experiences that are entertaining, engaging, boundary-breaking, and value-adding. Some are large and spectacular, others small and intimate. They include shows put on *for* customers, put on *with* customers, or sometimes created *by* the customers themselves.

Reinventing the Peppermint: Altoids

Originally a stomach remedy, Altoids was invented in the UK more than 200 years ago, during the reign of King George III. Although it has been sold in the U.S. since before the Revolution, for a long time Altoids was a niche player with a very small market share: just 2 percent in 1994 after it was bought by Kraft.

In the mid-1990s, a new marketing campaign (the "curiously strong mint" campaign) focusing heavily on show business elements changed all that. The result: throughout the 1990s, the brand grew an average of 40 percent. By early 2001, the brand's sales totaled $126.3 million and the brand was number one in its category, accounting for 35 percent of sales among breath fresheners. In fact, Altoids is now much credited for the packaging revolution that occurred in the entire category.

The original campaign started with billboards featuring taglines such as "Mints so strong, they come in metal boxes." Altoids played ironically with the old-fashioned packaging. Without losing the nostalgia value Altoids brought its image up-to-date by featuring jokes about bisexuality ("Bi-curious?"). This peppy campaign was integrated with an engaging web site, altoids.com, where visitors could make silly art work in tacky retro styles reminiscent of the 1950s era imagery of the ads. By giving Altoids lovers a place to express themselves and their feelings about the mint, Altoids welcomed the customers to take things into their own hands.

Altoids took the campaign to a new level by starting an underground media blitz in core urban markets. The new show used nontraditional media: magnets placed on street signs and subway cars, personal ads in local weekly papers, postcards and posters, all with just the address www.toohot.com. Curious customers, no doubt expecting a porn site, clicked their mouse and instead found a web site for Cinnamon Altoids, the newest extension of the brand. Greeting visitors was Sindy (think "sin"), Altoids's cinnamon babe, dressed in a Playboy-bunny-style outfit: a racy, animated spokesperson "hot enough to make the Devil jealous." The show again led customers themselves to pursue the brand and respond to the provocation. It got them talking and got them sharing stories and their own new ideas about the mints.

In the late 1990s, an Altoids customer's discovery hit the Internet and spread rapidly, becoming the hot topic on numerous chat sites. The discovery? "A few Altoids just before engaging in oral sex elevates the recipient's experience to the 'out of this world' category," according to the word of mouth.

The rumor must have reached Monica Lewinsky, because according to the Starr Report, she tried to work it into her own show on November 13, 1997:

> The President finally joined Ms. Lewinsky in the study, where they were alone for only a minute or two. Ms. Lewinsky gave him an antique paperweight in the shape of the White House. She also showed him an email describing the effect of chewing Altoids mints before performing oral sex. Ms. Lewinsky was chewing Altoids at the time, but the president replied that he did not have enough time for oral sex. They kissed, and the President rushed off for a State Dinner with [Mexican] President Zedillo.[3]

As they say, you can't buy this kind of publicity. The consumers themselves created it all—because Altoids had sparked their imagination and invited them to put on their own show.

By now, Altoids's retro-fresh, experience-rich packaging has been mimicked by the whole premium mint industry. Cunning tin boxes now line the shelves. But none of the imitators has even come close to challenging Altoids, and none has developed a show that provokes such customer loyalty. None of them has the potential of creating a similar "out-of-this-world" experience.

STOKING THE RUMORS: APPLE'S IMAC

Sometimes show business is all about building excitement for a climactic launch event. Apple Computers is a company that knows how to put on a great show for product launches. Twice every year, the computer company takes the stage at the MacWorld Expo and reaps a bevy of free publicity as newspapers, magazines, and TV lavish attention on the show. The charismatic CEO Steve Jobs is probably the only person in the world who can excite the mainstream press about an operating system upgrade.

One of Apple's greatest launch shows in recent memory was for the dazzling second-generation iMac. When Apple computers was finishing its design, with the swiveling flat screen and dome-shaped base, they knew they had a winning product on their hands. They also knew that the company needed to put on a great show to generate excitement for its launch.

For years, Apple has counted on its loyal customer community to help it build excitement and word of mouth for new products. Part of the show around any Apple launch is the rumor-mongering among its fans that starts months before every biannual MacWorld Expo. Fan web sites like Thinksecret.com, Appleinsider.com, and Spymac.com start generating buzz and speculation about what's coming down the pike. In this cat-and-mouse drama, insiders in the company smuggle out photos of the new designs that are posted on the Web until Apple's lawyers file the habitual half-hearted complaint—half-hearted because these fans are the ones out there generating the most excitement. But if the secret breaks too early, obviously the drama goes bust.

With the new iMac, Apple decided to run the show a little differently. Building up suspense for what would be its most dramatic new product design in recent memory, Apple goaded its fans, superseding their rumor sites by running its own buzz campaign. Instead of suing the customer sites, it staged a running taunt on its own corporate site: "Beyond the rumor sites. Way beyond." "Count on being blown away." As the Expo approached, apple.com began a countdown ("10 days. It's coming," "9 days. Can you feel it?").

Apple managed to keep the new design a complete secret. As a result, the rumors started to fly: There were stories of a detachable monitor with handwriting recognition, of new digital video devices, talk of a flying computer. Spymac.com even published video footage of an alleged (but nonexistent) hand-held device called the iWalk. It finally leaked out that the surprise would be an update of some kind to the iMac when employees at CompUSA deciphered a change in inventory code that indicated the end of the line for the original candy-colored desktop.

The final act happened on the first day of MacWorld's January 2002 Expo. Steve Jobs's keynote address was sold out, with lines you would expect at Madison Square Garden, and he took the stage like a rock star before the thronging crowd, entering to his personal theme music and in his trademark stage costume (black mock turtleneck and blue jeans).

These expo technology introductions are a melodrama whose elements are so worn as to have no chance at surprise. But that's the point: the fans know it's coming and get to ooh and ahh at the newest magical wonder. The previous year, Jobs had introduced the iPod with his trademark shtick of waiting till the end of his talk and then, as he started to walk off-stage, saying, "Oh, but there's one more thing…" He then launched into a whirlwind riff about the capabilities of his newest hardware device and surprised everyone by pulling the tiny iPod out of his back pocket.

This year, having built up so much expectation for the new iMac, the show was all about a sudden climax. Jobs went

FIGURE I-2   Apple's show business launch for the daring new iMac won the product front-page media coverage. Photo courtesy of Time Magazine.

straight for the big moment, striding on stage to give his speech before an enormous video screen that burst into images of the beautiful new iMac as it rose up from the floor in front of him on a pedestal (a touch from Broadway shows) to the wild applause of the audience. If you couldn't be there, there was always the

Web, where avid Mac fans were watching the whole show streaming to their computers worldwide.

Major news carriers like CNN had already been running stories in advance of the Expo about the mystery of Apple's newest arrival. By arranging a deal offering a prerelease test drive and an exclusive on the story, Apple got *Time* magazine to commit a cover story to the new flat-screen wonder, under the headline, "Flat-Out Cool!" The result of this carefully orchestrated show business product launch: a record-breaking 150,000 pre-orders in the first day.

THE BAG THAT LAUNCHED A THOUSAND CLICKS: BLUEFLY.COM

What would *you* do for a Birkin bag? That was the question that was asked of fashionable women entering Madison Square Garden for New York's annual Fashion Week, strolling the designer streets of Beverly Hills, or browsing the chic boutiques of Miami's most upscale fashion neighborhood.

If you don't know what the Birkin bag is, your answer probably wasn't what these shoppers said:

"I would streak naked down 5th Avenue!"

"I'd lay in bed with snakes."

"I'd walk around Beverly Hills with my facial mask."

"Just name the guy you want me to sleep with!"

Whoa! Who mentioned sleeping? This outpouring of offers of the ultimate sacrifice was elicited by a street show put on by Bluefly.com to launch its new brand and web site devoted to offering designer fashion at discount prices. The niche was new and promising, but to get their brand off the ground, Bluefly.com knew it needed to do something to get the attention of the right customers, and they certainly didn't have the budget to do it with advertising. So they decided to put on a show.

The company knew it had to offer something irresistible that would be a perfect match for the discerning customer who

FIGURE I-3   Bluefly.com took its show to the streets to ask customers how far they'd go for fashion. Photo courtesy of Renegade Marketing.

shopped regularly for designer brands. But what would these women covet above all else?

Enter the Birkin bag. Made by luxury design company Hermes, the Birkin bag normally sells for anywhere from $5,000 to $50,000 a bag. Even if you have the money, it takes connections to buy a Birkin bag. Without fame, you'll be lucky to make it on a six-month waiting list. The mystique of the fabulous bag had recently been the subject of an episode of HBO's hit show *Sex and the City*, as the ultimate fashion accessory.

The company somehow managed to acquire 12 of the bags, and then set up one in each of the three cities, inside a glass case with their web site on it and with a security guard on hand. Next to the exquisite display, a mock reporter stopped the passing fashionati, asked about their own passion for the bag, and recorded the conversations on videotape. After revealing the lengths to which they would go, each confessor was told the magic secret: by registering online at the Bluefly.com web site, they could enter a chance to win one of the 12 bags for free—no snakes. The show touched a lot of people that week—20,000 "bull's-eye influencers," as they called these targeted customers (they knew they were reaching the right crowd when 9 out of 10 interviewees knew what the bag was). Those 20,000 told more friends in turn. And to really spread the word, Bluefly.com made a video of the most outrageous customer comments and sent it out as a press release that was widely picked up and reported for its humor and topicality. Fox TV in Los Angeles devoted two-and-a-half-minutes of its morning news show to talking about the bag, the show, the company, and to urging husbands to go online and register if they wanted to show their love for their wives.

The results of the show were a windfall of more than just publicity. Bluefly.com received 160,000 new online registrants at their web site. More importantly, within two months, over 6,000 of them had become first-time purchasers at the site. From previous customer registration patterns, Bluefly.com predicted the number of new purchasing customers from the show to reach 16,000 within 12 months. That's show business that speaks straight to the bottom line.

SOMETHING OLD, SOMETHING NEW: THE NBC EXPERIENCE

When NBC decided to build a show business retail space in New York around their television brand, the company knew who their audience would be. There were already hundreds of thousands of tourists visiting Rockefeller Center each year for a tour of NBC's studios, which gave them a nostalgic look at the past (NBC's early days in radio, hand-made sound effects, and the transition to television) and a backstage peek at the studios of the present (*NBC Nightly News*, *Saturday Night Live*, and *Late Night with Conan O'Brien*).

After the tour piqued their curiosity, NBC wanted to create a store that would immerse the visitors in a total experience of the brand and then leverage the audience's attachment to it into sales of high-priced merchandise. So they created what they call The NBC Experience Store.

NBC had already discovered through research that there was a tremendous resonance in their audience for the network's 50 years of vintage programming. They wanted the experience in the store to put visitors back in touch with those memories and evoke a powerful nostalgic appeal. But they also wanted an experience that used leading-edge technology to point toward the future and to give visitors a chance to step into the screen and become a part of the NBC show themselves.

The store they created does all this and more. It is a never-ending spectacle, with a stunning multilevel interior design of mirrored steel, hundreds of TV monitors everywhere you look showing highlights of current programs, and a linoleum floor printed with black and white archival photos of NBC shows from the past. There's even the NBC three-note signal as you step across the floor. The centerpiece of the space is a two-story globe covered with 100,000 LEDs that provide 360-degree graphics. Inside the globe is a 40-seat 3-screen High-Definition TV theater that tells the history of the network.

Surrounding the globe in all directions are walls of merchandise in sections arranged by programming schedules: early morning, daytime, primetime, and late night. Branded t-shirts, mugs, key chains, and other standard fare are mixed in with television scripts, DVD collections of classic episodes, sitcom board games, and insider books that range from news anchors' memoirs to the lusty reflections of soap opera stars.

Visitors can spend their money not just on kiss-and-tell and coffee cups, but to jump into the show and become a part of the NBC brand. At special kiosks, staff assist visitors with TelePrompTers and blue-screen technology that allow them to virtually sit on Conan O'Brien's desk, give the weather report with Al Roker, or chat about sports with Bob Costas—and buy a video of their moment of stardom to take home and share with others.

FIGURE I-4   Inside the multilevel NBC Experience Store. Photo courtesy of Jack Morton Worldwide.

The show business of the Experience Store doesn't just convert NBC's steady stream of visitors into enthusiastic purchasers. It also returns the favor by helping promote the backstage experience of the studio tour, and it builds customers' connection with the brand in a powerful and affecting way.

FIGURE I-5   NBC's spectacle of high-technology and nostalgic imagery. Photo courtesy of Jack Morton Worldwide.

A PREVIEW OF THIS BOOK

Now that we have provided a clear sense of what show business is, we can start to look in detail at how it is done and the value it offers.

In Part I of this book we look at different types of shows, from shows staged as live events, to creative show spaces, to shows that use new and reinvented media, to shows that rely on the oldest of marketing tools, word of mouth and referral. We provide appropriate applications and best practices for each type of show so that you will know which type to use for which business situation.

In Part II, we examine the strategic tools available to show business. We show you how to keep your show on-brand, how to understand and engage your customer through show business, how to extend the impact of your show through PR and CRM, and how to measure a show's return on investment.

In Part III, we look at how to put on a show for your own employees and business partners. We examine best practices for internal shows, how they contribute value to a company, and the special issues that arise for this kind of show business. We will also look at how show business can be a part of leadership, and feature the leaders whose persona, myth, and ethos have shaped the experience of their companies.

In Part IV, we show how show business is not only transforming individual organizations, but entire industries and culture at large.

Along the way, we feature numerous examples of companies who have created experiences that entertain, engage, break boundaries, and deliver value, including:

- The Tie Me Up, Tie Me Down S&M and bondage party that launched a flurry of press for Casio's G-Shock watch and made it the darling of the influential fashion community
- SAP's E-Business Solutions Tour, a traveling, satellite-linked road show that shows off their enterprise software in a multimedia theater that can pull into their prospects' parking lots
- Vans's discovery of self-liquidating marketing, with an independent movie that put their brand in the hearts of their skateboarding customers while delivering a big profit at the box-office
- Crayola Works, the retail-store-art-studio-product-testing-lab-customer-playspace, which is helping move the Crayola brand from a product-only positioning to an experiential and solutions-focused brand
- The experiential dealer launch of the VW Phaeton, where Volkswagen introduced its European dealers not just to a new car, but to a new type of customer and the lifestyle which the Phaeton will be a part of
- Victoria's Secret's glamour show of supermodel fantasies, faux fashion shows, and boutique retail stores that

have captivated the imagination of their customers and transformed the apparel industry

- Oracle's Larry Ellison, the "James Bond of the IT world," a show business leader who talks the talk, walks the walk, sails the yacht and flies the fighter jet
- Vespa's buzz marketers, cruising the streets of California spreading the word about the return of this classic on wheels
- Intel's cyborgs on the streets, the interactive show that fired demand for its newest chip for laptops
- The Dallas Cowboys's plan to turn one of the world's three biggest sports brands into an interactive destination experience
- Jeep's, Saturn's, and BMW's participatory shows for customers, which give them a chance to experience and live their brands on the racetrack, on the off-roads, and in the factory

All this and more awaits us, so…

Let's get on with the show!

TYPES OF SHOWS

In Part I, we look at different types of shows:

- Shows staged as live events (Chapter 2)
- Creative spaces (Chapter 2)
- Shows that use new and reinvented media (Chapter 3)
- Shows that rely on the oldest of marketing tools—word of mouth and referral (Chapter 4)

Finally, in Chapter 5, using Victoria's Secret as an example, we show you how to integrate different types of shows for maximum impact.

1 LIVE SHOWS

T he invitations arrived in the mail, wrapped in black leather with a steel zipper. Inside was a vellum sheet and black stationery that read, "SUBMIT, FEAST, IMBIBE, DANCE, ATTEND— the Casio G-Shock Tie Me Up, Tie Me Down Party." Was this for real? S&M and bondage? For a wristwatch?

"Yes," was the answer, when 200 members of the press and 500 of New York's slickest models, fashion stylists, and entertainment industry people showed up at the packed event at the Roxy night club. The space had been transformed into an S&M homage to the most outrageous new brand in wrist wear—chains, leather, and Casio watches intertwined in the room's décor and in the revealing costumes worn by the evening's performers. The inimitable Grace Jones herself held forth as mistress of ceremonies while guests saw the new G-Shock watches being put to the test, strutting their resilience under crushing steps of stiletto heels. Exotic dancers dressed in full-body leather-and-G-Shock outfits spanked, tied up, and pierced each other's bodies on stages and while roving among the audience.

The carefully picked trendsetters in attendance fell in love with the show and the edgy new brand. The new G-Shock was broadly embraced by the fashion stylist community, and the party and other launch events helped to generate over 75 million

FIGURE 1-1   Chains, bondage, and wristwatches at the G-Shock Tie Me Up, Tie Me Down party. Photo courtesy of Renegade Marketing.

media impressions in the brand's first six months. *The New York Post* awarded Casio the Marketer Chutzpah of the Year Award for its audacity.

But why promote a watch with S&M? Casio knew when they created their new G-Shock that they wanted its brand to be chic, outrageous, and urban with an edge. They knew they needed to create experiences that communicated that brand to key customer trendsetters in order to succeed. "Casio said they wanted work that would really put the shock in G-Shock," said Drew Neisser, President and CEO of Renegade Marketing, who produced the show and a range of print and show business marketing for Casio. "We developed four ideas for a launch party—one where we tried to be as outrageous as we could imagine, and three others that we thought Casio would actually consider. We were surprised when they picked the first."

FIGURE 1-2 Latex and a playful spanking with your watch?
Photo courtesy of Renegade Marketing.

The G-Shock party highlights two key imperatives of show business: know your audience and break some boundaries to get their attention. Casio's boldness paid off. But it wasn't just a crazy gamble: the show was right for the brand and fit the audience—New York's fashion stylists and press at the wild end of the 1990s. Other show business events were created for different trend-setting groups, with appropriate themes for each of them: in-line skaters, snowboarders, and college music festival participants. In each, the gritty, edgy, provocative nature of the G-Shock brand found a way to reach its audience face-to-face. Customers who would not have been reachable by traditional advertising media became engaged by the show and helped to make the new brand fashionable and a strong seller.

THE POWER OF LIVE SHOWS

Live shows are just that—shows staged in real life. They can include launch parties, interactive product demonstrations, circus-like road shows, street theater performances, or brand-centered festivals for customers. They are used in industries as varied as beverages, automobiles, and enterprise software.

Live shows should be entertaining, thrilling, or amusing. They engage their audiences through the charms of live performance and are best when they get the customer to interact and take a part in the show. They should break boundaries of what is expected, or normally seen, to create an impression that stays with the audience long after the experience. They add value to the lives of customers, and, in turn, to the company.

Live shows are still a small part of the marketing pie compared with other marketing activities. But as traditional print and broadcast advertising have declined in recent years, more and more industries and companies are discovering the amazing and cost-efficient ability of a powerful live experience to build a brand and to reach customer targets.

In a 2002 study of 40 UK companies using events as part of their marketing mix, Jack Morton Worldwide found that 39 percent planned to increase their event budgets over the next two years, compared with only 23 percent expecting a decrease. *Event Marketer Magazine* estimates that event marketing was a $150 billion industry in 2001, with continuing growth expected in events for both business audiences and for end-consumers.[4] Much of the event industry is still committed to tradeshows and sales meetings, which often lack the creativity or branded experience to be called "show business." But those are the kinds of events that are facing the same decline as advertising, while more engaging uses of events as show business are actually on the rise.

The great advantage of a live show is its ability to deliver an engaging experience of a brand directly to a very specific identified audience. Good live shows are like direct marketing that delivers an experience to your key customer, rather than just a sales brochure. They hone in on specific customer groups who are desired for their influence on others, their value as repeat customers, or their ability to influence high-value purchasing decisions. Most important, live shows offer customers an experience that brings the brand to life and engages them in it directly.

Live shows are an excellent way for reaching audiences who are resistant to, or resentful of, traditional marketing because they are always an "opt-in" experience. Customers seeing a live show will have dedicated one of their most precious resources—time and attention—to this event. The voluntary nature of the experience means that they are much more invested in its message than is usually the case with traditional advertising.

Another reason for the effectiveness of live shows is the fact that they engage the customer over a considerable period of time, and thus leave a lasting impression.

Live shows are particularly effective because of the immediacy of face-to-face communication with customers and because the live experience typically is shared with others. This is what makes theater and ritual so powerful. In cases like the G-Shock party, participants are literally immersed in the brand and become a part of the brand themselves.

Great live shows are often interactive, giving the audience a chance to take a role, try out a product, or ask questions. By doing so, they get the customer involved in more meaningful ways and thus result in what marketers have called a high-involvement decision process.

As a result live shows can be used for much more than creating buzz in consumer markets and the press, as we saw in the G-Shock party. They can be effectively used for a wide variety of brands and for a wide variety of customers, including B2B customers. Let's take a look at another very different case, that of a live show for a highly educated business audience making very high-cost purchasing decisions.

SAP'S ROAD SHOW

SAP teaches a lot about quality production in show business. The global e-business solutions provider is well known in the technology industry for putting on outstanding shows at trade events, like its flashily staged SAPPHIRE conferences hosted around the world for SAP's customers, employees, and business partners. But despite their success in the trade show arena, there still were customers and potential customers whom SAP was not reaching. As a result, Marty Homlish, SAP's Global Chief Marketing Officer, decided to take the show on the road through a mobile live show called the SAP E-Business Solutions Tour.

The Tour is a mobile, interactive, satellite-linked showroom that's mounted on a 53-foot truck and has been touring North America since 2000. It allows SAP to take its best presentation to the customer—literally to the parking lot of their corporate headquarters, where it will set up shop and put on the SAP show for all the decision-making executives who care to enjoy it on their lunch hour. This road show is traveling onsite to existing business customers and new prospects, as well as appearing at e-business trade and educational conferences, and to targeted lifestyle and sporting events like the SAP U.S. Grand Prix auto race in Indianapolis.

The first-of-its-kind, mobile, experiential trade show is carefully integrated in its design with SAP's advertising messages. It is able, however, to show the kind of things no advertising campaign can—how their enterprise software products work.

Upon entering the exhibit, the customer steps into a true immersion experience. The first room is a five-screen surrounding theater that presents SAP's vision of the benefits of global, cross-enterprise collaboration. Next is a satellite-enabled demonstration space that provides an in-depth look at how technology solutions (in supply chain management, customer relationship management, enterprise portals, and e-marketplaces) can enable business success. In the final stage, SAP "solution architects" are on hand to present customized demonstrations of SAP technology mapped to guests' specific business needs.

The result is a terrific show that allows SAP to show off the benefits of an extremely complicated set of products and services for business, to make the process fun and interactive, and to take that show to the customers, wherever they may be.

The decision to build a mobile live show was made as part of a global strategy to build the SAP corporate brand by leveraging SAP's long experience and market position. The aim of this strategy was to position SAP as a stable brand of e-business solutions in an environment that included many newcomers—and a lot of failing IT startups. SAP's advertising messages at that time were very brand-focused, and so was the use of the Tour.

The company chose to invest part of their global marketing budget in a live experience because they saw that offering a unique and technologically superior exhibit would demonstrate their commitment to educating their customers. The Tour was also chosen to demonstrate that SAP was becoming a more market-driven company and one more focused on interacting with customers face-to-face.

When the Tour was renewed for a second year, the exhibit was retooled and its usage adjusted to reflect a shift in marketing strategy. This strategy was focused less on corporate brand building and more on penetration into the marketplace toward the generation of new customer leads. The show became more about demonstrating solutions and less about promoting the corporate brand. Though SAP Global Marketing continued to own the Tour property, other partners got involved. SAP U.S. Sales & Marketing became the lead sponsor, taking on a share of the operating costs in order to have the show come to their events and help attract their customers.

SAP has also developed important survey tools for measuring the impact of its show and the success of its marketing objectives. These measurements focus on purchase intent and the behavior of Tour visitors, and also on collecting leads and qualifying them—ranking their value on the basis of questions like, "Are you a decision maker for this purchase?" and "What is the timing until your purchasing decision?"

In its third year, the Tour focuses now on even more specific sales targets and on helping close deals, with more focused objectives for each prospect seen. To match the evolving strategy, SAP's metrics evolved to measure correlations between the timing of Tour appearances and progress in the regional sales "pipeline" (e.g., business closings). The result of these measurements was renewed support for the Tour as an effective marketing tool for SAP.

LIQUOR, GADGETS, AND CARDS: SHOWS FOR MASS CONSUMERS

Of course, live shows aren't just done for business customers or the press. They are also a great way to engage targeted customers for mass consumer products. The most interesting shows are experiential, interactive, and fun.

David Laks, President of DSL Global Event Marketing, which designed the SAP E-Business Solutions Tour, is also responsible for U.S. event marketing for Yu-Gi-Oh™, the new trading card game from Japan (similar to Pokemon), which is taking pre-adolescent American boys by storm. "Strategic trading cards is an industry that does mostly events and little advertising," says Laks, "because your success depends upon teaching people how to play the game so they will sample the product and then remain engaged over the long term." In this case, the product demands a hands-on experience to convince customers to buy. Typically, repeat customers convert their friends into customers, and event marketing is the best way to encourage conversions.

Another industry that has shown growing interest in live shows is consumer electronics. Nintendo is using invitation-only Cube Clubs—traveling all-day game parties—to entertain and attract avid computer gamers. Their competitor, Microsoft, launched its Xbox game system with a 32-city tour called the Xbox Odyssey, which brought a traveling circus-tent atmosphere to the customer: throbbing music and dozens of gaming stations with giant TV screens, all under a two-story inflatable black dome. Motorola launched its breakthrough V70 cell phone in Asian markets by throwing prerelease parties for fashion-conscious consumers where décor, costumes, and design shared the striking keyhole shape of the new phone and revelers were given the inside scoop on where to get this new must-have accessory.

Liquor companies, facing legal constraints in using traditional advertising, are also making a big push for live shows as a way to acquire new customers. Faced with an aging population of existing customers, brands like Chivas Regal have chosen live shows as part of their approach to luring a younger demographic, more used to beer, to consider their products. The Chivas Regal scotch-tasting events are part happy hour, part comedy hour, and part customer education, with comedian Sir Jeremy John Bell (the Knight of Toasting) providing entertaining lectures on the regionalisms of five competitor scotches as participants eat, drink, and get merry.

CUSTOMER FESTIVALS IN THE AUTO INDUSTRY

The auto industry has long been a source of high-end show business spectaculars at the major annual auto shows that introduce new models and prototypes for the future to industry audiences around the world.

Leaders in the industry have also pioneered the use of live shows as customer events to build brand communities. These festivals for their most brand-loyal customers are designed to help them bond as a community through their shared driving lifestyle. The aim is to build relationships with and between customers and turn them into evangelists for the brand.

Let's take a look at three shows in the auto industry: for Saturn, Jeep, and BMW.

In the early 1990s, Saturn built an enviable brand whose identity was folksy, family-oriented, and trustworthy. To create a sense of family among the customers of this "different kind of car company," Saturn invented the Saturn Homecoming, an annual two-day festival for owners at the Saturn plant in Springfield, Tennessee. The theme of the show was members of the Saturn "family" coming "home" from all over the country to the place where their car was "born." And come they did, tens of thousands in caravans from cities across the country bringing homemade buttons and t-shirts to swap and share ("My Saturn Saved My Life," "Who Cares about Mars—I've Been to Saturn!"), custom paint jobs to show-off, even fiancés to marry at the event. The folksy feeling was evident in the entertainment (parades, country music, fireworks, line-dancing, and speeches by astronauts and sports stars) and the contests (chili-making, karaoke, table tennis). Factory tours revealed the behind-the-scenes show of how Saturns were born, and customers vied for prizes for the newest Saturn, the oldest, the most miles, and the best essay about a memorable experience with their car.

The show business centerpiece of the Homecoming was a dance-drama spectacular called The Spirit of Saturn, which played both nights under an enormous tent. Its story traced the tale of a bewildered customer's discovery of the Saturn, through the inner workings of the plant and the live assemblage of a car, all played out onstage through high-energy dancing and drumming in the style of such popular urban dance shows as *Stomp* and *Tap Dogs*. This tale of automotive spirit and manufacturing genius incorporated audience participation, roller-blading, gymnastics, and vehicles and factory carts zooming on and off stage with musicians riding and playing atop them. The live action was enhanced by eight video screens showing footage of the history and philosophy of the car company. At the finale, the dancers cleverly made music out of Saturn's much-proclaimed pride in its scratch-proof finish by dancing about while beating out their percussive finale on the car parts themselves (all unscathed by the drumming). All in all, a great interactive show that immersed customers in the spirit of the brand.

Jeep, a much older car brand, has created a live customer show of its own, the Jeep Jamboree. These weekend events happen dozens of times a year across the U.S. and are built on the Jeep brand's promise of rough driving and rugged exploration of the great outdoors. What to do when most SUV customers have no practical need for the off-road capabilities of their gas-guzzling beasts? Well, Jeep created a show that helped them take a carefully supported step into the world of the brand. With a range of easy to nigh-impossible routes to choose from, Jeep owners from the suburban rookie to the Rocky Mountain cowboy can choose a Jamboree to suit them. Unlike Saturn's Homecoming, the Jamborees are all about driving; there's no time for chili contests or dance shows as you navigate the courses over boulders, streams, and steep inclines through (once pristine) scenes of natural splendor.

The BMW Ultimate Driving Experience is similarly all about the drive, but in a very different way that reflects its own brand. The focus of the show is on engineering technology and design and on discovering the BMW's capabilities for high-performance driving. Professional racers give BMW owners classroom instruction on driving dynamics followed by behind-the-wheel training. Customers learn about performance cornering, understeering and oversteering, and how to control a skid using the Dynamic Stability Control System. They also get to race each other, discover the experience of driving a BMW at top speeds on a closed course, and learn how to stop hard with the proper use of the Anti-Lock Braking System.

In each case, these shows give their companies a chance to meet their customers face-to-face, to immerse them in the world of their brand, and to interact, answer questions, and learn more about their most loyal customers—those interested enough in the brand to spend their weekend at this kind of event. This provides a chance to build a deeper brand relationship between the company and these customers, and also between the customers themselves.

TAKING IT TO THE STREETS: INTEL'S MOBILE MESSENGERS

In some cases, live shows take place not on a stage, at a trade show, or a private party or venue, but in the public realm. Intel, the computer chip maker, has shown how street theater can be used to promote even an item as unglamorous as the processor inside your computer.

As part of the launch of its newest chip for laptops—the Mobile Intel® Pentium® 4 Processor-M—Intel sent out more than 50 "human desks" across New York City to convey their chip's promise of "desktop performance on the go." Performers in bold orange-and-blue spandex body suits (the colors of Intel) strolled the city's streets, parks, and college campuses with laptops strapped to their chests, keyboards flipped down, offering a test-ride to pedestrians. For those who wanted a full demo with wireless Internet, the cyborg mobile messengers directed passersby to mobile experience zones, where Pentium-equipped laptops could be used to experience high-speed web surfing, music downloads, and digital photography. These branded orange and blue pavilions were set up for the day in Grand Central Station, Penn Station, Bryant Park, Columbia University, and leading computer stores. The day's events culminated in software giveaways, an Intel sweepstakes, and a free concert at Bryant Park with the multiplatinum selling band, Barenaked Ladies. For customers across New York, the performance of the latest laptop chips (hardly a product one stays up at night thinking about) was suddenly turned into an unforgettable experience.

This street-level show was part of a range of New York events for the launch date that were integrated with a $75 million global advertising campaign for the new processor on the theme of "powerful desktop performance without the desk." The campaign, a five-fold increase in Intel's advertising on notebooks, was the result of research that showed the notebook PC segment growing at more than twice the rate of the overall PC market. Intel had also learned from talking to customers that the move to notebooks was not just about business

FIGURE 1-3   Intel's mobile messengers took their newest products to street level to show customers. Photo courtesy of Intel Corporation.

travel, but a new acceptance of their use in the owner's life-style: 81 percent of surveyed laptop users were using them in front of the TV, 60 percent in bed, 54 percent while eating, and 48 percent undressed or in their underwear.

The Intel street show demonstrates three important principles for live shows put on at street level. First, identify the product or brand message that you want to show off and find a dramatic way to demonstrate it. Second, try to make it visual and theatrical; costumes and props are great. They don't have to be high-priced, just garish and visible. You need to catch people's attention for this kind of show. Finally, you have to go to where your target customers are, whether it's the great hall of Grand Central Station or the quad of your local college. Part of the key to street theater shows is finding the right location to reach your audience, one where they are already going.

This isn't always where you might first think to look. In India, for example, religious festivals have become a major focus of marketing initiatives. The biggest of all is the Kumbh Mela, which draws 30 million people to the confluence of the Ganges and Yamuna rivers each year. Marketers have already been offering their brands of hot tea to the pilgrims as they emerge from their ritual cleansing in the river; but recently global brands like Pepsi and Coke have realized the opportunity of this event to hawk their own wares. Reportedly the biggest congregation of people anywhere in the world, the local state government has touted the Kumbh Mela festival as "the best business opportunity of the millennium." What kind of live show could you imagine putting on there?

LIVE SHOWS AT TRADE SHOWS

Even though proprietary or single-company events of the types we've looked at so far are growing rapidly, the largest venue for event marketing is still trade shows. In the year 2000, more than 12,000 trade shows were held in the US[5], with more than 1.4 million exhibits created for 110 million visitors.[6]

Although many exhibits at trade shows lack any truly experiential elements to engage customers (brochures and a free tote bag are not show business!), the trade show is an important venue where companies can demonstrate leadership by putting on a real show.

In fact, a trade-show environment demands that companies deliver something truly extraordinary if they are to engage and hold the customer's attention because, unlike the live shows we've seen so far, the venue is not the company's own. A customer experience at a trade show thus has to stand out amidst a clamor of competing messages or productions attempting to claim the audience's attention.

However, a trade show can still be a very desirable place to produce a live show, if the audience is right. User-group trade shows, where the audience is drawn from current customers of a particular brand, can be particularly valuable. There is still competition from other companies offering services of value to users of say, Apple's computers (such as at the independently run MacWorld Expo, where Apple launched its iMac and has introduced many other new products). But the self-selected audience of a user-group event provides a valuable targeted demographic for marketers to reach. These kinds of consumer-focused events have continued to grow while more traditional trade shows have declined in many mature industries.[7]

The audience at trade shows tends to be educated and interested in details. They like being entertained, but they are looking for substance. They also expect something interactive and are eager to ask questions and be involved in a discussion, which is great for your show.

The best show business for trade show audiences focuses on getting people to experience what the company has to offer firsthand, to learn interactively, and to do so in a dramatic setting. J.D. Edwards put on just this kind of show at a user-group conference, with an interactive experience titled Corridors of Chaos. To illustrate the power of their collaborative global software applications, the company created a fictional scenario of a viral epidemic let loose in the United States, whose treatment required medicine from a rare plant in Costa Rica.

Audience participants started by zigzagging between 14 plasma screens that bombarded them with images of the everyday business frustrations of online commerce (your supply chain doesn't talk to your inventory, your services don't work with your software). From these opening corridors, they proceeded into a main theater where the story of the viral outbreak played out, exploring the communications and organizational challenges posed by the hypothetical crisis and illustrating, in human terms, how collaborative commerce works. From the theater, participants moved to ten interactive kiosks that allowed them to drill down into specific topics like order-processing, and to see characters from the story explain how their software worked. In the last phase of the experience, J.D. Edwards's guides led participants through hands-on tours of each piece of software described, answering their questions, and demonstrating possible solutions.

"Our goal was an experience unique enough that it would spread the word and everyone in attendance would hear about it," said Michael Trovalli of Jack Morton Worldwide, who created the show. The audience responded, with nearly 3,000 people choosing to see this intimate and interactive

FIGURE 1-4 After experiencing the dramatic story of J.D. Edwards's Corridors of Chaos, users learned more at interactive kiosks. Photo courtesy of Jack Morton Worldwide.

experience within 18 hours. Interviews of participants and the buzz among industry observers agreed: "That's it! This is what collaborative commerce is all about."

LESSONS LEARNED

As we have seen, live shows can be extremely varied in their format, style, methods, and goals. Some of the possible models for a live show include:

- Launch parties—like the G-Shock launch party or the iMac launch—where the aim is to spread excitement and buzz among key influencer groups

- Product demos—like J.D. Edwards's Corridors of Chaos and Chivas Regal's scotch tastings—where targeted customers can learn hands-on about the product, test it out, ask questions, and interact with the company

- Road shows—like the SAP E-Business Solutions Tour and the Xbox Odyssey—where the aim is to take a product demo to the customer's doorstep: a show business version of the old traveling salesman, or the carnival tent

- Street theater—like Intel's mobile messengers and Blue-fly.com's fashion frenzy—that takes the brand to the public domain to draw attention, spread word of mouth, and strut its stuff
- Customer festivals—like Saturn's, Jeep's, and BMW's—where brand loyalty and community is built among repeat customers who come to meet each other and immerse themselves in an experience of the brand

Like all show business, live shows need to be fun and exhilarating; they need to engage their audience, they need to break boundaries, and they need to add value. A great live show is an opportunity to show leadership—technological, creative, lifestyle—and to demonstrate your commitment to close contact with customers. It is also a great way to cut through the clutter of media overkill. To do that your show should be:

- **Right for the specific audience.** Like direct marketing, live shows can hone in on a targeted group. The best return on investment (ROI) for live shows usually comes from targeting high-value customers. Live shows are also good at reaching media-resistant or media-resentful customer groups because they are voluntary experiences.
- **Right for the brand.** Immerse your customer in your brand, integrate your brand essence and imagery into every element of your show's design, and coordinate your show with your other marketing messages.
- **Fun and substantive.** Live shows can present a service or product in a way that both entertains and communicates ideas (including sophisticated information that advertising media cannot easily deliver).
- **Memorable and interactive.** Live shows create a powerful and lasting impact because they last longer, communicate face-to-face, and are shared experiences. The best live shows give customers a chance to interact (try your product, ask questions, meet you, meet each other) and to build relationships.

Of course, to build an ongoing brand relationship with your customers, you should create an experience where customers can meet you, and each other, for more than a one-time great experience. Ongoing shows that take place beyond a single day, night, or weekend allow for the creation of branded environments of even greater depth and interactivity.

Branded environments offer long-running shows with live experiences that customers can return to, allowing brands to build relationships more deeply and interact more continuously. We call the best of these show spaces *immersionary* (immersive + visionary). Let's take a look at them in the next chapter.

2 IMMERSIONARY SHOW SPACES

In the Arundel Mills mall outside Baltimore, Maryland, there is a new space for customers that is a little hard to describe, but it could be a model and a portent for the future. Part retail store, part branded environment, part classroom, part playroom, part product testing lab—Crayola Works might be confusing to a traditional marketer, but to customers it's just plain fun.

From outside, Crayola Works catches the eye with its bright blotches of playful color; inside it is like being in a crayon box—with rainbow colors in flashing lights and patterns on the floor. Transparent pillars are filled with colorful crayons and a black-and-white Volkswagen Beetle is available for kids to color on with markers. The space includes a retail store that sells everything from basic Crayola crayon boxes to arts and crafts, kits, and board games, and offers ongoing product demonstrations. But the other half of the 20,000 square-foot space is dedicated to a creativity studio where up to 200 children and adults can do arts-and-crafts projects.

Nancy DeBellis, Director of Retail Development for Binney & Smith, the makers of Crayola products, says that they want to use Crayola Works "to develop a tighter relationship with the people who buy and use our products, and to learn what they are looking for from our brand." They do that by offering

FIGURE 2-1   Crayola Works greets visitors with a colorful playground for the brand. Photo courtesy of Binney-Smith. Allan Holm Photography.

an expanded range of products and by using the creativity studio as a learning lab for testing new products under development.

Zoogles, collectible plaster-cast characters that you paint, were being product-tested in the studio in late 2002 for release in March 2003. The Zoogles, whose characters each come with a distinct persona and biographical history, were available as a painting activity kit in the studio. A Crayola marketing team spent time with the kids and adults who were painting these special advance-release toys; they listened to customer questions, tested names for the characters, and fine-tuned the toys' instructions. "It was basically a 30-day customer focus group," says DeBellis, "which was an extraordinary opportunity."

Crayola Works is itself a testing ground—for multiple business models that the brand is considering deploying elsewhere.

FIGURE 2-2 Product playspace meets arts and crafts and kids' creativity inside the Creativity Studio. Photo courtesy of Binney-Smith. Allan Holm Photography.

There is the retail store, of course. And the studio, whose admission price is the purchase of one activity. These activities change each month, with an average of 10 available at a time for a range of prices (from $7.99 to $29.99) and for a range of ages. Friday nights have seen 15-year-old boys custom-painting their soccer balls as preschoolers sat at the next table using color wands. School groups are booked every day (as well as church groups and scouts) for Curriculum Connections, where art teachers customize programs that tie art across the fields of science, geography, math, and language. Birthday parties have been particularly in demand, as has the Made By Me program, a sort of arts-and-crafts child-care option for the mall. For $30, parents with their shopping hands full can drop off children aged 5–12 for 90 minutes, during which the lucky kids have a snack and make four hands-on creative gifts for their grateful family.

Crayola Works is a new space and a new experiment. It benefits from an array of engaging ways to delight and learn from customers, and it enjoys a choice location from which to attract them. Located in one of the top four retail markets in the U.S., Arundel Mills provides strong local and tourist demographics and a crucial educational market as well. The relationships formed in the store and studio are continued when customers leave the space too, via an email newsletter. The subscribers who tested products still on the drawing board (like glow-in-the-dark Model Magic clay) receive follow-up offers to buy unique products made only for the store. Responses to exclusive offers have been as high as 40 percent.

The Crayola Works show is part of Crayola's strategy to control its brand destiny by moving from a product-only positioning to a positioning as an arts and crafts brand that offers creative experiences. They aim to focus on positive feelings adults have for the brand and getting them to pass that on to their kids, and to give kids new and different ways to express their creativity through the brand. Moreover, they want to pursue part of the brand's core mission, which is to keep creativity in schools in the face of widespread cuts in arts funding. These goals are ambitious, but by creating an experiential space that is both extremely fun and participatory, the Crayola brand has created a terrific show that looks poised to achieve them.

IMMERSIONARY SPACE AS SHOW

When a space becomes show business, we call it *immersionary* (immersive + visionary). These environments create a show that completely *immerses* the customer in an experience of the brand, and offers a *vision* that links the brand to their own lifestyle and values.

Such experiences may be created inside retail stores, in nonretail play spaces, in branded destination experiences, or in brand museums or theme parks. In each, there is a unique opportunity to differentiate the brand, engage customers, and build brand relationships through an environment where customers can meet and interact with the brand on an ongoing basis.

The experience of an immersionary space lacks the sharp focus of a live show's dramatic performance. Participants tend to come and go, for longer or shorter visits, depending on their wants and needs. Each visitor's show overlaps with the others'. However, for building relationships, immersionary space shows have a particular advantage: they provide an ongoing live experience where companies can meet customers, and customers meet each other. Customers can come back to the show repeatedly, at their convenience, and can interact with the brand continuously.

The 1990s saw entries into creative retail space by a host of new players such as Nike, Disney, Warner Brothers, Nickelodeon, and the NBA. Many were extending their brands into merchandising for the first time. The mixed results proved that 3-D advertising in a showcase retail store is a tough proposition, and that themed merchandise in a themed environment is often not enough. What adds more value, and a higher ROI, is to provide a real experience, to make it a show—as we saw in The NBC Experience Store, which offers a mix of experiential retail and live interactions via its Theater and the linked Studio Tour.

The best shows created in customer spaces are hybrids that offer a range of interactions and value added and use their one-on-one experience to talk to customers. Like Crayola Works, these shows can be research and learning tools for companies: places to try out new merchandising ideas and get the kind of direct feedback that you can't get from selling products through other channels. Great immersionary space shows are highly participatory, even social environments.

Participatory shows need to understand that customers won't return unless you offer a variety of experiences or activities for them, accommodate their different needs, and continue to innovate. MRA International, which worked to develop the concept for Crayola Works, offers an apt set of guidelines for participatory show spaces:[8]

- Provide a mix of individual activity and group activity offerings (especially to appeal to weekday group visits such as school or tour groups).
- Provide both short and longer time-frame activities (for different types of visits and visitors with different attention spans).
- Provide guided and unguided activities.
- Provide a balance of sequential and product-oriented activities (e.g., making a toy bear) as well as nonsequential exploratory activities.
- Deliver both a fun experience and some take-away value (customers enjoy the process and they have something afterwards that encourages a return visit).
- Vary your menu of offerings regularly so no one—staff or customers—gets bored.
- Provide a mix of activities within spaces (e.g., kidcentered spaces need adult activities too, to keep the parents coming back, or even get them to come on their own).

Let's look at some more cases of shows that create an immersionary space and what lessons each can offer.

INTERACTIVE RETAIL SPACE SHOWS

In 1999, Sears decided to put on a show for its male customers interested in tools. Their advertising campaign for women ("Come see the soft side of Sears") had worked well, but Sears had a harder time getting men to make the trip to the mall to find out what Sears had to offer them.

They knew that a man's entry point to Sears is the tools department, and they wanted Sears to be branded as America's Best Tool Store. But they were hampered by customer perceptions that store personnel were not tool experts and by the misperception that Sears sold only its own tool brand, Craftsman—even though they sold other brands as well.

Rather than creating a new stand-alone show space, Sears invented what it dubbed Tool Territory, a playground for tool-loving men. This new show-within-a-store was tested in 13 stores in its first year, and by 2002 nearly half of 870 Sears nationwide had put on the show. The Territories are up to 10,000 square feet and offer row after row of power tools of every kind, each one powered up and ready to be picked up and tried. Browsing enthusiasts engage in small arms races over the voltage and power of handheld tools in a revamped product line that includes every major competitor brand, such as Makita, DeWalt, and Power Cable. A master craftsman is on hand, dressed in a black uniform with the Tool Territory logo and slogan, "Where Tools Rule." These craftsmen are genuine experts, with 10, 15, or 20 years' experience in the building or automotive industries. They instruct customers, answer questions, and demonstrate the latest in product innovations like strap wrenches, bolt-out tools, and reversing ratchet wrenches in a shop space called the What's New Center. The Tool Territory is open and visible to the rest of the store, and festooned with placards that shout out the mantras from its advertising: "18,000 tools in stock. Collect them all." "Finally, daycare at the mall for men." "The man who dies with the most tools wins." The show has allowed Sears to gain credibility by displaying a wider array of competitor brands, while using customer interactions to show off what it sees as Craftsman tools' competitive edge.

Its success has also been leveraged in nonparticipating Sears stores through an initiative known internally as Tool Territory Light, whereby lessons learned from the Territory are applied to marketing, merchandising, and pricing at other

FIGURE 2-3   Sears's Tool Territory: he who dies with the most tools wins. Photo courtesy of Sears.

stores, minus the interactive space, experts, and product demonstrations. Three years into the program, the results are a testament to the power of show business in a retail space: consistent improvements in tool sales have been measured in both cases, but with a significant advantage in Tool Territory vs. the nonexperiential Tool Territory Light.

Sears's show offers an example of how you can build a show space within a larger store, and provides two important lessons. First, the right staff is essential to delivering an interactive customer experience and immersing your customer in the brand. Second, a hands-on learning environment can transform your relationship with your customers and dramatically increase their interest in and understanding of your products.

A company in a very different category, Apple Computers, is using a remarkably similar approach to immersionary space. Apple began launching its new interactive Apple Stores in 2001, opening 53 stores over two years in key locations around the U.S. The Apple Stores are different from any other computer stores you have ever seen. They offer a participatory branded environment for customers to learn more about the brand's products hands-on, with the assistance of expert guides and tutorials. The Apple Stores reflect the design savvy that the company is known for in its products. Hardwood floors, white walls, curved shapes, high ceilings, and subdued lighting give it the look of an art gallery or a trendy futuristic bar. Half of the retail space is dedicated to demo stations where visitors can explore and play with products, making iMovies, burning CDs with iTunes, and using digital cameras. In the back is the Genius Bar, where you can sidle up to a local guru and ask your most intractable Mac computer question. And in case you stump the genius, there's even a special red phone to call headquarters for the answer (a touch supposedly lifted from an old *Batman* episode). The show also includes a theater with a 10-foot HDTV screen for product demonstrations, movie-making contests for local kids, and workshops like the Made on a Mac talks where professional photographers, CPAs, and video editors show off the brilliant work they do on their Macs.

The stores are part of Apple's overall marketing strategy to expand its customer base by recruiting first-time users to the Macintosh platform. With a current market share of about 5 percent, Apple wants its stores to be an important strategy tool for reaching out to the other 95 percent who are currently not considering a Mac. The strategy starts with a plan to ambush these customers by building the stores where the target audience is already spending time. The Apple Stores then use interactive show business to show off the Mac as the hub of a digital lifestyle. Apple prides itself on having the best platform for connecting a home computer to digital cameras, camcorders, and MP3 players. Showing that to new customers (and getting them to reconsider the non-PC alternative) requires a new kind of customer experience: a place where customers can play with the coolest peripheral gadgets and interact with staff who can educate, entertain, and attract new Mac disciples. The place and the players need to be hip but friendly, and the whole experience fun.

With its Apple Stores, the company has used show business to enter the retail category for the first time. With only a few dozen Apple Stores planned, compared with 3000 other retail locations nationwide, the scale of the stores is limited, but Apple has said it hopes they will soon be profitable, beyond their advantage as a marketing tool. Although it would have been less costly to provide a one-on-one experience through traveling events like Intel's mobile messenger show, this approach wouldn't have created a show that could pay for itself. Given Apple's strong cash situation at the time, their bolder choice seems smart.

THE FLAGSHIP STORE AS SHOW BUSINESS

Flagship stores sometimes attempt a kind of immersionary experience, but too often they're just the same-old retail in fancy dress. A few companies go beyond that to actually incorporate what we consider show business elements in a flagship store. A recent example is Prada.

Hoping to expand and strengthen its brand image, Prada has decided to complement its many small fashion boutiques with a series of super-sized stores in a few cities around the world. Building a show out of what Prada does best, they aim to extend the company's core competence in cutting-edge design and reflect it in the architecture of their new premier retail spaces. The New York superstore in SoHo was designed by world-famous architect Rem Koolhaas. The show was built to serve as a performance space for fashion events, as well as a store. The environment combines Koolhaas's high-concept design with hi-tech features like dressing rooms whose glass walls turn translucent with the push of a button. The spectacular glass elevator is designed to be completely transparent, without even any visible metal parts, just elegant sliding glass. Merchandise displays hang from ceiling grids, allowing for flexible redesign of their positioning above the beautiful pink resin shelves and marble floors. At the center of the store is "The Wave"—a central sloping set of broad steps that descends from ground floor to the lower level, and serves as either a dramatic display space for shoes or bleachers for a performance when the store hosts a fashion show.

Prada offers an unusual environment that immerses you in their brand. Though it remains to be seen what the benefits of this costly flagship store will be, the investment is a brand-building exercise, and certainly displays the brand in a mesmerizing way. But without a strong component of customer participation or learning, or customer interaction with staff, the spectacle of a flagship store may not deliver the depth of brand affiliation that show business makes possible, and thus may not provide the right experience.

BRAND MUSEUMS: THE WORLD OF COCA-COLA

Many show business spaces do not involve retail, however. Instead, the show is more like a museum or theme park about a company or brand. One such show is The World of Coca-Cola, located just three miles from Coke's headquarters in Atlanta.

Customers had been coming to Atlanta for years, asking Coke for some kind of tour or museum before the company decided on a plan and opened its show in 1990. "The aims," says Phil Mooney, Director of Coke's Archives Department, "were to help the city in its downtown revitalization, to be responsive and provide consumers something they said they wanted, and to make a landmark statement that, 'Atlanta is Coke's home. We've been here 100 years, and will be here for a long time more.'"

The show certainly is a landmark. Its entrance is presided over by an enormous suspended globe with a rotating neon Coke sign inside of it. Inside, the show business couldn't be better, as amusement and entertainment await in a world of Coke for visitors to explore. The immersionary environment is full of flashing videos, overlapping soundtracks, and sensory overload of interactive exhibits and video presentations. The galleries showcase the world's largest collection of Coke memorabilia and offer exhibits that trace the heritage of the 110-year-old company and its marketing. Visitors can watch vintage TV commercials, discover the evolution of Coke's packaging and vending (including the first soft-drink dispenser in outer space), and listen at a greatest-hits kiosk to advertising jingles sung by famous pop stars over the years. The Bottling Fantasy offers a mystifying show of zooming bottles on assembly lines that presents an aestheticized version of the bottling process: all machines, no people. Then there's the 1930s Barnes Soda Fountain, with a period jukebox of Coke songs and costumed staff playing the role of soda jerks who demonstrate how the drink used to be made. For a taste of something different, the popular Tastes of the World offers 18 thirst-quenching beverages from around the world made by Coke but unavailable in the U.S. (mango Fanta, anyone?).

The World of Coca-Cola is not afraid to be a little tacky in celebrating and encouraging its customers' zeal for the brand, either. Videos on display range from montages of global factories full of glistening bottles, to a faux-historical comic video, *The Search for Refreshment* with comedian Dom DeLouise, showing Socrates, Dr. Jekyll and others through the ages questing for the right beverage until Coke's miraculous discovery by Dr. John Pemberton in 1886. In the Take 5 history booths, the history of the United States is presented in five-year installments, each with a side note on the role of Coca-Cola in that period. The funniest show, though, is the futuristic soda fountain near the end: put your cup in place and an ultrasonic sensor triggers a series of sound effects and a stream of Coke that appears to bubble up through a column of flashing lights and leap in 20-foot arcs over your head before rippling down through a nozzle right into your cup. What show biz!

With a modest admission price of $6 for adults, The World of Coca-Cola is not intended as a revenue center. Nevertheless, the corporate museum, which is Atlanta's most popular indoor attraction, pulls in close to 1 million visitors a year, allowing it to recoup its substantial operating costs and clearly contributing to the city's tourism industry. The real success for Coke has been the brand experience provided for loyal customers and the museum's use as a public relations tool. The World of Coca-Cola has been featured on the History Channel and Food Network, during the Super Bowl and NASCAR events, and in NBC's live broadcasts of the Atlanta Olympics. It has been used for press conferences and photo ops, and has even been featured in the credits of local television newscasts.

Despite its successes, the company feels that even more could be done with a World of Coca-Cola. The exhibit space is fairly static, beyond changing the content of individual videos, and such. Because of a design choice to build the experience around a linear treatment of the brand's history, an issue began to arise by the mid-1990s of how the World of Coca-Cola could continue to evolve and follow the latest in the brand's history. Plans are now underway for the development of a second-generation brand destination in Atlanta, which will address these issues and provide an even greater experience.

BRAND DESTINATIONS

As we have seen, immersionary space can create a destination for the brand instead of a store. General Mills offers families visiting the Mall of America a Cereal Adventure immersed in the brands of breakfast cereal that the company has made famous. For a modest entrance fee, families can take a break from the mall to explore the Trix Fruity Carnival, walk through the marshmallow maze of the Lucky Charms Magical Forest, or slide down a giant spoon into a bowl of Cheerios. Other exhibits let you explore how breakfast cereal is made as you climb on a tractor, operate the controls at a make-believe factory, and walk through a giant cooker. In the Wheaties Hall of Champions, you can look through sport lockers full of vintage Wheaties boxes, sports artifacts, and information on Wheaties athletic champions.

Even brands that are not linked to consumer products have decided that they want to create a show business space for their brand. ESPN is taking brand play to "x-tremes" with a new series of skate parks, located inside shopping malls, that promote interest in its X Games programming by transporting visitors into the exciting athletic atmosphere of the TV show. The X Games skate parks feature facilities for in-line skating, skateboarding, and stunt biking, with halfpipes of all sizes, ramps for the beginner to pro, and a kids section with less daunting ramps. The parks will host ESPN events and currently offer classes and equipment rentals as well as lounges, video game areas, and retail outlets with X Games branded merchandise.

Sport brands that develop show space have an advantage in linking their brands to customers' lifestyle and social community because they easily relate to fun and engaging group activities. In these brand spaces, companies may try to offer customers a Third Place, the sociological term for some place between work and home that creates a sense of community, as discussed in Robert Putnam's book *Bowling Alone*. An ambitious show business destination of this type is currently being planned by the Dallas Cowboys as part of a proposed new stadium development for the Dallas/Fort Worth metroplex. The development, which would be anchored by a new stadium for the football team, would not only include new retail, dining, hospitality, and entertainment, but also a branded destination called Legend Square.

The idea of a destination experience for the Cowboys is appealing because of the strength of their brand (the biggest seller of sports merchandise in the U.S. and considered one of the top three sports brands in the world) and because the metroplex area lacks a significant "must-see" tourist destination for a city of its size. Legend Square would be a year-round place to experience the brand and celebrate both the Cowboys and a broader range of sports heroes. "We want to create a place where local, regional, and hopefully national heroes will be celebrated," says the Cowboys's Director of Stadium Development, Jud Heflin. "A place where other athletes will want to celebrate... and not just sports heroes, but other heroes as well. If you want to commemorate a firefighter or police officer or a local principal, this would be a place where they could be celebrated." Central to Legend Square would be the Dallas

Cowboys Fieldhouse, which, instead of just offering a Hall of Fame, would provide a place where fans can participate in sports on a variety of courts and playing fields, in amateur leagues from lacrosse to flag football. Corporate challenge courses (middle managers climbing around on ropes) would allow for subsponsorships (e.g., the Ford Explorer Course) that would help link the Cowboys brand to a broader consumer lifestyle. Competitive sport experiences would be offered for youth, and adults could participate in branded leadership seminars like The Cowboy Way, or make use of the building's meeting facilities.

This show may sound like brand extension gone amok, but the Cowboys have a track record of success in the area. By partnering with experienced real estate developers, they have already created two hugely successful upscale housing developments in the area, branded by the team's owners, Jerry and Steven Jones, whose names are synonymous with the Cowboys thereabouts. They have also built one of the nation's top-ranked municipal golf courses, the Dallas Cowboys Golf Course, in Grape Vine, Texas. This is the only NFL-branded course in the country, with carts named after famous players, the Cowboys star on every tee, and a story from Cowboys legend to read at every hole. With a guarantee of traffic from the adjacent stadium, Legend Square could be a show that creates as well as celebrates legends.

PURE PLAYSPACE: WHEN THE SHOW IS FREE

In what we call "customer playspace," there is no admission charge and often nothing for sale. These immersionary shows are rare, but they do exist. For customers, they are like a gift of pure play, an environment for interaction, fun, and learning through a brand—but no pressure to buy. For the business, the show can have rewards of its own.

PBS, the nonprofit public television producer, has recently announced plans to team up with the Mills Corporation

FIGURE 2-4   Nothing for sale in a studio for discovering and exploring the Shiseido brand. Photo courtesy of Shiseido.

(a developer of shopping malls) to create PBS Kids, a "themed play area" in malls nationwide, starting in Nashville. The play areas will feature popular PBS children's characters like Barney, Arthur, the Sesame Street characters, and the Teletubbies. They will include reading nooks, televisions with PBS programs, learn-and-play areas, Internet kiosks, and other displays. Events will include guest appearances by PBS stars as well as reading workshops and community events organized by local PBS affiliate stations.

There will be some sales of PBS merchandise at the sites, but PBS insists that this will "not be a store" motivated by sales, but a free playspace for families, a destination designed to develop its brand. Most of PBS's reward for this civic-minded space-creation will come from licensing its characters to Mills. For the real estate developer, the project is an opportunity to build a free attraction that will draw a prime demographic group (education-conscious parents shopping with

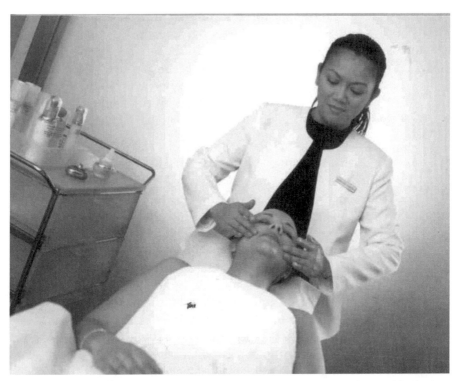

FIGURE 2-5   Shiseido's show of hospitality: interactive technology, personal beauty consultants, and free facial massage. Photo courtesy of Shiseido.

kids). That will raise the value of the retail space. Mills has pursued other creative partnerships as well (Crayola Works and the X Games parks are both in Mills malls), because they bring real value in a mall category dominated by shopping centers with nearly identical lists of chain stores.

Another version of a pure playspace opened in New York in 1999, put on by Shiseido, a market-leader for high-end cosmetics in Asia that is hoping to establish a stronger presence in the U.S. among trend-setting consumers. Their challenge was that their younger target segment was unfamiliar with the brand and perceived it as more "high end" than other similarly-priced competitors. Shiseido needed a new way to reach these customers and introduce them to the brand. So they created the Shiseido Studio.

At the Studio, customers are invited into a nonretail exploration space dedicated to beauty. Inside, they can play with and learn about Shiseido's entire line of beauty products. There are no pushy salespeople; visitors are greeted by a pressure-free environment and nonintrusive beauty consultants who are ready to answer questions and cater to their interests without thinking of commissions or sales.

Customers learn about Shiseido's 130-year history and its various product lines by inserting digital product cards into computer stations embedded in tabletops with translucent screens. Each catalog item is linked to related products with navigation maps, showing how products complement each other for optimal results. And if you're curious about the makeup but don't want to spoil the look you put on this morning, you can explore the Interactive Makeup station. It takes a digital picture and creates four different images of you with four possible makeup combinations. If you select one, the Navigator shows a video of how you could create that look and prints out information on the required products. Customers move between these technological consultants and the live beauty consultants on hand, testing out products and asking questions. They can also enjoy sample spa treatments like facial massages and sign up for free classes on skincare, makeup, and topics like "D-Stress Solutions" and "Fragrance, Experience, Meaning."

Some visitors are perplexed when they decide they're sold on the product and then discover that there's no cash register to accept their purchase. Instead, they are given a list of nearby locations where Shiseido is sold. The show at the Studio is all about engaging and luring the customer into the world of Shiseido. And the interaction and learning is mutual: customers have the option to register a customer profile and create a wish list. The resulting sales leads are linked with detailed profiles of customers' product interests based on their electronic explorations in the store. Shiseido uses this information in direct marketing that offers promotions tailored to specific product combinations customers have explored.

The nonretail show concept for the Studio came from a similar show called the Cosmetic Gardens in Japan. Starting in New York, the Studio has been replicated to 11 cities around the world. Almost 20,000 people visit the New York Studio each year. "Our goal is to educate people about the brand... the Studio is more about touching people, and building word of mouth," says Michelle Torio, the Studio's manager. "It ties to our corporate motto: teach others to live well and beautifully." Indeed.

LESSONS LEARNED

Immersionary space shows offer a wide variety of models for creating fun, engaging, extraordinary experiences for customers. As we have seen in this chapter, they include the following types:

- Interactive retail space—like the Apple Stores—where customers creatively participate, test products, learn, and interact with company employees
- Show-within-a-store—like Sears's Tool Territory—where an interactive space is placed within a larger retail venue
- Flagship stores—like the Prada superstore in SoHo—where boundary-breaking environments immerse the visitor in a visionary world of the brand
- Brand destinations—like the World of Coca-Cola or the Dallas Cowboys Legends Square—where a brand can be leveraged into a non-retail experience such as a museum, theme park, or athletic course, that builds relationships with customers
- Pure playspace—like PBS Kids or Shiseido Studio—where nothing is for sale and customers are free to play, experiment, and learn through the show
- Hybrids of these types—like Crayola Works—where playspace, product testing, customer-employee interaction, and immersion in the brand all come together

Great immersionary show spaces create new worlds for customers to experience and explore. Most important, they provide a brand experience that can be repeated. Immersion-ary shows should:

- Create an environment that completely immerses the customer in a fun, surprising, and memorable experience of your brand while offering options for varied levels of participation to suit the customer.
- Enable interaction with the customer and among customers to provide one-on-one experiences that can shape customers' perceptions of the brand, and that can be used to gather information about customers' needs and desires.
- Encourage visitors to sign up for continuing information; the customers most interested by your show space are likely to be high-value customers.
- Be innovative and flexible enough to incorporate new experiences and changes in marketing strategy.
- Partner, if advantageous, with other brands that will extend the relevance of your own brand for customers, or bring expertise in a new area (golf courses, retail stores, etc.).

Show business doesn't just happen in live performances or immersionary spaces. Quirky and unusual kinds of show business are appearing everywhere in new media and in old media rediscovered. These shows use invented and reinvented media that don't fall neatly into any marketing category. In the next chapter we will see unusual product placement in movies, a swimming pool used as a billboard, sandals that can imprint a brand all over Miami Beach, and how sticking a bra into your annual report can get investors' attention.

3 Shows for Invented (and Reinvented) Media

Anything can become a medium for show business. In some cases, show business invents new media out of ordinary objects (swimming pools, sandals, and splash guards). In other cases, by giving ordinary communication tools (documentary films, web sites, annual reports, novels) an unexpected and creative new use, media are reinvented to engage customers in their day-to-day lives.

One of the most successful independent films of 2002 was a sleeper hit called *Dogtown and Z-Boys*. This 90-minute documentary details the origins of skateboarding among a small group of California misfits in the 1970s who eventually became celebrities in this new alternative sport. The film was directed by Stacey Peralta, one of the original Z-Boys, and won several prestigious awards at major independent film festivals such as the Sundance Film Festival. What started as a limited initial release in three U.S. cities spread into a major phenomenon with the help of heavy and doting coverage in mainstream press like MTV and National Public Radio.

But except for one article in the business section of *The New York Times*, no one seemed to notice that this film was entirely financed (to the tune of $650,000) by Vans, the sneaker company whose shoes are the footwear of choice for the skateboarding subculture. This may sound like a lot to throw behind sponsorship of an independent artistic product, but Vans knew Mr. Peralta was a hero to their customers and saw his film as an opportunity to connect to them and their lifestyle by doing something less direct, less suspect, and much more valuable than a traditional media campaign.

In fact, Vans keeps a suitably low profile in *Dogtown*, which avoids making it seem crassly commercial. Their role as producers (Vans Off The Wall Productions) is mentioned only in the credits, and the product name appears only once in the film's dialogue. Instead, the camera does the talking, showing Vans on the feet of almost everyone onscreen in the entire movie. As a result, the film has been able to avoid the kind of criticism that overt product placement would likely bring in the alternative culture of independent film. But the real audience for the brand, the avid skateboarders whose culture it documents, noticed who had made it possible for their story to reach the silver screen.

Where does a shoe company get the idea to enter movie making? "It wasn't that hard an idea," according to Jay Wilson, executive producer of the movie and Vice President of Global Marketing for Vans. "Teens go to movies, go to skateboarding events. It was a pretty obvious connection." The concept started with a long profile of Mr. Peralta in *Spin* magazine called "Lords of Dogtown." When Peralta couldn't sell the idea to film his story to Warner Brothers, Vans stepped in. Wilson convinced his CEO to put up $400,000 to start, and then $250,000 to finish and promote it as their excitement over the film grew. Peralta directed the project, which remained his baby, and Vans got 80 percent ownership. With box-office totals at $1.4 million by year's end, the film has grown from a marketing coup for Vans to a big profit-maker, with more revenue to come from overseas distribution, DVD, and television.

Wilson calls this an example of self-liquidating marketing. "A friend in J. Walter Thompson asked me how I thought of it, and I said, 'You guys invented it!' Thompson's clients used to own their own shows, like the Burma Shave hours, the Gillette hours." Vans has been so pleased with the results of its first movie that they have already filmed a reality TV show with the WB network, leased out their Pipemaster's surf competition for the film *Blue Crush*, and invested heavily in a cross-promotion of an action film whose superhero also does a lot of skateboarding in Vans shoes. Meanwhile, Vans's profits have grown 66% between 1999 and 2002, driven by steep increases in U.S. sales.

SHOW BUSINESS IN ENTERTAINMENT MEDIA

In this chapter, we look at how show business invents and reinvents media. Show business can turn anything into a medium for communication: shoes, coins, even bicycle seats. Show business can also take familiar forms of communication and adapt them to powerfully communicate brand experiences.

The first place where show business reinvents familiar communications is our entertainment media: movies, TV, theater, novels. When brands become an integrated part of the entertainment that customers embrace and share with peers (i.e., a favorite TV show, not the 30-second advertisement that interrupts it) they can provide an experience that entertains and engages customers in the brand.

The boldest entertainment-media show businesses are producing content of their own—like Vans's film with Stacey Peralta, which celebrated and was celebrated by their core audience, the sports enthusiasts who use their products and serve as trendsetters for other customers.

In 2002, DaimlerChrysler's Dodge division teamed up with MTV to create a reality show called the *Fast Enuff Challenge*. The show began with casting calls and test drives in the summer to find 15 real-life drivers for a Dodge racing competition. The contestants were filmed as they trained in professional racing, lived together, learned together, and finally competed against each other and celebrities from MTV's other programs in a climactic racing showdown. The whole Dodge-centered story was then turned into a 1-hour reality TV show that aired at the end of the year.

BMW turned heads when it went into the movie-making business in 2001, producing *The Hire*, a series of short films with leading international directors—John Frankenheimer, Ang Lee, Alejandro González Iñárritu, Guy Ritchie, John Woo, and more. Each movie showed off the signature style of the director and featured major Hollywood stars (Gary Oldman, Don Cheadle, Madonna) and the recurring character of a driver behind the wheel of a BMW (played by Clive Owen). The movies were also unusual in that they could only be seen on BMW's website: a new form of advertising—and entertainment—for affluent target customers who weren't easily reached by television spots. Visitors online can watch the films, download the movies or wallpaper images to their desktop, order a DVD, read credits and plot synopses, or view trailers and shorts on the making of the films. This bold investment in online creative content has paid off in avid customer interest. More than 10 million films have been watched from BMW's website. More importantly, 2 million visitors have registered at the site, with 60 percent of those opting-in for continuing communication from BMW, and an amazing 94 percent making an online recommendation to a friend.[9]

In *Dogtown*, the *Fast Enuff Challenge*, and *The Hire*, Vans, Dodge and BMW took the lead to help create and produce original content that told a story with their brand in a central role. They were careful to partner with others with the knowledge or experience to help tell the story (Peralta, MTV, BMW's stable of Hollywood directors). Vans and Dodge also took the step of including the customers they were trying to reach in the process of making the story: *Dogtown* was a film for, of, and by the skateboarding community; *Fast Enuff Challenge* was a TV show made with and about the customers Dodge was trying to reach. This kind of show business collaboration brings close communication and bonding with customers.

PRODUCT PLACEMENT VS. PLOT PLACEMENT

Not all entertainment-media shows require a company to step into the role of executive producer. Where TV and film used to offer only static product placement to companies, new creative approaches are verging into a practice that we call "plot placement." As media buyers develop more and more sophisticated quantification of the impact and value of product placements, companies are discovering that having a product appear in the background of a scene is one thing, but to become a central plot element (à la Butterfingers candy in one episode of *Seinfeld*) may be worth ten times the cost of running a commercial in that same program. This kind of integration of a brand or product into a significant and engaging role in a storyline is what we call plot placement. Other recent and upcoming examples include:

- Award-winning English novelist Fay Weldon's use of the Bulgari brand in her romantic satire, *The Bulgari Connection*, in exchange for a sponsorship from the Italian jeweler
- The first production at the new Ford Center for the Performing Arts in Times Square: the historical American musical *Ragtime*, a tremendous popular and critical success that happened to feature a prominent role for Henry Ford and his story
- A three-month plot line on the soap opera *All My Children*, involving the cosmetics brand Revlon and thrilling corporate espionage
- The movie *The Italian Job,* in which a Mini (BMW's sporty new miniature car) plays a central and elaborate role in the title heist
- Television variety and talks shows where sponsors place their logos on sets and their products and spokespeople in comedy sketches, including Fox's *The Best Damn Sports Show Period* and a planned variety show on the WB Network that will have no interruptions for traditional commercials

We also expect to see traditional product placement continue and even increase as new technology allows product placements to be added after the fact, boosting profits on sports footage (with extra logos crammed in digitally onto empty playing field space) and syndicated reruns (Mary Tyler Moore drank Vanilla Coke?). But really, one has to ask: how valuable is it to slap your logo on the last uncovered inch of Michael Schumacher's elbow as he steps into his Formula One racecar? Show business brands instead will look to integrate their brand into the plot and deliver something enjoyable in the process.

With TiVo and other intermediary viewing technologies looming, we might even be looking at a technological "end of advertising as we know it" (i.e., stand-alone TV spots). In that case TV will likely go back to integrating programming and advertising as in the early days of the medium. Not just Lucy and Desi commenting on the smoothness of their Phillip Morris cigarettes or the Beverly Hillbillies conspicuously downing their Kellogg's Cornflakes; but all the way back to the Burma Shave and Gillette hours.

The prospect may sound dreadful (so does a lot of current TV programming), but really it's a question of how it is handled. If corporate sponsorship has to rely on crassly commercial product placements, it will be even less effective than today's advertisements. But if it can find a way to become so integrated and entertaining that people don't mind, or better yet, actually enjoy the affiliation of a favorite brand with a favorite story, the show will go on.

RABBITS AND INVENTED MEDIA

Another way that companies are creating experiences that reach the hard-to-reach is by inventing new media for their messages—quirky little shows that catch customers' attention (and hopefully stir their laughter) by popping up bizarrely in a corner of life where they are least expected.

We call this kind of invented media a *rabbit*. Rabbits are little surprises that are warm and fuzzy, or weird and funny. Our response to this is "Ah-ha!" or "How clever!" or "That's cute!" Like the rabbit that's pulled out of a magician's hat, a show business rabbit can be a pleasing, magical surprise.

The New York discount furniture retailer Basics Furniture used rabbits to help introduce its brand to a local audience when it opened its doors in the Chelsea neighborhood. They started by sprinkling 5,000 quarters around the streets of New York, the floors of taxicabs, and in the coin-return slots of pay phones. The quarters, which were real, were covered with stickers that had the store's phone number and the message, "Hi, Thrifty, we've got your furniture." The fiscally-conscious passerby who decided to retrieve the coin got a little "gotcha," but also a reward, and hopefully a smile, associated with the new brand in the neighborhood. At the same time, Basics was sending its customers home with shopping bags that read, "This is a shameless moving billboard for Basics Furniture," and included comical instructions on how to display it with correct posture. When Basic's newest tagline, "A cheap chair for your cheap ass," was introduced in both posters and on miniature signs on the back of messenger bicycles, the buzz began to spread. At one point, half the customers walking in the door said they had seen the "ass" ad, and several of the bike signs were reported stolen when customers became over-attached to the show.

"We find that the experience is exponentially increased when the right medium and the right creative work together," says Eddie Bamonte, co-creative director at STAIN nyc, who developed the Basics campaign. A good rabbit finds a medium that reinforces both the message (the bike seat) and the brand (quarters, for a "cheap, affordable furniture" company). Other creatively invented media seen recently include:

- A run-down public swimming pool outside London's Heathrow airport, repaired with support from Evian, who placed their brand on the pool's bottom, where it is visible to airplanes flying overhead
- Logos at the beach, including brand sand sculptures and a company that gave out free flip-flop sandals with

FIGURE 3-1 Rabbits appear in the unlikeliest of places. From the back of a quarter... Photo courtesy of STAIN nyc.

raised logos on the soles—leaving the brand imprinted in the sand with every footstep

- An imaginary movie trailer for an action movie called *Lucky Star*, starring Benicio Del Toro and the new Mercedes SL sedan, which was shown in theaters across Britain even though the movie never existed

- A host of brand placement options from Manhattan's GoGorilla Media, including rolls of toilet paper, fortune cookies, and dollar bills (talk about circulation!); clients can spread their message on the wrappers of condoms distributed at night clubs, or reach a male-only audience with branded urinal splash guards (yikes!)

Of course, this can all get quickly out of hand. The danger of rabbits is that when they become too popular they become an intrusion, another instance of advertising noise and clutter that customers will feel a need to retreat from. Do you really need an advertisement when you go to the restroom? In the worst cases, companies have shown disrespect for public

FIGURE 3-2   …to the back of a bike messenger. Photo courtesy of STAIN nyc.

environments by leaving marketing graffiti on streets and buildings without concern for how to get it off. IBM ran afoul of the law in San Francisco when it painted the logo of its "Peace, Love, Linux" campaign on sidewalks. They had planned for it to be done in biodegradable chalk, but when things got out of hand, the company wound up with a large fine and an unattractive perception of its brand.

The better cases of rabbits we've seen add actual value that the customer appreciates. Audi AG sent out teams to search the streets of Amsterdam and gave every parked Audi they could find a wash and a polish. The owners returned to find a sparkling finish and a note on the windshield, "Sorry, but we couldn't resist. Yours sincerely, Audi." In the case of Altoids, mysterious stickers advertising www.toohot.com didn't deliver their punch line until the audience participated and followed their lead, which added a nice element of interaction to a rabbit.

At a minimum, rabbits should genuinely entertain their target. Cleverness is of no use to a customer if it's not something relevant, and no use to a company if it doesn't generate customer interest in the brand. "Before it's even about the client, it has to be about the customer," says Bamonte. "If we don't catch their attention *and* bring them something that they like, then there's no point."

REINVENTING BORING MEDIA

Show business can also reach audiences by adding something creative and boundary-breaking to a familiar medium that audiences would normally not expect to find entertaining, let alone creative.

One standard medium that fairly begs for a show business reinvention is the annual report. To be sure, annual reports need to be informative and include technical information. But do they have to be boring and all look the same? Annual reports can be more than just financial documents that rattle off the same laundry list of strategic imperatives and core values: global, innovative, competitive. They don't have to include tacky images. By breaking boring conventions, they can express what's truly distinct about a company and communicate it with a much-needed spirit of fun.

One year Victoria's Secret's annual report came with a bra inside. Harley-Davidson's reports reflect the powerful brand community it shares with its customers, featuring pictures of the CEO in a leather jacket, an unpretentious look, black-and-white photography, and pull-out posters of their bikes of the year. One year the report included a recording of the distinctive "potato-potato-potato" sound of an idling Harley engine, which they were in the process of trying to patent.

The branding firm of Cahan & Associates has a specialty in these kinds of engaging, rule-breaking annual reports. Reports they've produced have read like a Boy Scout guide, a children's book, or—for a client that had received an inordinate amount of press that year—a newspaper, printed on newsprint. To explain the importance of Molecular Biosystems Inc.'s ultrasound imaging technology to investors, they produced a report that opened with full-page blurry photos and asked readers to identify what they saw. The story that unfolded helped readers understand the problem that MBI's technology solves for the medical profession, and not just what its current budget numbers were. This show business annual report generated 700 response cards, mostly from analysts and large investors (a skeptical audience).

"We break conventions, but never just for the sake of throwing away conventions," says Bill Cahan, the firm's founder and president. "Every concept has to come from a strategy that's signed off on by our client." Their work begins with research and interviews with everyone from senior management to factory-level workers to outsiders in the financial community, to get a full sense of the year's story for a company. They even use a Visual Rorschach Test™ to calibrate just how much show business a client is looking for ("Do something different!" can mean a lot of things). In the end, the report should tell a story that engages many audiences. "An annual report can be a sales and marketing tool, a PR tool, an employee retention tool," says Cahan. "It's an opportunity to do something unique and express why you should care about a company."

Even a direct mailing can be given show business flair if companies find a way to break customer's expectations and deliver something that speaks more directly than a glossy brochure. When Canada's major news magazine *McLean's* was creating a campaign to reach advertisers, they needed to address a misconception of the size and growth of their readership. So they took 100,000 copies of the magazine, tore them, beat them up, spilled coffee on them, and sent them to media representatives. The battered issues came with a message about how much pass-around *McLean's* copies receive (between friends, in an office, at home)—with an estimated three million actual readers of each issue.

SHOW BUSINESS ON THE WEB

With all this talk about invented media, what about the "new media?" Can the Internet be used to create an engaging experience for customers? Certainly the early attempts by companies were mostly failures: graphics-loaded sites that crashed dial-up users' computers and had little to say about the brand. As the dust settled after the Internet crash, most of the corporate sites that were still "sticky" (bringing customers back repeatedly) were ones that focused on valuable information and easy portals without a lot of frills—think of eBay, Amazon, and Barnes & Noble, or the best travel sites.

To find sites that really generate enthusiasm, interactivity, and community among consumers, it's best to look at sites that consumers have built themselves. Popular sites like televisionwithoutpity.com or the vastly popular slashdot.org have leaders who have organized the forum, but it is a large community of visitors who drive their content and direction. These are the kind of sites where you can find people connecting to each other more deeply via the Web.

One company we've seen tap into this kind of close-knit online community to add show business to their brand is the Swiss mobile phone company Orange. Orange discovered an existing graphic chat community that had been online for a long time, called Habbo Hotel. With a huge teen following, Habbo had grown from a web designer's pet project to a real online community by the time Orange offered to adopt it and sponsor the show.

The graphic design of the Habbo Hotel allows you to use an animated character to represent you as you move from room to room chatting with others from around the world, your instant-messaged words appearing as dialogue balloons as in a comic strip. Visitors dance or walk their way among the lobby, the Orange Cinema, and the game hall; walk up to other characters to meet and interact; or check into private hotel rooms to hang out with the friends they've already made. Visitors use the Hotel as an online messenger, email system, or chat room—which makes it a perfect compliment for Orange's brand and communication services. The Hotel is now linked from Orange's web site, and Orange customers can use SMS (mobile phone text messages) or Orange PrePay to buy their Habbo Credits—points used to decorate their hotel rooms and enjoy other perks. Orange not only gets to sell the site's premium services, but by tapping into an existing online community, it has extended its brand to a large and tech-savvy group of young mobile communicators. Just the kind of customers a mobile phone company's show should reach.

LESSONS LEARNED

Show business can create new kinds of experiences for customers by inventing new media for communicating or by reinventing more familiar ones. When these boundary-breaking experiences entertain and engage, they add value for both customers and companies.

The models that we've seen include:

■ Producing entertainment—like *Dogtown and Z-Boys,* BMW's online films, or the *Fast Enuff Challenge*—that delights your customers and grows out of their experiences with your brand

- Plot placement—like the Mini in *The Italian Job* or Bulgari jewelry in *The Bulgari Connection*—which integrates your brand or product into a significant and engaging role in a story-line

- Rabbits—like the Basics Furniture quarters or the Evian swimming pool—which invent new media that embody your brand and your message, and surprise and engage your customer

- Reinventing boring media—like Harley-Davidson's annual reports with bike centerfolds or the *McLean's* direct mailing of coffee-stained issues—to transform drudgery into entertaining experiences that convey what is unique about your business

- Web shows—like the Habbo Hotel—which foster real interaction with your customers by building on the communities they are already forming online

Each of these kinds of shows offers an ability to reach very targeted customer groups, and often at very low costs (or even a profit). But beware of low-customer involvement or the danger of being just more advertising noise rather than an alternative to it. To make sure your show really engages:

- Connect to strong customer communities by supporting their own creative initiatives or providing them resources to create a show or tell their own story.

- Discover opportunities to partner with customers or with experienced media producers.

- Don't plaster your brand on every square inch of viewing space—whether it's a football field or the sidewalks of San Francisco; mindless repetition is not going to make your brand mean something to people.

- Reinvent media as a way to add real value, not just to interject another piece of cleverness that you hope will "get past customers' defenses."

- Know your customers and aim your show to reach them where they already are: the TV shows they watch, the reports they read, the night clubs they visit, the web sites they love.

The best of these shows, like live shows and immersionary space shows, involve the customer in the experience, in its development, and in spreading the word about a company's brand. But how does that word get spread? Who spreads it? And where does that magical customer buzz come from? Shows that involve company and brand evangelists of all kinds, will be discussed next.

4 Buzz, Evangelistas, and Customer Shows

In this chapter we look at shows that use spokespeople—from hired enthusiasts to recruited customers to totally independent brand evangelists. These types of shows are increasingly important as consumers become less influenced by advertising and more reliant on face-to-face and peer recommendations. But when it comes to word of mouth, it's important to recognize that the show is not entirely in your hands, and that the wrong behavior can quickly spread the wrong buzz.

One brand which has used this approach successfully is Vespa. Vespa is an icon brand. The cool Italian fashion and laid-back riding experience of these legendary scooters is the kind of product experience that speaks for itself and gets customers to speak on its behalf. When Piaggio USA was preparing to bring the brand back to the United States after a nearly 20-year absence, they knew the key to success for the Vespa's return would be word of mouth.

To get customers to look at the stylish machines in action, the corporate marketing department first sent out street teams of beautiful people scootering around the fashionable streets of its key target markets. The show was meant to match the essence of the Vespa—it was all about looking good and being stylish. However, the show got some less than flattering press when it was alleged that the Vespa riders were flirting with customers over lattes and talking up the brand while disguised as everyday sexy café patrons.

Piaggio USA moved on to other approaches to relaunch the brand, but one California dealership, Vespa Riverside, decided to try street teams from a markedly different angle. "I don't hire models, I hire enthusiasts," says Ken Stansbury, Riverside's general/marketing manager. And the enthusiasts are trained through a rigorous boot camp that includes reading texts from the recent *Marketing Warfare*, back to Dale Carnegie's *How to Win Friends and Influence People*. The Riverside street teams are sent out not to be seen on their bikes, but to meet targeted leads face-to-face and talk to them about the brand. The teams are clearly identified by their Vespa dickey shirts and carry fliers with information about the dealership and upcoming test rides where customers can get a feel for a Vespa themselves. Rather than focusing on cool coffee shops and trendy young consumers, Riverside's street teams go where the purchasing power is. Yes, tattoo parlors get a visit, but more time is spent at doctors' and dentists' offices, talking to staff who can realistically afford the sticker price. The street teams don't even ride Vespas if they are targeting neighborhoods like East San Bernardino where customers are spread far apart and likely to be met indoors. Each rider carries with them a folder with business cards and notes on the leads they talk to. Back at the dealership, maps are drawn up with pins inserted to track each street team's progress across Southern California's inland empire.

"This is Navy SEAL marketing," says Stansbury. "There's a lot of reconnaissance involved, and the debriefing after each mission is intense." So far, results have been strong, with Riverside garnering press locally and in the *L.A. Times*, and sales leading the more established dealers in the region.

Meanwhile, co-branded street teams are being deployed by Piaggio USA's corporate marketing department, in conjunction with lifestyle brands like Armani Exchange, Skecher's, and Orbit chewing gum. Piaggio USA provides Vespas for the spokespeople who are handing out or talking up the partners' brands in urban markets, and local Vespa dealers join the team to spread the word about their own brand.

FIGURE 4-1 Vespa's loyal evangelists spread the buzz about the brand at rallies and group rides. Photo courtesy of Piaggio USA.

Yet, the greatest customer involvement has been generated by Vespa group rides, rallies, and owners clubs. The Houston dealership has organized "La Femme de Vespa," a riders group of women in their 40s and 50s who get together to go out, ride, and have coffee. In San Francisco, large Vespa rallies can be seen riding up and down the fabulous local hills, and riders come from as far away as Europe for the annual traveling AmerVespa rally. These events, and smaller ones, have often grown out of owners clubs that predated Vespa's recent return to the U.S. Vintage Vespa owners kept the brand alive for almost two decades while they had to go as far as Italy to get replacement parts for repairs, and now they've helped to form the core of a growing brand community whose enthusiasm is attracting new customers.

It's clearly been working: U.S. Vespa sales grew from 64 units per month in early 2001 to 1,000 per month by the end of the following year.[10]

STREET TEAM SHOWS

A great interactive show that focuses on word of mouth is street teams. Like Vespa's, these teams use hired spokespeople: not celebrity endorsers with golf clubs in hand as they pose with your product on television, but ordinary-seeming people who meet with customers at street level to talk to them face to face.

The first rule of street teams should be: always disclose. Under the moniker of "stealth marketing," there have been campaigns recently that used undercover spokespeople to pose as average consumers and act out a script to lure unaware customers. Sony and Ericsson received angry feedback for a ploy that hired actors to pose as tourists and ask passersby to take a picture of them with (surprise!) a Sony-Ericsson cell-phone camera. Microsoft tried to imitate Apple's "Switch" ad campaign with a story on their web site of a woman who had enthusiastically switched from Apple to Windows—but who was later found out to be a Microsoft PR staffer. Customers aren't stupid. Attempts to build brand equity by deceit only discredit marketing in general, and your brand in particular. Instead, build an honest enthusiasm among customers, then see what you can do with it.

A branded street team lacks the element of surprise, but it more than makes up for it with the ability to communicate deeply. "If you put a good-looking woman in a bar with your gadget, guys are going to talk to her, so why not put a Sony logo on her clothes somewhere?" asks Drew Neisser of Renegade Marketing. If consumers know they're speaking to a company representative, they are likely to ask more serious questions about a product. That kind of conversation and interaction is exactly what street teams are great for. "A body can answer questions in a way advertising can't," says Stansbury, who does

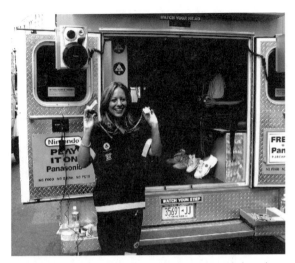

FIGURE 4-2   Kids climb inside the Panasonic Rescue Vehicle to play with the latest in electronic games and gadgets. Photo courtesy of Renegade Marketing.

street-teaming himself with his Vespas. On a recent trip to Palm Springs he found himself mobbed by young club goers early Sunday morning, just out from their all-night parties and eager to ask him questions about his scooter.

Neisser ran a street-team show for Panasonic in 2002 as part of a campaign to "Save Your Summer!" They turned three ambulances into Panasonic Rescue Vehicles that toured six major urban markets to engage young electronics lovers in conversation and to change their perception of the brand by showing off Panasonic's latest technology to prove they weren't just producing commodities. Inside each ambulance was a gaming and gadget testing room; outside, teams in EMS-like outfits wowed kids with demonstrations. One device was the size of a matchbox with a video camera, MP3 player, and digital camera in one; another was a miniature printer the same size. Rescue team members would take a kid's picture, print it out for them, and then put both devices back in their pocket—Wow!

GoGorilla Media put on a street-team show for Nescafé at the 2002 Winter Olympics to promote the launch of their Frothé beverage line. Street teamers wandered through the chilly outdoor crowds dispensing warm cups of Frothé from special thermos-like backpacks. At the same time, they answered questions about the product and handed out Frothé-branded maps of the Olympic grounds and events. The impact of the show was enhanced by the projection of a four-story-tall image of a steaming cup with Frothé's tag line, seen by thousands on the entrance wall as they arrived and exited from the awards ceremony. The story of the street teams was picked up in several national papers, and back at the Olympics the crowds were grateful for the warm pick-me-up.

"This kind of marketing is not new," observes Ken Stansbury. "Going out and showing your wares—in ancient times people did it with their pottery, in pre-Civil War people would hand out samples of their feed to farmers to try." Everything old is new again in show business.

RECRUITING EVANGELISTAS

Rather than sending their own trained team of staff out to spread the word about a product, companies sometimes get customers themselves to do the talking. You probably know the type of person buzz marketers always look for. They are the kind of consumer who is extremely resistant to advertising messages. But they are also passionate evangelists for the brands they love based on their experiences, and on recommendations from other evangelists. They are always arriving at a house or party with enthusiastic news of a new kind of oatmeal they discovered, or an affordable wine they got on a great tip from a friend. They are social and gregarious as well, so their recommendations are always circulated among a large network of friends and acquaintances.

We call these noncelebrity endorsers *evangelistas*—guerrillas of buzz, in the trenches, spreading the good word about your scooter, your movie, your car, your shoes. The enthusiasm of a small group of evangelistas can, if conditions are right, spark a chain reaction of word of mouth that will create broad interest in a new product at a fraction the cost of a traditional media campaign. Even though evangelistas have always been free spirits, choosing to endorse on the basis of what captures their imagination, companies have also come up with some novel strategies for recruiting them, and in some cases even organizing them. Using actual customers leaves a company with less control over the show, but gives greater legitimacy to their spokespeople.

Historically, the use of evangelistas has its roots in the music industry, where they have been used for years to promote bands without major recording contracts. Music street teams are kids recruited not with money but by the lure of free CDs, t-shirts, and concert tickets with backstage passes to see the band. Fans willingly join for the bands they discover and are enthusiastic about. Their job then is simply to spread the word about their favorite band—and spread its free promotional give-aways—at concerts, online, and among friends. Originally this was done ad hoc by the band members, their friends, and the groupies they managed to garner at their initial performances. Nowadays, up-and-coming metal bands like Taproot and Disturbed work with professional street-teaming firms like StreetWise, which recruit evangelistas and hook them up with the client bands whose music they like.

More recently, consumer packaged goods companies have taken to putting on shows with recruited evangelistas. For example, ConAgra Foods recruited 250 moms in 12 cities to be evangelistas for their Hebrew National hot dogs. These PTA presidents and community leaders of diverse ethnic groups promoted this all-American food at the grass roots level by forming Mom Squads that traveled around in Hebrew National SUVs, hosting back-yard hot dog roasts in their neighborhoods and handing out product coupons.

In other cases, companies have simply engaged in product seeding—giving out or loaning free samples to individuals they think will influence a targeted customer group. Calvin Klein is seeding its new Crave men's fragrance, Ford launched its Focus car with loans to trendsetting customers, and PowerBar built its sports bar brand by enlisting serious subprofessional athletes to promote and consume them. Aiming for a different audience, the Hasbro toy company recruited 1600 fourth- and fifth-grade children to act as evangelistas for the release of their POX handheld game. Their training was simple: the junior secret agents were given this hot new game for free and instructed to enjoy it, show it off to their friends, and thus generate interest and envy among game-loving peers.

One of the keys to successful evangelistas is finding the right customers to spread the word. They need to be enthusiastic about the product, but they also need to be well connected socially to communicate with and influence the right groups of people. Who your evangelistas will be depends on what you're selling and whom it will appeal to. Finding the right influencers to recruit as evangelistas may take some research. Reebok interviewed 1,000 women in Canada in order to identify 90 key influencers who received free pairs of its new U-Shuffle DMX women's shoes.

One of our favorite shows that has recruited customers to speak up for a product was the broadcast coupon promoted in TV ads trumpeting the arrival of Burger King's Chicken Whopper sandwich. The ads showed various customers clucking happily over the new sandwich and ended with a daring promise: if you clucked like a chicken at the counter when you ordered it, you'd get 50 cents off your Chicken Whopper. Soon you had Burger King customers all over America crowing like barnyard fowl at the counters of their restaurant, letting everyone within earshot know that they wanted this new sandwich, by God, and they wanted their discount. Not only that, Burger King had invented the best new system of tracking advertising impact since the Nielsen Company.

CUSTOMER SHOWS

Often the buzz for certain brands does not come from companies at all. Brand evangelistas also operate independently, sponsoring and endorsing the things that they love among friends. Sometimes they even go beyond just talking about their passionate enthusiasms and actually put on a show. We call these shows customer shows because they are truly of, for, and by the customer. Customer shows can be any of the types of show business that we've seen so far: live events, playspaces, rabbits, or street teams. What distinguishes these shows is that they originate with customers but are a show about a company's business or brand.

Examples include fan web sites like the Apple rumor sites that helped fuel the buzz for the new iMac, spontaneous rumors or word-of-mouth buzz (like the Altoids oral sex rumor), customer social gatherings (like the vintage Vespa owners group rides), or fan-created shrines to a brand (there are lots of smaller and more eccentric Coca-Cola museums in America besides the company's official one).

Customer shows are not only the hobby-horses of fans with free time; they can also be viable commercial enterprises run by outside parties targeting the communities interested in your brand. Independent user-group events are essential to communication with technology customers, like the annual Focus event that J.D. Edwards used to stage its Corridors of Chaos live show, or the Mac Expo where Apple launched its new iMac.

But some of the most passionate customer communities can be found at customer shows with little commercial or professional purpose. The extraordinarily devoted customers of Harley-Davidson put on fantastic shows for the motorcycle brand at rallies across America, a vital tradition where Harley lovers from all walks of life come together to ride and share their love for the bikes. Picturesque small towns like Westwego, Louisiana; Killington, Vermont; and Hannibal, Missouri, are suddenly transformed each year into meeting grounds for Harley riders when the regional rally comes to town. The largest such event is held in a tiny town called Sturgis—a rally that attracts 200,000 to 600,000 riders every August to make a pilgrimage to the remote Black Hills of South Dakota. You can show up for the rally on any other brand of motorcycle, we've been told—just don't expect to get out alive.

Of course the Harley-Davidson Company works hard to nurture its rider community. Sponsored by local Harley dealers, the Harley Owner's Groups (H.O.G.s, after the traditional name for the bike) boast 600,000 members at over 900 chapters worldwide. These local chapters host events ranging from Saturday hot dog bike rallies to dealer events that draw hundreds of members to their local dealership for the unveiling of the newest model. H.O.G. members are often very active in their community, participating in group events every month or more. (An Orlando dealership even boasts Harley-themed wedding services, for the truly hog-wild couple.)

A newer example of a customer show is cropping up in the unlikely field of plastic surgery: the botox party. Botox is the botulism-derived toxin that can be injected into your face, temporarily paralysing your muscles and thus removing frown lines and crow's-feet. This only lasts for a few months, though; after that a repeat treatment is needed. The recent craze for botox arose when the FDA approved its use for standard wrinkle-removal and gave authority for just about any cosmetician to inject it into your face. Immediately, botox became a way of taking care of yourself—akin to getting a facial or a manicure—for large numbers of customers. As the sting of serious medicine was taken out of this fashionable self-poisoning, consumers decided they wanted to get together socially to enjoy the experience. After all, the doctor's office does not provide the same experience as going with your friends to get your nails or hair done.

Enter the botox party. These parties are instigated by the customers, who host them at their own homes. Think of them as a Tupperware party for a confused age. In the posh pads of the Hamptons and Manhattan's Upper East Side, the well-to-do have started hosting parties at which women and men gather to share the experience of being botoxed together. Party guests spend most of the time gaily socializing and nibbling on finger food. One by one, each steps out to take their turn in a private room where a doctor waits with a needle. After a few pricks and warnings about bruising, the guest returns to the group for a shared laugh, and another quaff of Pellegrino. Not a soul in the room is frowning—because they can't! It's a new kind of initiation ritual and surely a new watermark in customer show business. The more intimate and personal a consumer product,

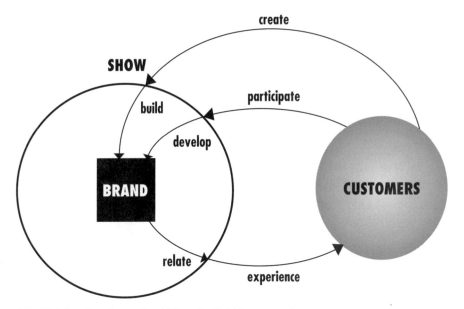

FIGURE 4-3   Show Business Brand Relationship Model for customer shows.

it seems, the more likely it is that consumers will want to connect and bond over it.

Customer shows are extremely important for companies for several reasons. Seeing a show created by their most involved customers can be one of the best ways for companies to learn about their own brand. Customer shows are also some of the best experiences for cultivating customer-to-customer communication. Although the company loses direct control of the communication in these cases, the information exchanged often has greater legitimacy and influence on customers than company-crafted information.

Customer shows complete the Show Business Brand Relationship Model that we first saw in the Introduction, by providing the arrow that allows a customer to build the brand by creating a show, just as company personnel do in other shows (see Figure 4-3). In fact, in customer shows, the company relates to and experiences the brand from the show just like the rest of the audience.

As audiences gain more independence in how they think about brands, and as they remain increasingly skeptical about corporate communications, customer shows are a crucial tool for every company that relies on a strong brand relationship with its customers. Companies like Harley-Davidson, Apple, and Vespa succeed by knowing how to encourage and support exceptionally loyal followers and by supporting the shows they put on.

WHEN CUSTOMER SHOWS GO BAD

Of course, not everything companies learn about their brands from customers is good news. Sometimes customer shows can be nightmares for companies. Think about organized boycotts and the "sucks" web sites (chasebanksucks.com, ticketmastersucks.com) where customers post their complaints. Companies need to know how to respond not only to positive customer feedback, but to negative as well.

Coca-Cola launched a $150 million promotional campaign (its largest ever) to promote reading to kids through a broad variety of events and messages, all centered around the characters of the popular children's book and film, *Harry Potter and the Sorcerer's Stone*. The initiatives taking place in almost 40 countries over three years include television ads, sweepstakes, charitable contributions, trip contests, and donations of more than a million books to classrooms and children's centers. The show also includes Story Traveler trucks, which travel nationwide promoting Reading is Fundamental Programs, the Harry Potter books, and, in more subdued designed elements, Coca-Cola. Sounds like a great show.

But not all the customers are biting (or drinking). Some parents and consumer organizations, like the Center for Science in the Public Interest, have been made queasy by this syrupy concoction of altruistic charity, Hollywood blockbuster promotion, and soft-selling of soda. Chiding Coke for using the beloved character of Harry to push "liquid candy" to kids, they have even put up a web site called SaveHarry.com, which urges visitors to share concerns with each other, mobilize in their schools, and tell author J.K. Rowling to take back her young sorcerer from the grasp of the soft drink giant.

Have you ever gotten a free trial CD in the mail from America Online? How about five or six? One a month, in a cardboard sheath? Or a metal box with no way to recycle it? After years of direct marketing that must have overflowed a landfill the size of Silicon Valley, a group of consumers finally got sick of AOL's blind blizzard of promotion and decided to put on a protest show. It has been running on the Web, with a site called nomoreaolcds.com, where those who have had enough can link up with each other and ship their stashes of unwanted discs to a special repository. Top contributors are listed on the humorous web site (over 3,000 sent in by Robotroonie in Germany), and when the total reaches 1 million CDs, the site's organizers say they plan to dump the entire pile on the doorstep of the company's headquarters. Given that they've already started to attract some media attention, that show could be a big hit.

It looks like the world's largest media giant may be listening, however. Jonathan Miller, brought in as AOL's CEO at the end of 2002, has said he plans on cutting back the lavish spending on mailings that pursue an ever-dwindling number of new online users. His alternative? Improve services to retain existing customers, and aim to raise profits by shaving costs.

Clearly, businesses need to know not just how to put on their own shows, but how they want to handle shows that the customer puts up in response. How you respond to a bad customer show may do a lot to determine its effect. Here are a few ideas:

- **Co-opt your enemies**. Listen to your critics, invite them in to see things from your side, and see if you can find a way to answer their needs. Even if you aren't able to satisfy a demand, the fact that you were open to meeting may make a difference in their perception of you.
- **Learn from them**. You may not be able to answer all your customers' requests, but if more companies looked at the postings on their "sucks" sites as report cards from customer experience consultants, they could use the lessons learned for real competitive advantage.

■ **Don't forget it's their brand, too.** If you want a brand to succeed, you have to pay attention to what customers feel about it. If the way they see it and you see it are not aligned, you need to start paying more attention to what they have to say.

■ **Get feedback before you launch a big show.** If you're starting a $150 million promotional campaign and charitable sponsorship, do some focus groups with the people who are emotionally vested in either you or your partner. You want to know if people will perceive your show as a great part of your company or as a crass attempt to sanctify yourself.

■ **Respect your audience.** Don't try to win them over by deceptive shows.

In short, don't neglect your audience. In the end, all shows are about your audience and what speaks to them—whether they are shows put on by your customers themselves, by your hand-picked evangelistas, or by your own staff.

LESSONS LEARNED

We've seen three models for shows that engage customers by talking directly to them, or having them talk to each other—shows that help to break the boundaries between customer and company, between audience and show creators:

■ Company street teams—like Vespa Riverside's dickey-shirted corps or the Panasonic Rescue Vehicles—that take your brand and your products to the customer to answer questions and build excitement

■ Recruited evangelistas—like Hebrew National Hot Dogs's Mom Squads or Burger King's Chicken Whopper cluckers—that you recruit to spread their enthusiasm on behalf of your brand

■ Customer shows—like the Harley and Vespa bike rallies or computer user-group events—that customers themselves create around your brand and their shared experience of it

Each of these types of shows can deliver a great experience—amusing, surprising, boundary-breaking, and value-creating—to customers in a way that builds interest and attachment to your products, services, or brand. To deliver the right experience, be sure to:

- Engage your customers. Talk to them; don't just expect them to see your product drive by and fall in love with it. Add an element of "wow" to the conversation you're initiating: a cool product demonstration, a rabbit (like the giant Nescafé projection), something funny. "Don't just tell me, show me."

- Give your customer a chance to get involved at the show—try your gadget, ride your scooter—or invite them to an event where they can get involved.

- Be real: let them know who you are (no posing) so customers will expect to really learn something from talking to you.

- Understand that the more personal a product, the stronger the feelings your customers may have and want to share about it.

- Accept that you're going to lose some control, but gain authenticity, when your customer gets involved in a show or takes the reins entirely.

- Remember that customer shows are your best research tool and opportunity to learn what your brand means to your customer, where you're measuring up, and where you're not.

The types of shows we have discussed in the last four chapters—live shows, immersionary space shows, invented and reinvented media, and buzz-building shows—all provide powerful tools to engage an audience. Many companies or marketers are content to attempt one type of show business as part of their communications efforts.

But why settle for putting on just one of these types of shows? Since they work toward the same goal, why not try to combine a few for greater impact?

In the next chapter we'll see how to do that and how to integrate the message of a variety of different shows in order to maximize their total impact.

5 INTEGRATING DIFFERENT TYPES OF SHOWS

Every marketer today knows the power of integrated communications. Even one-way, top-down, marketing tools like TV ads, print ads, PR, and sales promotion are more effective when they are coordinated and integrated into a single message. Now imagine what happens when you hitch the engine of integration to show business!

Victoria's Secret will give you an idea of how spectacular integrated show business can be.

THE VICTORIA'S SECRET SHOW

The retail clothing industry has been led into show business by the satin strap of a bra, by Victoria's Secret. The company, with $12.4 billion in sales, has a 15 percent share of the intimate apparel market, over 900 stores, a well-established catalog, and that rare thing: a profitable web site. Owned by Leslie Wexner's Limited Brands, Inc., Victoria's Secret is not a high-fashion lingerie house. What it sells so well is the fantasy of fashion and elegance.

The beginnings were modest: The Limited bought a few lingerie stores in San Francisco and dressed them up, then successfully took the concept national with the help of a sexy catalog. Since 1995, Victoria's Secret has gone from imitating marketing ideas of true luxury retailers to becoming the model for some of those same retailers by creating the truly inimitable Victoria's Secret Fashion Show. Every step of this dramatic progression has been pure show business—pushing the boundaries of fantasy and of taste, engaging (and sometimes enraging) audiences, and transforming an industry into re-imagining itself, like a teenager bonding with her first Wonderbra.

The show has been staged in retail spaces, in catalogs, in a ground-breaking series of live shows, on the Internet, and on prime-time television. In every one of these different types of show business, Victoria's Secret has kept its focus on a single theme expressed by the central item: the bra. Let's take a look at the script.

ACT I: THE BOOK

Even in its early incarnation, before the web site, before the supermodels, Victoria's Secret was all about fantasy. The product in and of itself was not that exceptional. Victoria's Secret bras and panties came in an unusual range of colors, and there were always a few rather risqué numbers, but the bulk of the offerings were not that different in style and price from what you'd find in a decent department store. The difference was in the fantasy, which was writ large in the store and catalog and encoded in the name Victoria's Secret.

Victoria: think upper-class; spoiled; British, perhaps; even slightly virginal—at least on the surface, and that's where the secret comes in. Fantasies are secret desires. The fantasy is Victoria's, and she is sharing it with you, exclusively. The implied intimacy was both reassuring and alluring, and, of course, entirely illusionary.

The Victoria's Secret image was built through the catalogs that arrived unsolicited in your mailbox, nestled next to L.L. Bean and *Newsweek*. Unlike the crass Frederick's catalogs or the chaste department store catalogs, Victoria's Secret hit the right balance: wholesome enough not to offend, but full of perfect female bodies in an assortment of colors and cup sizes, stroking a silky kitten, walking alone on a beach, arching languorously, or simply staring serenely into the distance. With its hint of auto-eroticism and its welcome to voyeurism, the catalog promoted the fantasy of being pampered, of being sexually irresistible.

The catalogs weren't designed for women alone. The images went just a little beyond what the respectable media would allow (the *Wall Street Journal* once rejected a full-page Victoria's Secret ad, advising them to put a little more clothing on the model). Still, a husband or visiting boyfriend could pick it up innocently enough. Toying with the borders of tastefulness, teasing and titillating, the catalogs magnified the fantasy by inviting couples to sift through them together, stimulating simultaneously the desire to be one of those girls and the desire to have one of those girls.

ACT II: THE BOUDOIR

It takes more than a good book to put on a great show. Back in 1995, Victoria's Secret was a step up from the department store, but in terms of design it was pretty much downscale retail—with stores sadly lagging behind the successful racy catalog. Realizing that the stores hadn't peaked in their potential, Wexner brought in the design firm Desgrippes Gobé to create a new identity for the stores and packaging, with pink stripes to make the brand contemporary and fun. As Marc Gobé remembers, "Wexner recognized that women were connecting to the bra on a deep emotional level. Their rapport was stronger than the brand was able to express." The brand had to catch up, to create a brand identity to match the level of aspiration that women were already investing the bras with.

The new design brought a revolutionary lifestyle approach to chain-retail space, encompassing larger stores, fresh signature decor, and a new line of bath products. Desgrippes Gobé's immersionary store designs helped reinvent Victoria's Secret as a strong aspirational brand, realizing the fantasy of the woman who can really only afford a $20 bra but yearns to be immersed in luxury experience. Victoria's Secret set out to make their pink trademark illusion of luxury experience available to every woman.

To see how far they went, we must look back into the history of the American bra-shopping experience. Before Victoria's Secret, the average bra-seeker was probably condemned to shopping in the lingerie section of the department store in her local mall. The area was usually off to the side as though its trade was slightly shameful. There was no sensory experience, there was no illusion—unless you count the smell of a stale dressing room and its ghastly aura of florescent light.

Men who liked to buy their women an occasional sexy something were even more to be pitied. They were lucky if they could focus on their errand under the watchful eye of the stern matron who usually sat guarding the dressing room door.

The Victoria's Secret retail show was a revolution: affordable bras in a faux-boutique setting. It was never a real boutique (not with those Sale: Get 2 for $15 signs), but it acted the part with real conviction. The stores became good show business: a convincing set, with the boudoir deep-pinks; little spiral staircases and balconies gracing the space; and small self-enclosed dressing rooms tucked into cozy corners (not arrayed—as those department store dressing rooms are—like stalls in a public restroom). There is a flow to the space: you can drift from little-girl-pink full-length dressing gowns to racier red-boa-trimmed bustiers. The lingerie sometimes hangs on small satin hangers or is arrayed in colorful profusion, like ripe fruit or fresh flowers in bloom. The "cast," or sales force, reflects the customers: mostly young, high school, college, or early-career women. You can pick any fantasy, take it to a smiling salesclerk and she will wrap it all up in tissue paper, then slip it into a signature shopping bag with that titillating name. On your return walk through the mall, you carry the sign that identifies you as a participant in an erotic experience.

ACT III: THE FASHION SHOW

Victoria's Secret had been infused with a new goal, a new lifestyle identity. But what happened next ensured that the Victoria's Secret bra was no longer just a sexy, affordable, decently made undergarment, but a full-fledged aspirational sex symbol.

It was Wexner's genius to make the connection between the bra and the self-expression/self-empowerment culture of the midlate 1990s. Whereas for the 1960s woman power was about burning your bra and letting your breasts swing low and natural, 1990s empowerment seemed to be about pumping them up, pushing them up (even surgically altering them), and baring as much cleavage as possible. Sexy lingerie represented a means of self-affirmation and a claim to high style. At Victoria's Secret, women's desire for aspirational transformation was set as the central theme for all touch points of the customer experience. But how to make this illusion real?

Ed Razek, Chief of Marketing for Limited Brands, Inc., knew that transformation requires drama and spectacle. In short, show business. He came up with a bodacious idea: the lingerie Fashion Show.

At the time, internal opposition was strong. Many in the company's Columbus, Ohio-based headquarters thought the idea was way too rash and wild. And who would these runway models be? Victoria's Secret had never been able to get top-name models for its catalogs (modeling lingerie could damage a gal's career back then). To make the aspirational goal a reality, Razek needed superstars. So he offered fees too huge to turn down and pursued every other necessary detail to make the show as much like haute couture as possible—except that he didn't hold it in a fashion house. He went for the Plaza Hotel in New York City and arranged a simulcast on the JumboTron, a gigantic display screen in Times Square.

The media went wild, and overnight the unthinkable became all the rage. The money spent to put on the show was nothing compared to the free advertising that Victoria's Secret got out of it, and the Fashion Show became a revenue-generator—in multiple directions.

Each year, more models signed on. Strutting in bra and panties was no longer going to kill your career: it meant big-time exposure. Claudia Schiffer, Naomi Campbell, Yasmine Ghauri, Karen Mulder, and Tyra Banks all joined up. Razek had a hit, and a new challenge: each year's fashion show had to top the one before.

In 1999 he took the act down to Wall Street, where lingerie-clad models strutted their stuff in the heart of the investment world. Billed as high fashion and set in the most expensive restaurant on Wall Street, Cipriani Wall Street, the show lured well-heeled brokers in droves, even if it was still ignored by the true fashionati. A few humorless critics complained that the show was more flesh than fashion. But Victoria's Secret knew what it was doing—this wasn't art, it was fantasy. The show was the ultimate staging of a dream of high fashion, and it was attended by the ultimate in fantastical celebrities, including Donald Trump and Sean "Puffy" Combs.

The show wasn't bound to one theatrical location; its extraordinary staginess overflowed into the real realm of the New York Stock Exchange, where the entrance became a huge advertisement for www.VictoriasSecret.com, and supermodel Stephanie Seymour rang the closing bell. Full-page ads in the *Wall Street Journal* had primed the audience.

That same year, the Fashion Show was Web simulcast. Reportedly, Broadcast.com added 120 servers to make a total of 1000 at the eleventh hour. Even so, it was a stunning display that challenged the potency of Wall Street: a reported 1.5 million hits crashed systems in the financial district, bringing brokers to their knees and making it all the more important to be there at the exclusive live moment.

The Web disruption generated a windfall of publicity, which in turn brought more publicity. Victoria's Secret reported that the show resulted in 500,000 consumers requesting their catalog. It also provoked the National Organization for Women (NOW) to chip in a little free publicity in the way of criticism. This seemed only to add an extra thrill to the fantasy. With all the sensationalism and furor, the Victoria's Secret show took on a life of its own.

The 2000 Fashion Show was held in Cannes and was a part of the American Foundation for AIDS Research's annual Cinema Against AIDS fundraiser, which Victoria's Secret hooked up with entertainment giant Miramax to sponsor (raising nearly $2.6 million for the charity). The Hollywood connection helped levy even more glamour and glitz. The supermodels were flown across the Atlantic in a Concorde jet with custom-painted pink logos. From bras and panties to the multimillion dollar pendants decorating their décolletage, every stitch the models wore received thorough publicity. A live broadcast on the Web and on the JumboTron in New York City was watched by over two million people.

Even a national tragedy couldn't stop the 2001 Fashion Show, which went on as scheduled on November 15. This one was held in New York City's Bryant Park, which adjoins the main branch of the New York Public Library and usually hosts such high culture events as lunchtime classical concerts and the annual charity haute couture Fashion Week show. Broadcast on Disney-owned ABC, announced with Super Bowl advertising spots and major sitcom plot tie-ins, it was a media tie-in extravaganza, with models appearing on ABC talk shows and a Regis Philbin special, *Millionaire: The Supermodel Edition*. The supermodels became Dream Angels, vamping down the runway with enormous feathered wings attached to their bras (a show-business tie-in to an entire Dream Angels campaign that included store displays, catalog spreads, and the new Victoria's Secret scent, Heavenly—you get the point: integration!).

The close timing after 9/11 got the critics in an uproar. At a nearby Victoria's Secret store, NOW staged a protest against the show's hypersexualized images of women. Then the show scored this priceless scolding by *The New York Times*: "...the folly of what can only be described as soft pornography on a television network couldn't have come at a worse time." "With its bells and whistles, artificially pumped-up cleavage and outright commercialism," (using sex to *sell* things—how shocking!) the article went on, the show was, "less a cultural phenomenon...than an hour-long infomercial, a combination of ABC, QVC and T-and-A." Setting out, quite redundantly, to expose the depravity of the display, the article included a titillating condemnation of the surgically enhanced models who were "hitting their paces hard so breasts bobbled atop demi-brassieres in time to the music."

Crass? Or sexy? Well, let's just say the 2001 show was an unequivocal victory of good marketing over questions of taste.

FIGURE 5-1   The Victoria's Secret Fashion Shows have catapulted the brand into superstardom. Photo ©Dan Lecca.

Tickets to the show were auctioned at as much as $25,000 a pair to raise money for various charities. The broadcast attracted 12.4 million viewers, besting ABC's usual 9 p.m. performance. "Believe me, ABC was pleased," Razek told the

Times—despite hundreds of viewers' complaints that flooded the Federal Communications Commission (which ruled that the show was not obscene) and letters to Disney and to advertisers from members of the American Decency Association, the Parents Television Council, Concerned Women for American, and NOW. Clearly, the protests were what we call a bad customer show. Was any of the fuss worth listening to? Grace Nichols, Victoria's Secret Stores President and CEO, says, "We're a lingerie brand. We respect people's right to have their own opinion about what is sexy. We also know that we have a wide audience. You don't get over $2 billion in lingerie sales if people don't like what you're doing."

The 2002 Fashion Show (which was briefly interrupted by anti-fur protestors who were edited out before the show aired) was hosted by Viacom-owned CBS, which put up a smashing Fashion Show web site with skin-baring video clips and, to give it all a legitimate fashion-world feel, biographies of the stars (highlighting their self-directed careers and their charitable projects), as well as backstage interviews. And how's this for an integrated experience: every single supermodel interviewed backstage (hair in rollers, assets concealed in a dressing gown) gave an "unrehearsed" version of the same line on the exploitation/pornography issue: the show was about women feeling powerful, expressing themselves and their sexuality, feeling good about themselves. The Fashion Show was for, by, and about women.

ACT IV: THE FANTASY GIFT, THE FANTASY FRAGRANCE

Once you've created so much excitement, how do you keep a brand from peaking and then petering out? The answer is in the mix. While Victoria's Secret launched an additional show, the Swim Suit Fashion show in 2002, they kept the action going between the extravaganzas with cunning innovations. There is the scent, Heavenly—tied in with the supermodel Dream Angels theme and currently a leader in the fragrance market—and a prospering cosmetics line. Victoria's Secret also began to offer exclusive Fantasy Gifts, including jewel-studded bras and super-luxury safari travel adventures. Improbable and outrageous, these gifts weren't really proffered as purchases, but as a new imaginary realm that would bring the Victoria's Secret fantasy world to dizzying heights. The Fantasy Gift brought a little bit of the fantasy Fashion Show to the web site and to smaller live events that helped plump up brand power.

The Fantasy Bras, jewel-studded and worn by supermodels, helped buoy the buzz between Fashion Shows. Tyra Banks graced a Harry Winston Bra worth $3 million. Daniela Pestova was supported by a $5 million number with 77 carats of rubies and 330 of diamonds. The 1999 Millennium Bra made the leap to $10 million, and was modeled by Heidi Klum. She also rounded out the 2001 Heavenly Star Bra, a concoction of some 1,000 pink sapphires, with platinum and diamonds, designed by the jeweler Mouawad and weighing in at $12.5 million. Giselle Bundchen breasted $15 million worth of diamonds and rubies to the opening of a new Victoria's Secret store in Manhattan.

The greatest pleasure and publicity comes from giving, as when Victoria's Secret extended its Hollywood connection by awarding Diamond V Bras (valued at a mere $1,500 apiece) to the 2000 Oscar winners for Best Actress and Best Supporting Actress. It has become a yearly PR ritual, with talk show hosts asking Oscar nominees how they'll wear the bras, and Victoria's Secret sizing up their cup measurements.

Is this over the top? Undoubtedly. That's part of the fascination—crossing the threshold of taste, laying it on too thick. Taste remains a mystery, which is why transgressing its borders brings such delightful fascination. Whether for sheer absurdity or freedom of fancy, Victoria's Secret strives to expand the horizon of desire, and keep people participating—talking, emailing, dialing the toll-free number out of pure desire to believe.

ACT V: THE WEB SITE

A bit slow on the uptake—especially for a business whose sales are driven by visual appeal—Victoria's Secret launched its web site in December 1998. But what a launch. The site was preceded by a simple "splash page" set up to capture email addresses of potential customers—approximately 500,000 signed up, according to Victoria's Secret. The only problem, initially, was handling all the traffic the site drew. But within a couple years, it was fast, efficient, and seductive to meet demand. It has become the fourth most visited retail apparel site on the Web (according to Media Metrix data).

From the start, the site was not envisioned as an alternative to the catalog, but as a whole new extension of the fantasy. It included an interactive Bra Salon, a Glam Lounge that screened the latest Victoria's Secret television commercial, a photo gallery with information on the catalog's popular models, and an area of exclusive Fantasy Gifts. The interactive part of this, though not as wild as a Fantasy Gift safari or as glamorous as the fashion shows, offered a good healthy erotic escape for the desk-bound: tender little videos with soft music, images of women in every imaginable PG-rated pose. Even the error message page continues the fantasy, with a peeved-looking full-bosomed blond wearing only a black lace demi-cup bra and matching thong (one guesses) panties, kneeling tautly before an open laptop.

MEANWHILE, BACKSTAGE, BEHIND THE VELVET CURTAIN...

Okay let's get really sexy. Come on and take a peek behind the dressing room curtain and see what's wooing the return customer. Some supermodel in her undies? No, it's CRM, mainframes, a call center, and a big warehouse. Not sexy? Guess again. Remember, this is about customer empowerment, and the customer doesn't feel like a powerful, sexy goddess unless she is being pleased and pampered.

Generating expectations this outrageous, how did the brand keep up? It's one thing to hitch a juggernaut to your brand; it's another for the brand to hold together over the ride—and emerge larger and more powerful than the juggernaut itself. As an aspirational brand, Victoria's Secret had high potential for multiple channel sales, but a confused customer interface could have spoiled all that. The customer experience, in which fantasy played such a crucial role, needed to be smoothly consistent at all touch points.

By launching new fashions and products in all three retail channels simultaneously, Victoria's Secret heightens the sales kick. With delivery within 24 hours to most parts of the world, the latest lacy nothings hurry into customers' hands before their fashion arousal can fade. Brand managers can count on ready and seamless customer service. Just imagine the rush they must get, free from dependence on distributors and dealers whose mishandling most manufacturers must endure with no possibility of direct influence!

No great show happens without a great backstage crew to support the dramatic action. This means a management team that understands how to cultivate customer experience—and Victoria's Secret has been able to attract the best, including Grace Nichols and Robin Burns, former president of Estée Lauder. No less important, we argue, are the salespeople and call center crew who add intimacy to the fantasy, and the integrated systems to back everyone up.

The pair of lovers cuddling behind Victoria's Secret's great earnings growth are fashion and low inventory—and you can't pull off that coupling without terrific integration. Victoria's Secret's distribution system is efficient to begin with because the company uses the same mainframe and the same distribution center for web and catalog orders. That makes it possible to integrate style, price, and retail performance, so there's less confusion for customers and more consistency in availability and delivery time.

Repeated gratifying encounters and confident expectations of performance go along with creative little innovations that pique the customer's interest—like the online gift reminder service that uses email to help lovers keep special dates in mind. Understanding that irksome delays can dilute desire and brand resonance overnight, Victoria's Secret never jilts a customer. The company has developed consistent and sensitive OOOO! (that's Online One-On-One, darling) with customers so that it can even cushion the occasional disappointment. If an item is temporarily out of stock, you'll get your "Unavailable" note with a seductive little suggestion for a substitution in another color or style. Try a little tenderness to transform brand resonance into brand relationships.

EPILOGUE: HOW TO KEEP THE RELATIONSHIP FROM GETTING STALE? THE TOUCH FACTOR

While staying true to their core, every few years Victoria's Secret gets a makeover to refresh her look. Victoria's Secret's parent company is also getting a facelift, having changed its name from The Limited, Inc. (associated with chain stores selling affordable clothes) to Limited Brands, Inc. in a self-proclaimed effort to reposition itself as a portfolio of life-style brands. (It also owns Bendel's, the renowned New York City luxury clothing store.) So what's in store for the Victoria's Secret supershow?

The Victoria's Secret flagship store, which opened in New York's Herald Square in November 2002 (the day before the 2002 Victoria's Secret Fashion Show), previews a new elegance for the brand and an updated commitment to immersionary retail space. The $15 million store is located on one of the world's busiest street corners, with 10,000 pedestrians passing every hour. Go inside the store, though, and all the hustle and bustle dissolves behind you. The store's subdued color tones and marble and terrazzo floors create a sophisticated stage for the glowing lingerie. The look is more modern, less Victorian. The entrance way is quite grand, a supremely uncluttered high-ceilinged space that Victoria's Secret calls the "decompression zone," where the customer is allowed to clear her mind and enter a mood of receptivity for the pampering that awaits her.

With square footage going at astronomical rates in this part of town, how can Victoria's Secret afford the illusion of having space to squander on serenity? It's done with show business resourcefulness by minimizing storage space (deliveries happen round-the-clock, so the ratio of storage to retail space is impressively low) and using new brand extensions. Special premium-priced one-of-a-kind lingerie (as costly as anything at La Perla or Bendels) has its own luxurious section of the

FIGURE 5-2 Victoria's Secret's latest show business environment: the flagship store heralds a bold new look. Photo ©Peter Aaron/Esto.

store. There's also Victoria's Secret's beauty line, comparable in price to Lancôme and the other luxury brands, which can generate excellent sales volume in just a fraction of the retail space needed for lingerie sales.

The growth of the fragrance line also illustrates another way that Victoria's Secret understands show business. There has been barely any advertising for this new line, whose revenue, nonetheless, has risen by double digits at a time when other companies are seeing a drop in fragrance sales. The new line has been marketed largely by translating the sexiness of the lingerie to the stores' fragrances and cosmetics.

Victoria's Secret also focuses on enhancing the customer experience in-store. Sales reps are chosen and trained with an emphasis on the "touch factor": their ability to create rapport while being sensitive to customer receptiveness. Special pampering, like a lip makeover or a hand massage given with a test of hand lotion, helps nurture sales and customer relationships.

Victoria's Secret knows that real value comes from dialogue and relating with customers and employees. Nichols and other executives make a point of connecting with customers in the stores to find out what they are looking for and where they're willing to move next. By talking to customers in Southern Florida stores, Victoria's Secret discovered the hip-hugging stretch panty known as the Brazilian tanga, and marketed versions that helped spark an international trend. "It's very up close and personal," says Nichols, "It happens on the floor. You can't get this from a focus group in a clinical office setting."

Victoria's Secret makes a point of being by, for, and about women. Nichols, one of three women who hold the top positions in the company, has been known to work a shift at a selling station just two days before Christmas. Having your female CEO on the front lines during the holiday rush is a great morale-boosting show for employees, as well as a great way to get a taste of the customer's shopping experience.

Victoria's Secret believes in using a show business approach for executives as well. Quarterly sales meetings are designed to be entertaining, featuring special video compilations of the brand's best new press coverage. "When Conan [O'Brien] mentions the brand and says something outrageous, it works for us. It's a great thing to get people laughing at a quarterly briefing," says Nichols. Experiencing the brand's celebrity-hood helps enhance associates' pride and sense of fun and spirit. Inside and out, Victoria's Secret is spectacularly integrated.

MORE EXAMPLES OF INTEGRATION

Victoria's Secret is not the only brand we've seen that combines and integrates different shows and different types of show business. For example:

The NBC Experience combines a live show (its behind-the-scenes tour of the network) with an immersionary store space.

Apple Computers has used show business in its new stores (immersionary space shows) and in its product launches that combine live spectaculars with customer shows on the Web.

In addition to making a show out of its documentary film, *Dogtown and Z-Boys*, Vans has bought up or created from scratch six triple crown sport competitions (live shows) for the six "core sports" at the core of its brand. It has even leased out these shows for use in other people's movies. (More profit from show business!)

Intel has done more shows than just the Mobile Messengers launch event with street theater and live concerts. It has also put on a traveling "digital dorm tour" with Microsoft that takes an immersionary experience of the joys of computing to college campuses. And it sponsored and created an experiential pavilion for the *Area: One Music Festival* (with artists like Moby, Outkast, and Incubus) that traveled to 17 different cities. The pavilion included a digital music zone where the audience could use computers to remix samples of the bands' own music and post their creations on the Web. Fans also lined up to email friends digital pictures taken of themselves in the crowd by Intel (spreading the word of the brand and the show).

LESSONS LEARNED: INTEGRATING MULTIPLE TYPES OF SHOWS

If you have the money and the personnel, use show business in a range of different types: combine a spectacular retail environment with live pageants, or festivals with groundbreaking and amusing new media, then reinvent your web site with an interactive game that gets customers talking and spreading the word. By using a range of show business, companies can break through the clutter of advertising and differentiate whole brands in the minds of their audience.

Integrating these shows is absolutely crucial for a company to leverage the real impact of variety itself. Shows should reflect the essence of the brand, share a common sense of style and humor, and develop overlapping themes, bringing these all together like the different acts in a play or musical.

As we have seen in this chapter, Victoria's Secret does this spectacularly. Their shows have varied broadly, but each has found a balance of entertainment, taboo- and rule-breaking, and ways to engage the audience. They have also all been integrated around a central set of themes and an identity for the brand and the company, Limited Brands, Inc. In combining them all, this show business whirlwind has managed to redefine the category.

The possibilities for integrated show business are just beginning to be explored. Of course, creating even one good show is not an easy task. Beyond the creative side of developing an experience that will delight and engage customers and break the boundaries of their expectations, show business also needs to be successful for a business.

In the next section, we cover strategic issues of show business and show you how to make show business a business success.

II HOW TO MAKE SHOW BUSINESS A BUSINESS SUCCESS

In Part I, we looked at different types of shows and provided best practices for each type. We now look at the strategic management issues of show business that will determine the success of a show business project.

These issues include:

- How to keep your show *on-brand* through each stage of its development so that the show reinforces your brand, builds brand equity, and moves your brand in the right strategic direction (Chapter 6)
- How to understand your customers so that your show will build profitable relationships (Chapter 7)
- How to extend the impact of your show to achieve the maximum possible reach (Chapter 8)
- How to budget for your show and measure its return on investment (ROI) (Chapter 9)

In this part, we draw on the cases we have introduced in the previous chapters of this book. As we return to them, we learn how the companies achieved their strategic objectives and delivered business value.

6 EIGHT STEPS TO KEEPING YOUR SHOW ON-BRAND

This chapter presents an eight-step framework that keeps your show aligned with your brand. Alignment ensures that your show will reinforce rather than confuse the identity of your brand. This helps your show to become part of your brand strategy and a tool for building brand equity.

The eight steps of this framework can be seen below in the *Eight-step framework for keeping a show on-brand*. Moreover, each step is illustrated in *Cases of the eight steps to keeping a show on-brand* (on page 94) with 10 cases that we introduced previously.

EIGHT-STEP FRAMEWORK FOR KEEPING A SHOW ON-BRAND

1. Know Your Brand Identity
2. Know Your Brand Strategy
3. Know Your Target Audience
4. Know Your Strategic Challenges
5. Identify Show Objectives and Expected Outcomes
6. Implement, i.e. Put on the Show
7. Integrate With Other Marketing
8. Measure Brand Impact and Alignment

CASES OF THE EIGHT STEPS TO KEEPING A SHOW
ON-BRAND

CASE	**Intel**
1: IDENTITY	Performance leader in computer processors
2: STRATEGY	Build demand for chips in laptops
3: AUDIENCE	Mass consumers
	Business consumers
	Investors
	Press
4: CHALLENGES	New product
	Product not visible
5: OBJECTIVES	High visibility experiences
	Demonstrate theme of mobility
	Lifestyle appeal
	Increase traffic to retail stores
	Generate media coverage
6: IMPLEMENT	Mobile laptop teams
	Product demonstrations
	Custom concert
7: INTEGRATE	Coordinated advertising campaign
	Retail promotion
8: MEASURE	Media impressions
	Investor response
	Traffic to stores
	Face-to-face interactions
	Quantitative and qualitative surveys
	Cost per sample measurement

CASE	**SAP**
1: IDENTITY	Stable provider of e-business solutions
2: STRATEGY	Leverage experience and market share
3: AUDIENCE	B2B enterprise software users
4: CHALLENGES	Convey complex products
5: OBJECTIVES	Demonstrate commitment to educating customer
	Show market-driven focus
	Interact with customers
6: IMPLEMENT	Mobile showroom
	Theater space
	Guided demos

7: INTEGRATE	Integrated with ad messages
8: MEASURE	Purchase intent and behavior
	Lead collection on suspect basis
	Correlate timing to closings
CASE	**Crayola**
1: IDENTITY	Creativity, learning, childhood
2: STRATEGY	Move from product-only positioning to providing experiences and solutions
3: AUDIENCE	Children aged 2–15
	Parents
	Educators
4: CHALLENGES	Untapped brand equity
	Insufficient brand affiliation
	Need to understand customer needs
5: OBJECTIVES	Brand immersion and affiliation
	Link to arts in schools
	Interactive "third space"
	Customer insight
6: IMPLEMENT	Varied creative activities
	Product testing
	Expanded product range
	Immersionary environment
7: INTEGRATE	Crayola Factory show
8: MEASURE	Customer feedback
	CRM registrations
	Direct marketing up-selling
CASE	**Vans**
1: IDENTITY	Worldwide leader in core sports
2: STRATEGY	Create inclusiveness for all sports and all levels of athletes
3: AUDIENCE	Serious sport participants
	Periodic participants
	Emulators
4: CHALLENGES	Limited sponsorship opportunities in some sports
	Customers resistant to traditional advertising
5: OBJECTIVES	Leadership in competitive events for all core sports
	Become the customer
	Collaborate with customer
6: IMPLEMENT	Create/sponsor media to document community

7: INTEGRATE	Suite of triple crown competitions
8: MEASURE	Face-to-face interactions
	Event response
	Film response

CASE	**Vespa**
1: IDENTITY	Iconic style and ease
2: STRATEGY	Capitalize on referral ability and user evangelism
3: AUDIENCE	Upscale professionals
4: CHALLENGES	Brand relaunch
	Limited resources
5: OBJECTIVES	Generate customer evangelism
	Partner with matching lifestyle brands
6: IMPLEMENT	Street teams
	Owner's groups
	Rallies
	Test rides
7: INTEGRATE	Corporate marketing for brand awareness
8: MEASURE	Face-to-face interactions
	Lead generation

CASE	**G-Shock**
1: IDENTITY	Chic, outrageous, urban style
2: STRATEGY	Build brand awareness and involvement among trendsetters
3: AUDIENCE	Fashion professionals
	Sports enthusiasts
	College music scene
4: CHALLENGES	Crowded competitor environment
5: OBJECTIVES	Edgy one-on-one customer experiences
	Unforgettable press launch
6: IMPLEMENT	Multiple events targeted at different audiences
7: INTEGRATE	Matching tone in print campaign
8: MEASURE	Trendsetter adoption
	Media impressions

CASE	**Sears**
1: IDENTITY	"America's Best Tool Store"
2: STRATEGY	Build customer expectation for Sears as best tool store

3: AUDIENCE	Male tool-buyers
4: CHALLENGES	Unfocused appeal to males Male resistance to mall location Perceived as one-brand house
5: OBJECTIVES	Get men in the door Compete on all brands Offer expertise (authority) Make it fun (playful)
6: IMPLEMENT	Interactive space within store Expert staff
7: INTEGRATE	Integrated advertising "Tool Territory Light"
8: MEASURE	Detailed sales tracking vs. control stores
CASE	**Bluefly.com**
1: IDENTITY	Affordable designer goods
2: STRATEGY	Build brand awareness among likely customers
3: AUDIENCE	Fashion-conscious consumers
4: CHALLENGES	Hard to reach Price appeal may weaken brand
5: OBJECTIVES	Offer irresistible sweepstakes Generate media coverage
6: IMPLEMENT	Live event at key locales Online sweepstakes
7: INTEGRATE	Video release to drive press coverage
8: MEASURE	Number of face-to-face interactions Number of sweepstakes registrations Number of new purchasers
CASE	**Shiseido**
1: IDENTITY	Hospitality, teach others to live well and live beautifully
2: STRATEGY	Build brand with younger women
3: AUDIENCE	Younger women
4: CHALLENGES	Perceived as high-end vs. same-price competitors Limited control of sales channels
5: OBJECTIVES	Consultative environment Mix of human and hi-tech Free and nonpressured experience

6: IMPLEMENT	Consultation
	Interactive kiosks
	Treatments
	Classes
7: INTEGRATE	Database linked with website database
8: MEASURE	CRM registrations
	Anecdotal referrals
CASE	**Basics Furniture**
1: IDENTITY	Affordable furniture at friendly store
2: STRATEGY	Build brand awareness among likely customers
3: AUDIENCE	New York residents in discount price category
4: CHALLENGES	Brand launch
	Limited resources
5: OBJECTIVES	Convey price positioning with relevant humor
6: IMPLEMENT	Humorous rabbits
7: INTEGRATE	Integrated print ads
8: MEASURE	Customer word of mouth

STEP 1: KNOW YOUR BRAND IDENTITY

The first step in creating a show is to understand the identity of your brand and to align the show with the brand identity. The identity of a brand includes its core image and personality. That is, what does the brand currently mean, both within your company and to the various external constituents who interact with it (mass consumers, business customers, investors, press)?

In each of the cases of successful show business that we have seen so far, the company began with an understanding of its own brand in planning what kind of show to put on. After all, any show should be an expression and reinforcement of the identity and meaning of your brand, in addition to any other marketing objectives it may fulfill.

In the case of SAP's E-Business Solutions Tour, the show was carefully designed to express its brand identity as a stable, highly experienced provider of e-business solutions in a post-dot-com economy. For Intel, the mobile messenger show and events for the Pentium 4 Processor-M chip were a new way to prove once again that their brand identity is about being the performance leader in computer processors. For the Vans athletic apparel company, its shows in movies (*Dogtown and Z-Boys* and others) and in hosting competitive events were designed to further its brand identity as the worldwide leader in core sports.

STEP 2: KNOW YOUR BRAND STRATEGY

As brand managers know, however, the identity of a brand is never constant. Brands are in a perpetual state of flux and change. Therefore, a brand strategy must always address the question of movement: where do we want this brand to go? This could include a broadening of consumer awareness, a deepening of customer involvement, more community building, or leveraging the brand into a new product category or in a new market. Any show therefore needs to be aligned with the overall strategy for its brand. When generating concepts for a creative show that will deliver value both to customers and to your business, understanding your overall brand strategy is the best way to start looking for ideas. Do you want to create an event to build a stronger brand community? Or an experience that will increase awareness or support a brand extension?

In the case of Crayola, a strategy had been formulated to tap into unused brand equity by moving the brand from a product-focused positioning to a brand that provided experiences and solutions for creativity to children and adults alike. It was this strategy that led directly to the concept of an experiential space devoted to customer creativity and interactions. For Vespa, relaunching its brand in the U.S. market after many years and with limited resources required it to capitalize on user evangelism and the product's referral ability—hence the various shows to promote word of mouth and group riding. Intel's strategy was to respond to research forecasting strong growth in the notebook segment by introducing a new processor chip for mobile computing and building demand for it among personal and business consumers. The Pentium laptop shows were designed to generate local excitement for the new chip's launch in tandem with traditional advertising.

STEP 3: KNOW YOUR TARGET AUDIENCE

In order to turn a brand strategy into a show business plan, companies need to know the target audience. Much more than traditional advertising, show business tends to focus on specific customer groups and therefore needs to know who are the most valuable or crucial customers.

For SAP, the audience consisted of key decision-makers in the purchasing of enterprise software solutions, an educated audience who would demand sophisticated information as well as compelling experiences from their show. Vans identified three tiers of users to appeal to in each of the core sports: serious athletic competitors, periodic participants (e.g., seasonal snowboarders), and lifestyle emulators. Then Vans built its shows to provide close interaction and identification with all three groups, and also to avoid any hard-selling that would weaken a sense of community between the brand and the customers. For Sears's Tool Territory show, the targeted customer was the male tool buyer who should have been viewing Sears as his best store.

We will return to the subject of knowing, learning from, and building relationships with your customer in greater depth in Chapter 7, *Creating Relationships Through Show Business*.

STEP 4: KNOW YOUR STRATEGIC CHALLENGES

Next, it is important to identify the key challenges or obstacles to achieving your strategy with that particular audience. Knowing these challenges will help you to focus the objectives of your show and increase your chances of success by helping you address your greatest risks.

For Vans, the challenges included a customer group that was extremely resistant to traditional advertising. Thus, the show had to support their enthusiasms and provide the right activities rather than hard-selling the brand and its products. Crayola's biggest challenge was insufficient brand affiliation by adults and a limited understanding of its customer's needs.

For Sears's Tool Territory, the key challenges included not only male customers' dislike of its mall location, but the perception that the store carried only its own brand of tools. This last challenge was a particularly onerous one if Sears was going to truly embody its brand promise to be "America's best tool store," and required the company to drastically rethink its approach to merchandising and pricing of tool brands.

STEP 5: IDENTIFY SHOW OBJECTIVES AND EXPECTED OUTCOMES

The next step is perhaps the most critical step. Here we develop specific objectives and expected outcomes out of what we have learned thus far. The objectives for the show will identify the kind of experiential impact that the show should have: what will the show demonstrate about products? What will it communicate about the brand? What kind of customer interaction will it provide? What kind of value will it provide? What should people remember or talk about after they see the show?

These are specific tactical objectives for the show itself, but they need to develop out of the prior four steps of this framework. A show's objectives must develop: *from* your brand, *toward* your strategy, *for* your audience, and *in response to* your challenges. The objectives also help define the spirit of the show. This is where you identify what the experience should feel like; in other words, how the show will be entertaining, engaging, and boundary-breaking.

Objectives should also be linked to expected outcomes, which can be used to measure the show's success. What will this show hope to achieve? What will it change?

For Intel's show, the objectives included demonstrating the theme of mobility in a funny and interactive way by linking laptops to a lifestyle appeal of both mobile computing and popular music and culture. Expected outcomes based on these objectives included media coverage and increased traffic to key retail stores for the launch.

SAP's objectives for its Tour were to demonstrate a commitment to educating its customers by creating a theatrical and thrilling show that demonstrated the market-driven focus of the company. Expected outcomes were increased sales from new customers. For Crayola, key objectives included creating an environment for brand immersion and affiliation through creativity, and linking the brand to school arts initiatives during a time of school budget cuts. Expected outcomes were new models for future retail space development and new customer insight for product development.

STEP 6: IMPLEMENT, I.E., PUT ON THE SHOW

The sixth step of the framework is implementation: to put on the show. The implementation of the show will be based on the objectives you have set for it (and thus, it will be aligned with your brand, strategy, audience, and challenges). The heart of implementation is the creativity of the people who are designing and enacting the show.

As this creativity runs its course, you will want to ensure that your brand is integrated throughout the implementation of your show.

This may seem like an obvious rule, but surprisingly it is one that is inconsistently carried out when many companies attempt to reach customers by something other than traditional advertising. Integrating your brand's meaning into an event does not mean hanging a giant logo over your stage or trade show booth, or making sure that your new retail store uses the colors of your brand's visual identity. It means injecting the spirit and character and design elements of your products and services seamlessly into the creative execution of your show at every level.

This is not just creativity with a banner up top. Think of the press party for Casio's G-shock brand. The design of its watches was what they were trying to link to an edgy brand identity; so the watch design was incorporated every step of the way: from the black-leather-clad invitation (the text was laid out in the shape of a wristwatch), to the S&M floorshows at the party (where the performers' costumes wove together watches with chains, leather, and latex), to the product demonstrations where G-Shock watches were subjected to crushing and grinding by black stiletto heels.

Another example of thoroughly integrating the brand into a show is the concert by the Barenaked Ladies which capped the day-long show to launch Intel's new laptop chips. Usually, when a known rock band appears under the sponsorship of a company, the brand is limited to banner appearances and more signage outside the venue. In this case, because the concert was a custom event, Intel had much more control. The concert stage was designed by Intel to incorporate the mobile computing theme: instead of the standard big screens on either side of the stage for the more distant audience to watch, Intel built giant mock laptops to display the footage of the band. The band itself got involved too, to a degree unheard of in a standard sponsorship relationship. Having been given information on Intel's product and the customer lifestyle it was supposed to be a part of, the Barenaked Ladies decided to create an original song for the event that included references to the marketing messages for the launch and to customers' use of the product (for digital video, audio, games, etc.). Toward the end of concert, when the 70 mobile messengers arrived as a group at the edge of the audience, the band greeted them with banter and jokes about their costumes as well.

All of which makes us wonder about the *non*-show-business model of music or sports sponsorship, where sponsors like Visa pay high fees for very restricted associations with an

FIGURE 6-1   The Barenaked Ladies not only rocked the house at Intel's launch party, they wrote their own song about the brand. Photo courtesy of Intel Corporation.

event. How much is the sponsor really gaining from its association with the performers? If companies saw artists and celebrities less as marketing tools to be bought (like time slots on television) and more as partners with whom to find creative ways to collaborate, a show business model of sponsorships could provide more value for companies and for customers.

STEP 7: INTEGRATE WITH OTHER MARKETING

The seventh step of the framework is to integrate your show with all other marketing communications used to promote your brand. Show business does not happen in isolation, and in most cases companies putting on shows are still relying on traditional marketing communications tools as well. Therefore, one important part of managing the brand impact of any show is to assess what your company's overall communication mix is and find ways to enlist or utilize those other resources. If your company makes a lot of use of broadcast advertising, then try to arrange for some of it to promote or draw attention to your show. Or at least, look for ways to link your show's themes to the brand messages in current media campaigns.

Because show business tends to happen on a very local level, its relationship with other marketing tools is often "local vs. global." In these cases, advertising and other tools are often used to create broad brand and product awareness across demographics, whereas show business can be used to approach more targeted customer groups, and to give them a much deeper experience of the brand, products, or services. Coordination needn't be very rigorous between the two for them to complement each other. In the case of Vespa, Piaggio USA's initiatives have focused on this kind of broad brand pro-motion, while the local dealers have initiated the street teams, events, and riders groups that have brought the brand to cus-tomers close-up.

Other examples of marketing integration for shows we've seen include:

- Intel's national advertising campaign to launch the Pentium 4 Processor-M chip, with the same theme as the launch events: "desktop performance without the desk"
- SAP's careful coordination of the E-Business Solutions Tour's messages with their advertising messages and their theme that, "The best run e-businesses run SAP"
- Sears's use of billboards and TV commercials that stressed the identity (playful + authoritative) of Tool Territory, with themes like, "Daycare at the mall for men," and "18,000 tools in stock. Collect them all"
- Casio's print advertising for the G-shock brand, which carried the same edgy personality, though with differ-ent themes for various target audiences

The example of G-Shock raises an important point, which is that integration should focus on coordinating the meaning of a brand and the spirit of its expressions. Integration of exact slogans, wording, fonts, and visual identity can be necessary at a certain level for large organizations and brands, but should be handled with care so as not to squelch the vitality of local brand expressions, especially in show business.

"We've seen that the Integration Emperor has no clothes," says Drew Neisser, who designed both advertising and show business events for G-Shock. "If you try to integrate a brand visually and verbally across all audiences and across all media, you will end up compromising all the media, to their lowest common denominator."

STEP 8: MEASURE BRAND IMPACT AND ALIGNMENT

The final step of keeping a show on-brand is to measure and evaluate its results after implementation. We suggest that you measure both the alignment of the show with the brand and audience (Did the experience match the identity and strategy for the brand and its target audience?) and its impact on the brand (in terms of audience awareness, perception, and bonding with the brand). We have listed measurement as a step after implementation, but in fact, for any measurement of impact, there will need to be a benchmarking measurement done before the show occurs.

Brand measurement needn't be expensive. For some goals, it can be achieved by adding a qualitative or attitudinal component to an exit survey or even by informal gathering of customer feedback through face-to-face interactions at an event. In most of the cases we have seen, brand impact and alignment is measured in only the most informal and anecdotal of ways. We would advise that such informal measurements could benefit from a regular process of recording and tabulating customer impressions that relate to the brand. At the least, brand alignment ought to be measured internally. Part of any project assessment should include ratings by managers who were involved in the show or observed it, regarding brand alignment and impact.

We will return to the topic of measurement and its relationship to budgeting and ROI for shows in Chapter 9.

BE PREPARED TO EVOLVE (YOUR BRAND, STRATEGY, AND SHOW)

As we discussed earlier, brands and brand strategies change. As a result, shows must be able to change as well.

If you are putting on a single-event live show, or other show with a short lifespan, brand evolution is not a real consideration. But if you are building an immersionary brand space or an expensive property for a traveling road show, and your space or property may be used for two or more years in order to maximize the return on the investment, you need to plan for changes in strategy.

Longer-term shows need to be designed at each step with flexibility to change in the future. Design components should be modular, content should be easily updated, and multiyear budgets should plan for significant overhauls rather than just maintenance repairs.

The SAP Tour has been used for shifting marketing goals each year that it has been in operation, with new deployments and sponsorships by differing SAP companies. What started as mostly a show to bring home a global branding campaign has evolved into a more sales- and lead-generation-focused marketing tool. This shift has come about mostly because of changing strategies on the best use of the property, but also because the success of SAP's global branding campaign in the first year meant that the Tour resource could be freed up for other marketing goals.

In other cases, a show will need to shift in order to remain in alignment with marketing communications (the challenge facing The World of Coca-Cola), or to remain in alignment with a brand whose identity or overall strategy is changing. Lastly, a long-running show needs to be capable of changing in response to the feedback it generates from customers. Since the experience is supposed to be for the customer, responsiveness to what they say about it is critical. As we have seen, one of the most important aspects of show business is its ability to help companies learn from their customers.

ON-BRAND OR ON-CUSTOMER?

This brings us to another challenge. The focus of this chapter has been on how to keep a show on-brand, which is extremely valuable. However, companies shouldn't just look inward toward their brands, but also outward toward customers. They need to align show business with both the brand and the customer.

To do that, companies need to move beyond the basic identification of customer segments and needs that we described in step three of this framework. A great show offers the possibility to progress from this initial kind of customer understanding to dynamic interaction and dialogue with the customer. This is the way toward building true relationships with customers that will deliver lasting value to a company. We show how to do this in the next chapter.

7 CREATING RELATIONSHIPS THROUGH SHOW BUSINESS

Catch any performer after a performance and one of the first things they'll talk about is "the house." What kind of crowd was out there? Were they hot or cold? Fast or slow on the uptake? Was the energy out there a lift or a drag? What worked, what got laughs, what got applause, what got a rise out of them? Most performers have to figure this out as they perform. They set foot on the stage without so much as a prior glance at the audience, the people who matter most to the success of their act.

Performers in business shows are in a better position. They have prior knowledge of the audience. This knowledge might come through a variety of sources: marketing research, segmentation schemes, customer relationship management (CRM), reports from salespeople or service providers, or even directly in the form of a show developed by the audience itself.

THE UPDR MODEL

Show business needs to begin from a point of understanding and targeting its audience and, ideally, should move from that starting point to the goal of attracting and engaging customers, and to creating relationships with them.

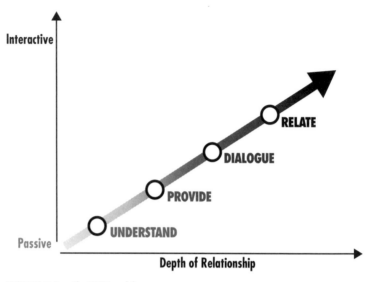

FIGURE 7-1 The UPDR model.

The Understand-Provide-Dialogue-Relate (UPDR) model (see Figure 7-1) schematizes this process: *understand* the audience; use this understanding to *provide* an experience; use that experience to *dialogue*; use that dialogue to *relate*—that is, to create further show business or consumption experiences.

This model also displays the interchange between the customer and the brand. Customers begin with an initial understanding of the brand. They are motivated by the provision experience to provide concrete information about their wants and needs; they are stimulated to dialogue, to discover and communicate needs or desires that they may not have been fully aware of. Through this process they are encouraged to relate to the brand, to form a relationship that affords the brand special privileges: frequent purchase, relative immunity to price considerations, loyalty that may be extended to brand extensions or licensed products, and so on.

Along the way, show business can enable personnel and customers to create relationships among themselves, even forming communities—communities that can blur the boundaries between internal and external. If you want customers to relate to your brand, you must relate to them, you may even "become the customer." Show business is one of the best ways to facilitate that kind of brand relationship.

In this chapter we will show how this happens, and we will identify the different types of information that are exchanged between a company's personnel and its customers when interaction takes place.

Here are some illustrations—using cases from the previous chapters of this book—of how the process of Understand-Provide-Dialogue-Relate works.

UNDERSTAND

Understand in the UPDR model means the kind of knowledge that comes from passive, one-way information gathering: data-mining, information from salespeople, market research, lessons about comparable products/services.

One of the first steps to creating a show, or to building a brand, is to understand your customers and what they want. For Bluefly.com, the audience targeted is the female customer who pays premium prices to shop for designer clothes, but is interested in finding a better price. The question Bluefly.com asked in developing their show was, "What do these particular women really covet? What can't they get anywhere else?" When they discovered the elusive and much sought-after Birkin bag, they knew they had the basis for creating their show.

Another crucial issue to understand about your audience is the history and culture of the customer group they are a part of. Jay Wilson says that the roots of *Dogtown and Z-Boys* were in the history of the surf and skateboarding community that the film documented. "This industry was born and driven by videos—videos about skateboarding, surfing. Not fancy material," just showing, "how to do it." The brilliant idea to fund a movie about a sport subculture was not original, Wilson says, "The real model for *Dogtown* was Bruce Brown's *Endless Summer I and II*." Those movies, about surfer guys wandering the world in search of the perfect wave, have made $30 million. Producing a subculture film that could make a profit while giving powerful unobtrusive promotion to a sporting brand—this was Wilson's new twist on the surfer dude classics.

In the realm of understanding, it is also important to find out what the customer knows about you. Your audience will have varying degrees of familiarity with your brand. The more you know about the knowledge base and experiences of your audience, the better you will be able to develop your show around concrete goals of audience engagement and relationship building. The Vans audience knew the shoe, so placement could be cool, unobtrusive, just another part of the excitement of the sport.

As part of understanding their customers, companies need to understand what types of customers they may be interacting with, or should be interacting with, in order to build brand relationships. There are three general customer categories for brand relationships: high value customers, high difficulty customers, and high demand customers. Each category includes subtypes, resulting in eight customer types (which sometimes overlap):

CUSTOMER TYPES FOR BRAND RELATIONSHIP BUILDING

High Value Customers
- Current users (frequent, repeat, loyal)
- Large-purchase decision makers
- Influencer groups

High Difficulty Customers
- Media-resistant customers
- Media-resentful customers
- Micro-niche customers

High Demand Customers
- High-knowledge customers
- High-expectation customers

HIGH VALUE CUSTOMERS

Marketing experts advise a balance of expenditures on acquisition and retention of customers, seeking ways to minimize the cost of customer acquisition (which typically offers a low return on investment). Brand management experts advise investing in the highest-value customer first. The three basic types of high-value customers are current users (especially frequent users, repeat, and loyal customers), large-purchase decision makers, and influencer groups.

J.D. Edwards's interactive Corridors of Chaos presentation was a show aimed at *current users* attending their annual global user-group conference. Who better to sell to than existing customers? By building a relationship with them and educating them about the capabilities of collaborative commerce, J.D. Edwards is able to sell new products and modules to complement those already in place. To pursue this high-value customer group, they have made this conference their single largest marketing budget item.

Large-purchase decision makers are simply customers who are influential in the decision of a very expensive purchase. For most companies in consumer packaged goods, for example, this customer type would not exist. However, if you are SAP, selling enterprise software solutions, it makes sense to invest in a high-value-added show experience for your customers, like their E-Business Solutions Tour, if you are using the show to target qualified customer leads and to help close high-value sales.

Influencer groups are the customers who are most able to spread buzz or word of mouth about your brand through networks of other customers. For Casio's G-Shock brand, this included the fashion stylists and press whom they invited to their Tie Me Up, Tie Me Down party. Panasonic chose to team up its roving Save My Summer street teams with Nintendo's events so that their brand could reach avid electronic gamers. The reason was not that these customers would purchase lots of games (that's what Nintendo sells, not Panasonic), but that if they became excited about the Panasonic brand, their opinion would influence others. Research had shown that gamers tend to be the experts whom peers and parents turn to for brand recommendations when making purchases of products like televisions or VCRs (which Panasonic does sell).

HIGH DIFFCULTY CUSTOMERS

In building brand relationships, companies also need to understand which customers they are going to find more difficult to reach. *Media-resistant customers* are ones who are not easily reached by traditional media channels. This may be from a lack of media-exposure; the Nickelodeon TV channel found it difficult to communicate directly to advertising agencies because of the small number of trade publications for advertisers. Instead they used rabbits such as branded giveaways and free cappuccino carts placed inside the agencies to increase their brand awareness. Customers may also be media-resistant simply because nothing short of a hands-on experience can convince them to try a new brand. It would be a mistake to try to build a relationship with this kind of customer through traditional advertising. "We used to do work for Wizards of the Coast [the largest company in the trading card category]," says David Laks of DSL Global Event Marketing who is currently creating live shows for Upper Deck Entertainment's franchise of the Yu-Gi-Oh™ card brand. "But they've now been bought by Hasbro, who is less focused on events as a medium." Will Hasbro change its marketing mix? Or will it find out the hard way that these customers are not so easily reached?

Media resentful customers are difficult to reach by traditional media because they are suspicious of it, resentful of its omnipresent saturation, or simply too cynical after years of often crass advertising ploys. This type of customer is often courted by companies trying to build a brand with young consumers. A blitz of media exposure will get you nowhere with this customer type. To build a brand, companies need to approach these customers on their own terms, toning down the commercial nature of messages, and adding real value to the customers' own activities or lifestyle. Vans's approach to building its brand with core sports enthusiasts shows just this kind of brand-building: sponsoring and creating sporting events, and documenting the sports' history, with Vans's role in that history represented but never underlined.

A third type of customer that is difficult to reach is *micro-niche customers*. This is a group who is so specifically defined that even the narrowest-bore media-buying plan is not likely to target them effectively enough. So show business becomes an important option for building a brand with them. Often it is a smaller brand that may go after this size of an audience. But all sizes of brands may be interested in targeting a micro-niche when it is an influencer group for a larger customer population; for example, the New York fashion stylist community who was the target of the G-Shock party. Similarly, GoGorilla has created sidewalk stencils for clients trying to draw attention to their booth at a small but very influential trade show for electronica enthusiasts.

HIGH DEMAND CUSTOMERS

In addition to customers who are of high-value and customers who are difficult to reach, companies need to be aware of those customers who are harder to impress. Certain types of customers simply demand more from an experience.

High-knowledge customers are extremely well informed about your brand, your products and services, and your competitors. They also value knowledge. They thus require special care and respect in your interactions. "The Internet is a major part of this," says Carsten Wierwille, VP Client Services at Plumb Design, who developed the interactive Thinkmap® technology for the Shiseido Studio. "Nowadays, customers are much more knowledgeable than in the past, which places big demands on sales representatives—they walk into Radio Shack and may know more about products than people working there." For companies like SAP and J.D. Edwards, communicating to business customers with varying knowledge about a very complex product category, it is imperative that the experiences they create provide a lot of learning.

Some customers also have high-level demands when it comes to production values in their interactions. These *high-expectation customers* are common in certain industries like automobiles where show business has been around longest and customers are used to being delivered real entertainment and a real experience when they interact with a brand. "Car dealers are an audience that has long been used to experiential marketing," says Lois Jacobs, Executive Vice President for Europe and Asia-Pacific, Jack Morton Worldwide, who recently helped launch the VW Phaeton in Europe. "There is a long tradition of seeing truly theatrical stuff at car shows. So they have higher expectations. You have to do something different."

TARGETING AND LOCALIZATION

For a variety of reasons, as mentioned earlier, traditional mass marketing that built brands in the last half of the 20th century is losing its effectiveness. Media fragmentation and the proliferation of consumer choices, the well-informed consumer, the increased power of retailers, and the growing level of resistance to mass-marketing appeal are all factors.

Marketing efforts that use smart localization are getting some of the best returns on investment. Show business can optimize localization efforts because it borrows from and enters the local culture that is being targeted. The audience experiences their culture through the brand (sometimes in very subtle ways) and feels the affinity between their culture and the brand. Many of the preceding cases demonstrate how show business, which is entertaining, creative, and interactive, can be used to create special memorable experiences to build brand relationships.

Targeting is all about understanding who your real brand customer is. And it may not be the youthful crowd that most advertisers try to pursue. "Hitting tattoo parlors and coffee shops is okay, it helps buzz," says Ken Stansbury of the Vespa Riverside dealership, about his street teams. "But who we want is professionals who aren't going to bat an eye when they see the price, who are going to take a Vespa and strap it onto their motor home." His street teams spend more time in doctors' offices than in bohemian hang-outs.

Because show business is experiential, it tends to occur in a specific time and place. Although this limits the breadth of audience engaged, it is ideal for targeting specific groups and for localizing your brand to adapt to the culture of each group that a show touches. Targeting is particularly important when going after micro-niche customers. Examples of highly targeted shows include a variety of rabbits developed by GoGorilla:

- Clarinex-branded tissues distributed at private gyms (research had shown this health-conscious group to be a good demographic target for the prescription allergy medication)

- A promotional rabbit for Verizon's "lifeline"—a discounted phone service offered to lower income people—which was used in unemployment centers

- Russian-speaking street teams with Russian-language rabbits and give-aways, used to promote an international calling plan in the Russian immigrant neighborhoods of New York City

If targeting is about going after very specific groups, and the right groups, localization also takes into account their context and changing culture. S&M and bondage are not themes that typically can be used to sell customers a wristwatch, no matter how edgy the brand. But the G-Shock party hit the zeitgeist for New York's fashion community that year, and they loved it. As Drew Neisser of Renegade Marketing said of the party, "This concept was *not* scalable to a broad consumer audience. But it was right for the brand, at that moment in time and history, with that crowd."

PROVIDE

The second step of interaction with a customer after developing an initial understanding of their needs, interests, value, and culture, is to provide something to your customer.

By provide, we mean give information and experience. The provision opportunity sets up carefully designed occasions where customers can get information, try products, or experience the brand in some meaningful way through a structured environment or activity. Note: This is not a promotion. You are not giving away the product or making it cheap. You are enhancing its value by immersing it and the audience in an entertaining experience.

The provision experiences we focus on are all some sort of show business and are usually shaped around maximizing dialogue between and among consumers and personnel. This is significant because most provision experiences are designed using existing information about the customer group. Enough information to target the group, but not, perhaps, information that goes very deeply into the customers' needs and desires. Thus, provide can be a bridge to go from an initial understanding to a more interactive and meaningful dialogue.

CUSTOMER VALUE FROM EXPERIENCES

To provide an experience that will maximize interaction and create dialogue, you need to know what your customer values and what you can do to provide value to the customer. The six types of value that can be provided for a customer through an interactive experience are:

SIX TYPES OF VALUE ADDED THROUGH SHOW BUSINESS EXPERIENCES

- Service or product
- Entertainment
- Learning
- Participation
- Social interaction
- Self-actualization

The first type of value a show business experience can provide is a *service or product*. However, this should not be the service or product that you sell. As we said, this is not a conventional promotion. An example would be the facial massages that Shiseido provides for customers when they come to its Studio to learn about Shiseido beauty products. The service offered connects to the brand and is presented in a way that links it to the brand. Shiseido's massaged customers learn that the Cutaneous Biology Research Center (a Shiseido partnership with Harvard and Boston's Massachusetts General Hospital) has concluded that facial massage is the proven best anti-aging method because it provides toning exercise for face muscles, is relaxing and destressing, and helps to balance and detoxify skin. Providing this sort of ancillary service or product can interest a customer in interacting with your company and also makes an effective springboard for dialogue about your brand.

Experiences can also provide *entertainment* value for customers. In fact, if they are show business experiences, they have to! This entertainment value can be the experience of fun (Coke's museum), fascination (SAP's interactive high-tech Tour theater), luxuriousness (Shiseido's customer treatment), glamor (the Vespa), or titillation (think Victoria's Secret). As we have said from the beginning, the first thing that makes show business reach customers is that it is something they enjoy. If they're not enjoying it, you need to rethink your show.

Many customers especially value experiences that provide *learning*. "To keep business people coming to trade shows," says Michael Trovalli of Jack Morton Worldwide, who worked on J.D. Edwards's user-group show, "You increasingly need to offer real value they can demonstrate to bosses, such as something they have learned." High knowledge customers in general get their best kicks from learning. Learning can be about a customer's industry or category (like J.D. Edwards's collaborative commerce show or Shiseido's beauty and relaxation classes), or a chance to try out a new product (like the trading card events), or a product they already own (BMW's instruction in high performance driving). Learning is part of the thrill of the experience.

Many of the best shows also provide an opportunity for customer *participation*. In shows like the automotive customer festivals (Jeep, BMW, and Saturn), or Sears's Tool Territory, or Crayola Works, the company provides an experience in which the customer can take an active part: racing their cars, playing with power tools, or creating artwork and customized products. The customer's physical experience of your product will strengthen their memory and help generate physical desire for more experience. Participatory experiences also provide the highest level of interaction between customers and company personnel and are terrific for producing dialogue because there is something immediate and exciting to talk about.

A show business experience can also provide customers a setting for *social interaction* with their peers, family, or community. Customer show spaces like Crayola Works offer creative, family-friendly environments for mall customers. The "third place" between work and play is an attractive setting where parents can interact with their children, children can interact with each other, or children can interact under supervision while the parents shop elsewhere.

In some cases, show business experiences can even offer customers *self-actualization*—valued ways to experience and learn about themselves or a group which they identify with. Vans's show business is an example. By producing a documentary movie about the history of the skateboarding and surfing community that was directed by a community originator and sports icon, Vans brought customers a way to learn from and experience their own history, and to build excitement about it. Sponsoring and creating the triple crown competitions for core sports enthusiasts is another way that Vans creates experiences through which customers express and realize their shared identity and community. The ability to provide this kind of experiential value for customers is extremely powerful, and is part of what other high-involvement brands like BMW, Jeep, and Saturn are trying to create in their community-building events. If your show can create an experience that provides self-actualization to your customer, the dialogue you create with them will lead to the strongest of brand relationships.

DIFFERENT LEVELS OF PROVISION

The key difference between the levels that we call *provide* and *relate* lies in the depth of understanding and interaction with the consumer and in the outcome of the experience. Provision starts from the basic notion of marketing a brand identity and attempting to line that up with the needs or desires of the consumer, based on a basic level of market research. The provision experience is controlled by the marketing team. Relating responds to a more complex, high-level dialogue with the consumers and gives the audience much more of a role in running the show. Providing mostly heightens brand identity, recognition, and associations. Relating is about establishing brand relationships among and between consumers and personnel.

Some show business events might offer opportunities for both provision and relating kinds of experience, approaching an audience that has different levels of familiarity with the brand, and letting individual members of the audience choose what level of engagement they are ready for. A simple way to look at it is that you can control a gift, but you can't control a relationship. You can't really script it; you can only stimulate and nurture it through long-term interaction. We'll talk more about relate later.

DIALOGUE

Dialogue involves asking, listening, and then asking and listening again. This is not passive information gathering such as the typical exit survey. Surveys offer a pretty much fixed set of questions to enable a one-way flow of information. They tend to invite and value responses that can be easily categorized. Typically, surveys can't do much with nuanced or creative responses that might actually be more valuable. That's why we need dialogue to really stimulate or relate to one another.

A tremendous range of potential possibilities for creative dialogue is just beginning to emerge with technological advances. But technology alone won't suffice. Not all the dialogue opportunities we will discuss use technology. Those that do use it to exploit its possibilities for creating an experience, not simply as a means of data-gathering. Show business aims for dialogue that is entertaining, experiential, interactive, and that stimulates and nurtures relationships between customers and companies and within companies and customer groups.

Tools for dialogue with customers can include marketing teams, show business staff, salespeople, and CRM that has an interactive or experiential interface. The goal of dialogue is always customer feedback, to find out more about your customer, what they want, value, believe, what they are looking for. By being interactive, dialogue can also help the customer learn and realize what it is that they desire, but couldn't yet describe—perhaps because it doesn't yet exist and is waiting to be created.

FACE-TO-FACE INTERACTION

The best forms of dialogue involve face-to-face interaction with customers, which is sometimes complemented by technological interaction. Show business is the best way to stimulate the kind of energetic face-to-face interaction that produces dialogue and valued customer feedback.

Figure 7-2 illustrates the different kinds of information that can be exchanged between a company's personnel and its customers through dialogue and interaction. In face-to-face show business, the company provides both rational (learning, service, or products) and experiential (participation, entertainment, social, self-knowledge) value to the customer, and in return the customer provides both rational (where I live, what I buy) and experiential (what I like, how I feel about your brand, how I want to feel) information to the company.

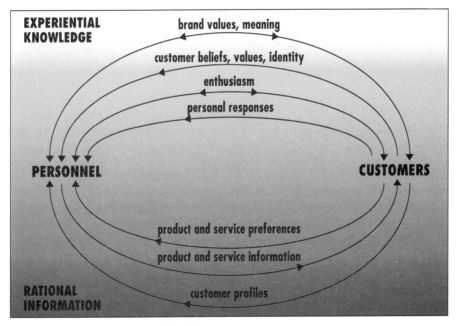

FIGURE 7-2 Customer interaction value model.

Because face-to-face interaction happens between live people, it can provide for deeper analysis than web questionnaires or CRM interactions via telephone centers. Mike Rubin, President of MRA International, which helped develop the concept for Crayola Works, notes that interactive space is "better for deeper analysis of customers with feedback that you might apply more broadly. There's a limit to the kind of questions that can be asked on the Web; it's a design issue." Crayola Works sees 500,000 customers a year and estimates that 10–15 percent of them engage in real dialogue with brand representatives.

If you are speaking live with a customer, the dialogue can go deeper and can resolve the ambiguities that come out of a lot of market research. It can elicit more meaningful responses and more honest answers by affirming to the customer that their answers matter. By contrast, dialogue with no face-to-face component is rarely able to provide the same value or to gather experiential information.

THREE MODELS FOR CUSTOMER DIALOGUE

Dialogue can come through a wide variety of interactions with customers and through all kinds of shows that build brands. The shows we've seen so far offer three models for creating dialogue with your customers: interactive show-and-tell, product play, and just dialogue.

In the *interactive show-and-tell* model, the show uses entertaining experiences to demonstrate the brand and its products and services and to engage customers. The show also provides customers a chance to ask questions and give feedback. This model can be accomplished without the use of technology, but it is often used either to enable the demonstration (plasma screens, satellite-linked theater rooms) or to provide follow-up information (registering online for product information or promotions). Customer feedback may come from a separate exit survey, but it is valuable to gather it through face-to-face dialogue with the customer as well. In both the SAP E-Business Solutions Tour and in J.D. Edwards's Corridors of Chaos a tech-enabled "show" is followed up by a face-to-face "tell" as trained staff guide the audience through further exploration of the software.

In the *product play* model, the focus of the show is squarely on the customer's experience of trying out the product in depth, with company personnel on hand to interact with them. Crayola Works's use of its creativity studio as a product testing lab is an example of this model, with close dialogue between staff and customers providing the invaluable feedback of a 30-day focus group for prototypes coming out of Crayola's product development teams. Trading card events are also product play.

In some cases, product play can generate a dialogue that combines face-to-face and tech-enabled communication. You could call it F2F + CRM. At the Shiseido Studio, customers move back and forth between live beauty consultants and Thinkmap® kiosks that provide a dynamic interface to an interconnected database of product and usage information.

The technology can serve as an icebreaker to facilitate the customer's comfort in what might otherwise be an awkward conversation about a skin problem, for example. At the same time, the kiosk technology is gathering information about the customers' interests, preferences, and needs through the questions they are asking (putting a name and contact information to that profile remains optional for the customer). The result is a seamless integration of face-to-face communication with technology-enabled communication within the same immersionary show space.

The model of *just dialogue* is used less often because it does not include an in-depth experience or demonstration of the product or service for the customer. But there are cases of good shows that focus primarily just on talking in-depth with customers about a brand that has already acquired a level of importance or allure for them. The Vespa street teams often follow a model of just dialogue, with the street teamer engaging in enthusiastic dialogue about the brand with customers while a scooter sits parked by his or her side. Or in some cases parked out the window—as the street teamer spreads the word to targeted professionals in their offices about an upcoming Vespa rally or group ride that they may want to participate in.

In each of these cases, face-to-face communication, with or without a CRM or survey format to complement it, provides a chance for dialogue in which companies can ask customers questions, listen, and ask again. What they do with the results is where the next stage, relate, comes in.

RELATE

The final stage of the UPDR model is to relate. This includes relating the brand to the customer and relating the customer to the brand. Relate grows out of dialogue and the learning that dialogue provides.

By relate we mean customer-to-brand interactions that actually help shape a product, a service, or the brand itself; or that shape the way these are experienced by customers. At its lowest level, this might include certain types of consumer-engaged product development—having customers vote on the color for a new M&M candy piece is a simple example—but it doesn't need to be that concrete and it should be a whole lot more life-altering. Relating goes beyond participation in a contest or poll. It enters the realm of mutuality, adding value that customers have requested and deepening their sense of participation in the life of the brand itself.

Customers can shape a brand by relating with it in experiential face-to-face product testing. Here a real consumer environment enhances new directions in product development. Again, Crayola Works is a great example, whose learning lab reaps feedback that is much deeper than "a. not satisfied, b. satisfied, c. very satisfied." Deeper feedback helps the brand relate to customers and inform product and brand innovations.

Customer input can also shape the show business experiences that a brand provides. In some cases, customer input may provide the core concepts for a show that a company will create for them. The idea for Crayola Works came from feedback the brand had gotten from customers via its web site and at the Crayola Factory, another immersionary show for customers that had already been opened. Coca-Cola's impetus for the first World of Coca-Cola brand museum was the voluminous requests it got from brand loyalists asking for some place to visit and learn about the brand when they were in Coca-Cola's hometown. Sears's planning for its Tool Territory was shaped in response to careful research of customer perceptions of the limitations of Sears's existing retail space and offerings.

BECOME THE CUSTOMER

When a customer relates to a brand and helps shape it, that customer is no longer just a statistic or a voter, but becomes an actor in the brand drama. The best relate shows will be the longest running ones, and their effect is to break down the internal/external boundary between employees and customers. In companies with truly close brand relationships with their customers, the boundary can disappear, and your employees are your customers.

Jay Wilson, Vice President of Global Marketing for Vans puts is this way, "The biggest mistake of brand managers and marketers is that they try to speak to, talk to the customer. You need to *become* the customer. Our guys making surf ads and skateboarding ads, surf and skateboard. The company is a reflection of who our customers are." Another example of this philosophy can be seen emerging in Piaggio USA (which sells the Vespa brand). Since the reintroduction of the brand in the United States after a 20-year hiatus, the company has recruited vintage Vespa enthusiasts to join their staff. These are the same brand loyalists who kept the flame burning for Vespa during the dark years of trips to Italy for replacement parts, and who are now key to the group rides and rallies that are helping to spread the word of Vespa's return.

"Becoming the customer" is facilitated through show business because at shows, employees and customers share the same interactive experience and form relationships. Shows can also help with recruiting. A customer who is a product enthusiast visits a great show and gets a taste of the experience, maybe even hears first-hand from an employee there about how great it is to work for your company. (This doesn't come as programmed proselytizing, but arises from the dialogue.) That customer is much more likely to think of your company as a place they'd like to work than if they saw even the best-written lure in the Careers section of a newspaper or your web site.

As we saw in the chapter on customer shows, building brand relationships is not just about communication and response between customers and company personnel. In order to truly relate, companies need to encourage customer-to-customer (C2C) communication about the brand.

This can be done at shows your company is producing: J.D. Edwards encourages its prospective customers to go to the Focus users conference not just to see its own show there, but to talk to current users about the brand and their own honest experiences with it.

C2C communication can be encouraged when you reward your customer evangelistas for spreading the word about your brand. The Vespa Riverside dealership uses customer referral clubs, whereby customers who bring in other sales are given one-of-a-kind branded merchandise and prizes (state laws prohibit paying money to nonlicensed salespeople). Vespa's corporate marketers are working to encourage C2C communication through their behind-the-scenes support for events put on by riders' clubs.

The high level of customer relationship that happens when customers independently communicate and form a community with each other through a brand is why customer-run shows are so valuable, and why companies need to flow with the partial loss of control of the brand that goes with customer-run shows.

FACE-TO-FACE THAT'S NOT IN YOUR FACE

If there is a Golden Rule to building a deep relationship with customers so that you become a part of the customer culture itself, it is this: No Hard Sell.

If you want to build a relationship with your customers, you cannot be aggressively pushing purchases of your products and services. You have to help them experience the brand and make the decision on their own. That's why Vans chose to use such a soft touch in the placement of its own product in a movie for which they put up 100 percent of the budget. If they had insisted on a scene where Stacey Peralta interviewed the athletes about the history of Vans and why and how they always wore them, it would have stunk of commercialism to their core audience. Peralta would have lost status for having "sold out." And Vans didn't need to do this anyway: the customer community that knew Vans (those high-value repeat customers and influencers) experienced it as part of their own world. This is not lost on viewers who want to emulate that world.

Likewise, it is important to be very sensitive when getting involved in customer shows. The customers who create them can be very sensitive about autonomy issues. When Vespa returned to the U.S., many of the vintage Vespa riders initially had animosity toward the newbies who had just discovered the brand. But that faded quickly, in part thanks to the support that the company gave to the vintage riders' rallies as one way of encouraging old and new customers to mingle. "Our involvement in scooter rallies is very grass-roots," says Costantino Sambuy, President of Piaggio USA. "We view rallies not as a chance to promote ourselves as a corporate entity but rather as an opportunity to support and pay homage to the true enthusiasts who kept the Vespa brand alive in America during our 15-year hiatus." That low-key support may include putting on a barbeque, providing goods for a raffle, giving out t-shirts, or just paying for the gas (pennies for a ride!). This approach is what allows a brand relationship to stay mutual and to grow.

CONCLUSION

Show business, or any business, needs to understand, interact with, and learn from its audience—the customers—if it wants to build a real relationship between them and a brand.

The four stages of the UPDR model—understand the audience, use this understanding to provide an experience, use that experience to dialogue, and use that dialogue to relate—are how a brand moves toward more experiential communication and learning from the customer and a deeper brand relationship with them.

This is not to say that every show needs to progress to the level of relate and achieve self-actualization and community building among its audience. Some shows are great successes at the provision level (Bluefly.com's, for example). The real success of a show is whether or not it achieves its marketing objectives, and this can happen at each level of the UPDR model.

A lot of show business interactions happen locally, but their reach does not have to be local. The next chapter will show how to extend the reach of your show to broaden its impact.

8 EXTENDING THE IMPACT OF YOUR SHOW

The core strength of show business is that it breaks the boundaries of traditional communications and finds ways to engage audiences in interactive or face-to-face experiences. Many shows, however, will not reach as many customers as traditional broadcast advertising does. There are two main reasons for this. The first is geographical. Most shows are situated in a specific place: immersionary space shows are built somewhere; live shows and evangelista shows target areas with specific audiences, and so on. The second reason has to do with capacity: live shows must limit the number of participants if the experience is to be truly interactive (even shows as large as the Saturn Homecoming, which hosted 30,000 customers a day). The same is true with immersionary space shows as well, though the one-time capacity is amplified by the length of time that the space stays open for business.

How can we overcome these limitations? The first way to address them is simply by doing more shows. If your show is a success, you can increase its reach by taking it on the road or changing its scale. A live show can be taken on tour by designing the physical show property for travel (like SAP's Tour and Microsoft's Xbox Odyssey), or by hosting a series of events in different locations (like Jeep's Jamborees, or Chivas Regal's tasting parties). An immersionary space can be replicated in multiple locations (like Sears's Tool Territory and the Apple

Stores). Evangelista shows or rabbits can likewise be done in multiple locations or markets (like Vespa's differing evangelista and customer shows by different dealerships) wherever target audiences are located.

But beyond that—beyond increasing the frequency or scope of your show—how else can you increase its impact? Beyond those who see it directly, how can you make sure that others also know about the show? Beyond the show itself, how can its vitality and creativity be leveraged for additional impact? And once the curtain goes up and the show is over, how can you continue a relationship with the people who experienced it?

There are successful models for doing each of these things:

- Promoting your show
- Syndicating, or leveraging the value of your show's content and creativity after it's over
- Following up using CRM, or marketing your show business after the actual event

That's what we mean by extending the impact of your show.

PROMOTING YOUR SHOW

If your marketing objective is to acquire new customers, face-to-face shows with customers can be an effective but somewhat expensive form of lead acquisition. In cases where the per-customer value is high (e.g., expensive consumer items or business products), the show's effectiveness may easily justify the expense. However, for shows for consumer packaged goods and other industries, it is imperative to try to reach more people with your show. In general this can be done by promoting the show to increase its attendance or by targeting audience members who will spread the word about the show after experiencing it. There are four specific approaches that accomplish these goals.

The first approach is to use other marketing tools, including traditional advertising, to drive customers to your show.

Intel used radio to promote free tickets for its Pentium 4 Processor-M launch concert, and direct marketing to invite business customers to the events. Sears used billboards and TV advertising to promote the opening of its Tool Territory show. Even with the best location or timing, shows will need promotion to draw attention.

The second approach is to partner or co-brand with another company to drive attention to your show, ride the coattails of an event they are producing, or combine promotional resources. Panasonic's Save Your Summer events for customers gained larger audiences by being done in conjunction with a larger event campaign by Nintendo. Vespa extended the reach of its street teaming by sending evangelistas out in partnership with teams for Skechers and Orbit. Vans's movie *Dogtown and Z-Boys* gained substantial publicity from its distributor Sony Pictures Classics.

A third approach to promotion is to target customers who will in turn influence other customers. As we have seen, these influencer groups can greatly increase the value and impact of your show. Bluefly.com and the Panasonic events both targeted customers who had influence in other circles (designer fashion purchasers, and home electronics purchasers). The additional customers with which these influencers network will not actually experience your show, but they will hear about it and be touched by its impact.

The fourth approach to promotion is to target the press. The use of PR and the media to amplify the news of a show business event or location is often a critical part of the return on investment for a show aimed at mass consumers. The amount of press attention and media impressions generated by a show can often determine whether it will be a mixed success or a breakaway hit. In the case of Bluefly.com, 20,000 customers were touched directly by the show, but 19 million on-air impressions helped drive the number of web site registrations to 160,000. "If we had done the Bluefly.com campaign just as street level events to the key audience in three cities, but without the PR, it would not have reached the numbers they got," says Drew Neisser.

PR AND THE MEDIA

Clearly, in planning a show, companies need to consider what the press might want to feature. The standard approach to generating media attention and PR is to have news, to create news, or do both.

Some shows manage to "have news" by linking themselves to something that will be covered in the press, such as sports or music events. Vans's creation and sponsorship of triple crown sporting events for core sports enthusiasts ensures that they will receive coverage from sports media. Intel's interactive show at the *Area: One Music Festival* benefited from press coverage of the festival.

Often, companies are urged to include something noncommercial or charitable in their sponsorships or events in order to attract media attention, but charitable sponsorships have to be handled properly. If they are insincere or trifling, they will easily be perceived as publicity-driven. Shows can benefit from community or social ties, however, if they are part of a long-standing involvement by the company. Certainly, part of the strong PR generated by The World of Coca-Cola (including appearing in the nightly credits of Atlanta newscasts) is owed to Coca-Cola's long commitment to its home city and the contribution The World of Coca-Cola has made both to the neighborhood it helped revitalize and to the city's overall tourism. The Dallas Cowboys already enjoy unmatched network coverage of their Thanksgiving game and half-time show, where they host the annual kick-off of the Salvation Army's kettle drive (a charity the Cowboys have long supported). Including the Salvation Army in a future Legend Square development could be a way to do good and to draw attention to their show at the same time.

When it comes to creating news, companies usually do well with three approaches:

- Keep your show of-the-moment.
- Be ludicrous, even outrageous.
- Create real entertainment content.

The first two are well displayed by Bluefly.com's video press release, which created strong media coverage of their Birkin bag giveaway show. By tying it into current pop culture (the glowing depiction of the unattainable bags on an episode of HBO's *Sex and the City*) and by offering the media something truly ridiculous to report (women who will sleep with snakes or run naked down Fifth Avenue to get these bags), they hit a surefire formula for press coverage. The movie *Dogtown and Z-Boys* is an example of real entertainment content—a 90-minute documentary—that got the kind of press coverage other shows can only dream of: radio interviews, director profiles, and a half-hour special about the film on MTV.

SYNDICATION

The second way to extend your show is to find a way to leverage more value from the show's content, creativity, and lessons after the show has run its course. We call this approach to show business extension *syndication*, after the practice of TV programming. Syndication can reuse some of the best in a show in the form of another show or in a non-show-business application.

In some cases, it may be appropriate to do a smaller, scaled-down version of your show after the first one has run its course. J.D. Edwards did just that with its Corridors of Chaos show created for its annual user-group meeting in Denver. The show had been created on a scale that would not have been cost-effective to replicate at other events, but they did find ways to create a scaled-back version of the same live presentation at a smaller international event in Australia for the Asian market.

In other cases, a scaled-down version of a stationary show may be taken on the road to reach more consumers. The immersionary Shiseido Studio provides an in-depth interactive learning environment for customers that could not be easily transported on a trailer or bus. In addition, Shiseido has developed something called Shiseido Studio On Location to bring the Studio experience to customers far from the New York and Santa Monica Studios. Studio On Location started two years after the first

Studio opening, and travels to the 860 channel stores where the brand is sold in the U.S. The syndicated show visits retailers for lengths of a week to a month and brings local customers some of the same educational and consultative experiences as the original show, including technology like the Multi-Micro-Sensor, which uses magnified and polarized images of customers' skin to determine skin type, exposure, and needs.

The creative content of an interactive or face-to-face show business experience can sometimes be incorporated into a static medium for further use as well. J.D. Edwards got the most syndication out of its Corridors of Chaos show via the CD-ROM it created, which included all of the video and interactive multimedia elements of the show and its story. The CD-ROM has been distributed around the world in sales calls to potential customers and in 50,000 copies distributed as free gifts in an issue of the magazine *Line 56*. The CD-ROM has actually become one of the most requested pieces of software J.D. Edwards ever produced. A CD-ROM alone would never have produced the impact the company wanted at their annual user-group event with key customers. As an extension of the live show, however, it was a perfect complement.

Another way to leverage the value of a show is to apply the lessons learned and customer insight gained from it to other non-show-business parts of your business. This can include using customer interactions to influence product development, as done by Binney & Smith with their Crayola Works show. Or it may include merchandising lessons like those taken from Sears's Tool Territory and applied successfully at other stores without the experiential environment.

CRM AND AFTERMARKETING FOR SHOW BUSINESS

A question that has drawn recent attention from marketers is, what do you do to market to customers after you have gotten them to buy? This subject, called "aftermarketing" focuses on how to maximize value from repeat customers and, as we have seen, this is one of the most important marketing goals that show business can fulfill.

But in extending a show, we have to ask a slightly different question: what do we do with (or for) our audience after the show? More specifically, how can we continue the interaction, dialogue, and relationship that a show business experience can help to build, and how can we leverage this into greater customer equity—that is, sales? "After your show" is one of the many places where the old razzle-dazzle meets new technology in show business, as one of the most important tools is customer relationship management (CRM). The use of CRM database technology allows companies to track large numbers of customers and potential customers with whom they have interacted through show business experiences and to communicate with them via direct mail, call centers, and online media in a customized way. This use of CRM is less personal than show business but can still incorporate some of what customers have shared about themselves during or after the show.

Of course, in order to use CRM after a show, you need to use the show to collect information about your customers. One approach is to collect contact information from customers at the event, which should always be optional for the customer. The last thing you want is to make your experience appear coercive (we're giving you this only if you do that for us) or to collect profiles on customers who aren't genuinely excited by the experience. In other cases, companies may promote a web site at a show, encouraging customers to go there later to register themselves. Companies may also want to encourage customers who see the show to tell their peers and colleagues to register at the same place—increasing the net number of profiles collected, but including customers with less connection to the event, and possibly your brand.

To collect a customer's contact information, you will need to offer something of value that will make them want to receive future communications. This can be information, such as a newsletter or a catalog with products they may not have seen. Or it can take the form of a financial opportunity—special discount offers, or sweepstakes (like Bluefly.com's chance to win a Birkin bag). You can also reward registering customers by offering them special opportunities: invitations to future shows or product exclusives.

CRM is important to show business because it helps to secure the up-selling profits that are one of the main goals of providing experiences for your customers. They are also an important justification for show business because of the quality of customers whose names are collected as part of putting on a show. Crayola Works got a 40 percent response rate to an offer of exclusive Zoogles toys to kids who had test-marketed the products, and other companies like Panasonic have found that customers reached through their live events have a low opt-out rate on follow-up communications. The interactivity of shows can also provide for much more detailed profiles of customers than is possible with simple paper or online registration forms (age, family income, do you like designer shoes?). Because the Shiseido Studio uses interactive technology to assist visitors seeking consultations, it is able to collect extremely detailed information about their product interests and personal needs that it can use if customers choose to register their contact information. The same database of interconnected product information that runs their kiosks is at the back-end of their web site, and Shiseido uses it in follow-up communications to offer customers product promotions targeted to their specific personal needs.

CONCLUSION

Show business is mostly a localized approach, but its impact can also be increased by three types of extension.

First, companies can promote the show itself or target influential customers and the press. Second, companies can syndicate or leverage more value from a show after it is over. Third, companies can gain greater value from a show by extending their relationship with the audience after the show is over, via CRM.

All these approaches to show extension are important to manage because they can directly impact the final return on your investment (ROI) for your show. But how do you determine ROI for a show? How do you get a budget based on your particular ROI? How do you prove that your show actually achieved what you said it would? We'll take a look at these questions in the next chapter.

9 MEASUREMENT, BUDGETS, AND ROI

As we have stressed from the first chapter, show business is not *just* about creating an entertaining, engaging, boundary-breaking experience for customers. It also has to add value to your business. So how can you budget for show business? How do you know if you've achieved your objectives? How can companies measure the return on investment (ROI) of a show?

THREE QUESTIONS FOR BUDGETING SHOWS

There are three questions that any company must answer in order to budget for a show business project:

- **What are the objectives and expected return on investment (ROI) for this show?** Your objectives for a show and the value you expect it to deliver to your company must be linked to an overall strategy for your company. The importance of your show's expected ROI within that strategy will determine what portion of your budget should be devoted to a show. For example, a show that builds long-term relationships with existing valued customers will receive a larger share of budget within a company that has ranked relationship building as its primary objective for the year, versus a company that is focusing first on new customer acquisition.

- **What is the extent of your resources, and what other resources could help defray your show's costs?** The size of a budget will depend not only on the strategic importance of the show's ROI, but also on the overall size of the budget itself. Some of the types of shows we have seen could only be attempted by large organizations with substantial marketing budgets, whereas others can be carried off by even small entrepreneurs. But show business managers should also look to resources beyond the basic marketing budget that may help to cover the costs of a show.

- **How effective has this kind of show been in the past?** To gauge the value of a show as a business tool, you need to know not just the type of ROI it will deliver, but also how much. Once a company has had some experience in show business, the success of previous projects will become invaluable in determining how to finance future ones.

The last question shows us why measurement is critical for show business. The only way to determine the success of a show business project is to measure its impact. The impact of show business can be very wide-ranging, from brand awareness to customer acquisition, from relationship building to repeat customer sales. Any measurement of a show's effectiveness will therefore have to be designed to fit its particular marketing objectives.

Let's look at how a company can answer each of the three questions for creating a show business budget.

SETTING OBJECTIVES AND EXPECTED ROI

The first step to managing the scope, budget, or measurement of a show business project is to determine the objectives and expected ROI for the project. In most cases, a show is expected to deliver on more than one marketing objective for the company. It is thus important to identify each of them and their relative importance to the project. As each ROI is identified, it is also necessary to find metrics and tools that can be used to measure it effectively.

Show business projects tend to generate one or more of four types of ROI:

- Broad-based brand development
- Customer retention
- Sales and customer acquisition
- Marketing research and customer data

In *broad-based brand development*, a show may aim to generate awareness or enthusiasm for a new brand or to affect the perception of an existing one. For some shows, such as The World of Coca-Cola or the Shiseido Studio, this is a major component of the expected value of the show. In these cases, customer education about a brand may be the company's key objective. In other cases, affecting customer perceptions may be secondary to other objectives such as stimulating sales. Both brand awareness and brand perceptions can be measured through a variety of market research tools.

Customer retention is a growing marketing priority for many companies as they realize the importance of existing customers in adding value to their revenue stream. Customer retention is usually the key objective of shows that aim to build relationships between brands and their existing customers, such as the Jeep Jamboree, Saturn Homecoming, and BMW Ultimate Driving Experience. Measurement for customer retention focuses on categorizing brand loyalty (and changes in loyalty) on a spectrum from the most loyal customers to those customers who are available for easy defection to other brands. Measuring the ROI for customer retention also requires a model for customer equity as well: You need to know not just what the probable time span of a customer's loyalty is (and how marketing changes that), but what their probable purchasing rate will be over that span of time.

Sales and customer acquisition is often an objective for shows, as was the case with the show for Bluefly.com, or the use of SAP's E-Business Solutions Tour at sales events in its second year. Some shows, like Bluefly.com's or the Panasonic Save My Summer tour, focus on driving consumers to register online and become potential customers via follow-up CRM. When possible, closing a sale at the show allows for much clearer measurement of the sales impact of show business; for example, a mobile phone company puts on a live show at which customers can subscribe for the company's service. In most cases, the value of sales is easy to measure, but its correlation to any marketing program (including show business) can only be approximated. When measuring ROI from the acquisition of new customers, it is important to again use a customer equity model to estimate the lifetime value of future purchases by that new customer, in order to gauge the return on your show.

Because of its close interactions with customers, show business is often used as a tool for *market research*. When customer feedback is collected and utilized in a systematic manner, the responses provide substantial ROI by delivering the kind of insight and information that marketing departments normally acquire through expensive market research.

Surprisingly, many companies seem to miss much of the opportunity to capitalize on the feedback value of customer interactions. By enabling research in the customer's natural habitat (or something like it), show business that is face-to-face with customers can generate very valuable insights for service, product design, and brand delivery. Crayola Works is an example of a show that makes a priority of fully capturing the value of this information; this show with customers is a true product-testing lab and on-going customer focus group. To measure the ROI on customer feedback, companies should compare the results with the costs for comparable research through other marketing resources (outside agencies, focus groups, etc.). More companies, especially those doing brand relationship building like the automotive community events, should focus on training their personnel to elicit live customer feedback during the course of the show and document it carefully for marketing purposes after the show. This will allow show business to become a significant tool for increasing companies' responsiveness to customers.

ASSESSING BUDGET RESOURCES AND COSTS

Once a company has determined the expected sources of ROI for its show, it should assess their relative importance within its marketing strategy to determine what share of its marketing budget to invest in show business.

The actual size of the show's budget will therefore depend significantly on the size of the overall marketing budget, which will depend both on the size of the organization and on the importance of marketing in its priorities. But the budget share for show business may also depend on cultural factors within an organization that do not necessarily reflect strategy as much as tradition.

Many companies still invest heavily in traditional advertising, in part because that is what they know best. Some industries, like automotive and some areas of the information technology (IT) industry, have more history in pursuing creative experiences like show business for their business partners, and in some cases, end consumers. The consumer packaged goods and consumer electronics industries are in the midst of a significant shift away from traditional advertising and are becoming much more interested in the show business approach to reaching customers.

For most companies, the budget for a show business project comes from an overall marketing budget or a joint sales and marketing budget. In some cases, a subcategory within marketing, such as "corporate events," may provide a home for a show business project (this is the case with J.D. Edwards, which makes the show at its users conference its single largest annual marketing budget item). In other cases, different departments within a company may jointly fund a show. The SAP E-business Solutions Tour was paid for entirely by SAP Global Marketing in its first year but half of its costs were covered by SAP U.S. Sales & Marketing in its second. The Sears Tool Territory was financed and managed jointly by the Merchandising Department (which handles buying) and the Strategic Marketing Department. In rare cases, such as The World of Coca-Cola, an ongoing show will run on its own line of profit and loss, with start-up costs coming out of general corporate funding.

As your resources for a show business project become clear, you should keep in mind that the shows we have seen come with a very wide range of price tags attached. For example:

- **Street teams** and **evangelista shows** can start for a few thousand dollars. GoGorilla provided Nescafé's beverage- and map-distributing team at the Olympics for about $3,000 a day. Vespa's support for vintage owners' rallies may cost as little as putting on a barbeque or providing free t-shirts.

- **Rabbits** also start at low costs. Nescafé's projection on the wall as crowds entered and left the Olympic awards ceremonies cost $6,000 a night (much less than a targeted billboard). Basic Furniture's humorous quarters campaign cost only 60 cents per stickered coin ($3,000 for 5,000 coins), plus agency fees.

- **Live shows** range widely based on their scale and technology. The G-Shock S&M party for 700 key influencers cost less than $400,000, but the Bluefly.com street level show (which touched 20,000 people) was much, much cheaper ("super cheap" says Drew Neisser). J.D. Edwards's high-tech Corridors of Chaos cost $300,000 to stage with kiosks and plasma screens and had significant additional costs for content and media development, but the total remained under a million.

- **Invented media shows** can run anywhere from the cost of an affordable book deal up to the high cost of producing a TV show like Dodge's *Fast Enuff Challenge*. Vans produced the successful documentary film *Dogtown and Z-Boys* for $650,000 including promotion—

with costs kept down because the movie was a labor of love for the customer-turned-director.

- **Road shows** run higher costs than other live events because of the expense of the physical property, but deliver a show that can be taken to customers repeatedly all year long. A well-made road show like SAP's will run about $2 million a year to operate and maintain, with an additional half million the first year to build it.

- **Immersionary space shows** have probably the highest costs, with square footage and location having the largest impact on price. The Shiseido Studio's relatively small (3,800 square foot) but well located (New York's SoHo neighborhood) and high-tech space (custom-designed interactive databases) was estimated by industry sources at $2 million in construction and $600,000 in annual operating costs. A much larger show space like The World of Coca-Cola would be more, but immersionary space shows usually generate revenue as well.

Costs for shows vary a great deal depending on how they are implemented, of course. If the show creates a great experience and is strategically managed, it will always give back more ROI when you invest more. A show will reach more customers, build more relationships, acquire more leads, or generate more customer feedback if it can be financed on a larger scale, for a longer time, or at multiple locations.

EXTENDING YOUR RESOURCES

Having determined what kind of resources may be available from a marketing budget, managers developing show business projects should also consider what resources might be available from other departments, or from outside their own company, to contribute to the budget and scale of their show.

An example of successful cost-sharing within an organization can be seen with SAP's E-Business Solutions Tour. The Tour was commissioned in its first year by SAP Global Marketing, which still owns the Tour property. It was paid as a pure advertising expense and used as a global marketing tool for the brand. In the second year, half the cost of the show was defrayed by SAP U.S. Sales & Marketing, who paid for its use at their sales events for the new objectives of lead generation and pipeline acceleration (closing deals). SAP Global Marketing still carried the other half of the budget, but had much less cost to keep using the Tour as a tool for their goals of brand awareness and consistent messaging.

In other cases, partners outside an organization can be used to sponsor and support a show business project. SAP has received sponsorships in barter or cash from companies including IBM and Compaq who share customers with SAP and gain value from attaching their brand to the show ("The SAP E-Business Solutions Tour, brought to you by IBM"). Similarly, the Dallas Cowboys plan to offer sponsorships for parts of its proposed Legend Square development (e.g., a Ford Explorer competitive course).

Sometimes, companies put on shows in which "usage sponsors" are actively involved in the production and the interaction with customers. Vespa has done this with its joint street teams with Orbit and Skechers. Intel's college campus tour with Microsoft offered a joint show business experience for the two companies' joint customers.

The other major way that resources can be extended for show business is when the show generates revenue of its own. In some cases, the revenue may even match or exceed costs: self-liquidating marketing! Shows earn revenue from retail sales (at immersionary show spaces like those of Sears, Crayola, and Apple), admission fees (at The World of Coca-Cola), or from revenue on a show like Vans's movie *Dogtown*—which has already made a profit from theater sales and will continue to earn derivative revenues (overseas box office, video, DVD) for years to come. The possibility of revenue and even profit from a show can offer a crucial argument for the allocation of internal marketing resources.

Another scenario for show business that generates revenue is when a show is hosted by another company and adds value to the host company's services. Mills Corp., the mall owner and developer, helps develop immersionary show spaces like Crayola Works and the PBS Kids environments (which Mills sponsors) because these entertaining family-friendly spaces make the malls uniquely attractive to high-value shoppers. That differentiation in environment adds value to the mall property and a premium to what Mills can charge all of its retailers. Not a bad way to pay for a show.

True integration of external funding for show business can be seen in Victoria's Secret's fashion shows. By partnering with charities, movie studios, and TV networks, the company has raised millions for charity and turned its fashion show into prime-time programming that the major networks pay top dollar to purchase.

MEASURING SHOW BUSINESS SUCCESS

The third question that companies must answer in budgeting for a show business project is how effective has this kind of show been in the past. Which brings us back to the subject of measurement.

The measurement of the impact of experiences is something that many companies are keenly interested in as they consider allocating marketing resources from traditional advertising to show business, but there is an air of mystery about the subject. "Measurements and metrics is the one area that people are most interested in, but it is very difficult," says Kerry Smith, publisher of *Event Marketer*. In fact, measurement of show business is difficult, and it also isn't.

It is difficult because the wide range of possible ROIs that can be generated by show business means that there can be no one-size-fits-all methodology to measurement. "Clients have different objectives—which require different metrics," says Smith. Additionally, accurate measurement is constrained, as with any other marketing tool, by the fact that show business does not act in isolation. The same customers who experience a show are also being influenced by a host of other factors and often by other marketing tactics from the same company. (Did she buy a Jeep again because of the Jamboree? Or was it the zero percent financing?)

On the other hand, measurement of show business is also significantly easier than measurement of mass marketing communications: in show business, you are likely to have more precise knowledge of, and direct access to, the exact customers who were touched by the show.

Once you know who they are, a variety of data collection techniques are available, including qualitative and quantitative exit surveys, conversations with customers at the show, coupons to track store purchases, online registrations, and CRM tracking of follow-up communication and sales.

MEASUREMENT TOOLS

Show business can be measured with a variety of tools that match different ROIs. Some tools are "soft" (qualitative) and others are "hard" (quantitative), and many can be used for a variety of purposes. Four main types of measurement that these tools provide are:

- Qualitative feedback or observation
- Customer contact generation
- Perception and motivation
- Sales generation

Qualitative tools can include gathering various types of customer feedback at shows. Coca-Cola collects customer stories at The World of Coca-Cola about how Coca-Cola has played an important part in their lives ("I met my wife over a Coke," "I was so happy after crossing the Gobi Desert to see a village grocer selling Coca-Cola"). Crayola Works collects customer responses in testing products in its studio. Any show that involves face-to-face interaction with customers should include collection by personnel of comments by customers about the brand, products, services, or their own needs and circumstances as a consumer. Qualitative tools can also include generalized observations of customer behavior: Casio informally monitored the adoption of G-Shock watches by fashion stylists in New York after its launch party to see the impact of its show for this targeted audience. In that case, Casio was indirectly measuring a presumed impact on sales (presuming that stylists influence broader consumption); but usually qualitative feedback measurements are used for brand-building and relationship-building ROI.

Tools for measuring *customer contact generation* are more quantitative. One simple tool is to measure the number of customers touched directly by a show, for example, to see how much traffic to an event was generated by word of mouth. The number of contacts can also be used to calculate the show's cost per contact, which is a nice hard number but of little value in isolation, since what is important is the ROI achieved per customer contact (which will vary tremendously depending on the customer and the experience). Another way of touching customers is through media coverage of shows. Longstanding metrics for media impressions can track how much media coverage a show garners and calculate an estimated value. This is an important tool to measure ROI for broad brand awareness if that is an objective for your show.

Lead generation is another kind of contact generation that can be measured, providing a metric for estimating ROI for sales and customer acquisition. Registering customers on-site or online (as done by Shiseido, Bluefly.com, and many other cases) is one way of tracking lead generation. For business customers, whose individual value is higher, companies like SAP will perform "lead qualification," whereby the value of each lead is estimated by asking them questions that include the length of time until their company's purchase decision and their degree of influence on that decision. Companies measuring lead generation should also ask the leads about their purchase intent, which falls under our next category.

Tools for measuring *customer perception and motivation* tend to be quite qualitative. For measuring sales ROI (as when tracking lead generation), these tools will include various measures of customer intent, especially purchase intent. For measuring ROI in brand building, these tools may be used to measure brand awareness (do they recognize the brand?), brand perception (how do they perceive the brand?), brand affiliation (how do they feel about the brand? what relation-ship do they have with it?), or brand loyalty (how readily would they consider switching to a competitor?). Changes in each of these levels of branding (awareness, affiliation, loyalty) can lead to approximations of changes in customer value if a customer equity model is applied.

Tools for measuring *sales generation* from show business tend to be quantitative, but often very approximate. Although they are much sought for shows whose ROI focuses on generat-ing customer purchases, they are often the hardest tools to use accurately. In some cases, a portion of sales generation can be directly tracked if sales happen at the show itself, such as retail sales at an immersionary space or sales closings at trade shows.

In other cases, the best approach may be to look for corre-lations. This may include correlating qualitative data on a show's impact on purchase intent with spikes in sales in nearby retail outlets (assuming no other significant marketing effort took place in the region). Or it may involve comparing business sale closings within a certain span of time after a show business event versus closings during a comparable period without a show business event. Sears succeeded in per-forming a detailed analysis of the sales impact of its Tool Terri-tory shows on both tools and other product lines by tracking performances of stores with and without the Territory before, during, and after the show's launch, and using the non-show-stores as a control to account for other trends affecting sales (other marketing efforts, competitive climate, pricing, etc.). The results allowed it to gain a very clear picture of the large-scale ROI of its show, without attempting to measure the impact on individual customers.

If measuring sales generation fails, it is usually because the company simply cannot track sales efficiently, as is often the case if it is selling through independent channel distributors. "[Retailer] Best Buy is not going to collect data for [manufac-turer] Upper Deck or Sony on sales rates of each of their toys—their focus is total sales in their stores on given days," observes David Laks of DSL Global Event Marketing. "In cases like these, I have actually resorted to sending people in to stand in stores and watch how many people buy a given item off the shelf in a fixed stretch of time." Another approach, used by Panasonic, has been to give out coupons to customers at its shows and track their redemption through retailers. Similar tools could be used by companies like Shiseido to measure sales generation from their shows.

Most of the measurement tools we have looked at require that the measurement begins before a show opens. Post-show measures like brand awareness, retail sales, and purchase intent are meaningless unless compared against a meaningful benchmark measurement conducted beforehand.

Don't Cut the Metrics!

Let us enter a parting plea to companies: Don't neglect the measurement component of your shows.

A recent study of 40 companies using event marketing found that 84 percent feel it is "helpful to have an event agency offer metrics," but only 38 percent say that they would pay for it. Time and again, in talking with agencies producing show business projects, we have heard the refrain, "All clients say they want metrics, but it's the first thing they cut from the budget."

This is, as the old saying goes, "penny-wise and pound-foolish". Without measurement, there can be no ROI on a show. The limited savings achieved by cutting measurement end up wasting resources because there is no way of knowing how well the show worked or what its value was.

Some agencies have taken to bundling at least part of their measurement into the total project cost (while disclosing the research they are planning within their Scope of Work documents). But companies should recognize the importance of measurement on their own and insist on it as an essential part of their show business investment.

We suggest as a guideline that a show should spend 10–15 percent of its budget on carefully conducted measurement (to ensure the other 85–90 percent doesn't go down a hole), with 5 percent as a bare minimum.

Measurement needn't be expensive. There are web-based measurement tools that can measure responses of 5,000 customers for $15,000. Even on a tiny project with, say, a $50,000 budget, at a minimum, a company can have its show biz personnel (the street teamers, Mobile Messengers, etc.) write reports on customer feedback each day and have a manager (preferably outside the project) evaluate the project and synthesize the customer feedback reports at the end.

Depending on your ROI, your measurement can be soft, but don't let it be anecdotal or ad hoc—"when a customer says they saw our show, we usually mention it to the manager." Quantitative measurement can be valuable even when approximate, too. A company will not likely use a complex customer equity model and detailed analysis of acquisition values for a small show—but a simple model along these lines can be developed internally by a skilled marketing department (How much is our average new customer worth?), and can be extremely useful in setting marketing priorities for show business and beyond.

CONCLUSION

To determine an appropriate budget for a show business project, managers must address three issues. The first is to determine their marketing objectives and expected return on investment for the show. The second is to consider the extent of marketing resources, as well as resources for the show from other departments or outside sources. The third issue is to estimate the impact of the show and actual ROI that may be delivered on its marketing objectives.

Understanding the impact of any show requires measurement. Measurement presupposes that marketing objectives and ROI have been identified. With these objectives in hand, a variety of tools are available—quantitative and qualitative—for measurements relating to brand equity, customer equity, and sales generation. Despite the temptation to save money on measurement, it is senseless to attempt a show business project without some carefully planned method—however frugal—to evaluate how it did or didn't succeed.

In the next section, we show you how to put on a show for your own employees and business partners. As we did for external shows (see Chapters 1–5), we examine best practices for internal shows and how they contribute value to the company. We also look at the relationship between show business and leadership and, in our Show Business Leadership Hall of Fame, feature extraordinary leaders who have used extraordinary show business.

||| THE SHOW BUSINESS ORGANIZATION

In Part III we look at how show business can be used inside an organization.

In Chapters 10 and 11, we look at how to put on a show for your own employees and business partners. We examine best practices for internal shows, how they contribute value to a company, and the special issues that arise for this kind of show business.

In Chapters 12 and 13, we look at how show business can be a part of leadership, and we look at the leaders whose persona, myth, and ethos have shaped the experience of their companies.

10 INTERNAL SHOWS FOR EMPLOYEES AND PARTNERS

External customers are not the only audiences for show business. Internal audiences are crucial as well. These internal audiences include a company's employees at every level as well as business partners—channel sellers, independent sales agents, and franchise owner-operators, for example.

Opportunities for internal show business happen in every company, but are often overlooked. Too many companies regularly assemble personnel for communication or morale-boosting with no sense of how to use the opportunity to deliver a great show. They pay to hire a major event organizer to organize a big, expensive, and boring meeting—without a thrilling experience. "If you get 9,000 people together for a sales meeting, then you have to spend the time to create an experience that lasts and stays with them," says Kerry Smith of *Event Marketer* magazine.

Of course, not every internal event can be an occasion for a boundary-breaking, engaging, and entertaining experience. Even at Vans, the snowboard-riding marketing team can't hold every meeting on the slopes. But when planning a major internal event, or a major design project for a headquarters or production facility, or a major intranet development, it makes no sense not to look for a way to create an experience that is compelling, creative and participatory.

WHY INTERNAL AUDIENCES NEED
SHOW BUSINESS

Internal audiences play a critical part in the life of any company and in the way its brands, products, and services are experienced by external customers. This is why internal audiences at every level need show business.

The importance and benefits of creating an internal show can be seen in three types of return on investment (ROI) that internal shows generate:

- Education
- Motivation
- Brand alignment

Show business education makes more of an impact on internal audiences for the same reasons that it makes more of an impact on external audiences: because it is entertaining, interactive, participatory, boundary-breaking, and adds value. Experience makes a lasting impression. This is true whether your company needs to educate employees, managers, or channel sellers about new products and services, new business processes, or about how to improve the quality of the work they are already doing. Show business is also valuable when educating internal audiences about strategic aspects of your business, including understanding who your customers are and how to serve them better.

Show business motivation makes a great tool for sales meetings and business partner summits that aim to boost morale or win buy-in for corporate change (e.g., after a merger). Show business can help your company earn greater support from internal audiences and business partners by making them feel involved, by communicating values through an engaging experience, and by showing the audience that your company is committed to earning their support.

Show business is also a uniquely powerful way to align internal audiences around your brand. Through show business, customers can experience the brand and feel a part of the brand. After experiencing the brand themselves, employees are prepared for their essential mission: to make the experience of the brand available to customers.

Internal show business has another important audience: business partners, who may be delivering the brand on the front lines. Automotive dealers are one example, as we will see in this chapter. Another is the owner-operator of a McDonald's franchise, who acts independently but is largely responsible for a customer's actual experience of the brand. The biennial convention where owner-operators meet with the McDonald's corporation is just the kind of event where show business is needed to bring a brand to life and communicate it to those who will carry it forward.

INTERNAL BRANDING AND SHOW BUSINESS

If the different groups responsible for a company's brand—marketing department, senior management, product developers, retail channels—are not aligned with the same understanding of the brand, they will fail to communicate it effectively to the customer. Building a brand for customers begins with building it for internal audiences.

Experience matters just as much for internal audiences as it does for customers. Companies wouldn't dream of conveying their brand to customers by sending them memos, handbooks of inspirational reading, and posters to tack on their walls. But many companies seem to feel that this is sufficient for communicating their brand to their own employees. No wonder employees don't respond.

This point was well shown in a study that Kings College, University of London, conducted on the impact of an internal show used to build support for a new brand identity after the merger of two long-established British banks, Lloyd's and TSB. The new company, Lloyd's TSB, not only brought together two cultures that had competed for hundreds of years, but asked them to transform themselves into a modern, customer-centric banking brand. To help build internal support for this transformation, the new company invited 5,000 pathfinding employees to a show business event that communicated the brand through peer employee storytelling and dozens of interactive exhibits.

After the show, the pathfinders went back to their departments with word of what they'd learned and with the handouts, visuals, and forms that usually are used for internal brand alignment. The Kings College researchers found that the campaign resulted in a strong increase in employee buy-in to the new direction for the company, but the improvement was consistently stronger among the employees who had experienced the show. For example, when asked if the merger meant that there would now really be "one new bank," the general response for employees went up from 77 percent yes, to 85 percent after the campaign, but for those who attended the show, the yes response rate was 96 percent.

INTERNAL LIVE SHOWS: VW PHAETON AND MAZDA

Show business for internal audiences can be staged with all the same types of shows we have seen in show business for customers, including live events.

When Volkswagen was preparing to launch its new Phaeton luxury car brand in Europe, it decided that it needed to put on a different kind of launch event for its dealers. Their audience was used to truly theatrical experiences; Volkswagen wanted the Phaeton launch to be truly exceptional. They also wanted to communicate differently to their dealers because they needed to educate dealers about something more than just a new product line. Namely: a new kind of customer. The Phaeton was designed for more affluent consumers than Volkswagen had ever sold to. At their launch event, Volkswagen wanted to educate and inspire the dealers regarding the possibilities of the car, but also to help them to understand this different target market, who they were, and why they would buy the Phaeton.

The Phaeton show was experienced by 400 dealers a day over a run of two weeks. The site was chosen to be at Dresden, a city emerging as an international hub in post-reunification Germany and home to the *Gläserne Manufaktur* (Transparent Factory), the brand new, state-of-the-art, transparent production facility that had been built especially to make Phaetons. Invited dealers arrived at the airport and were welcomed with an elegant, low-key presentation of the car and its features. Afterward, they were given a test drive of the Phaeton on a route that ended at a Grand Prix circuit and then taken on a tour of the luminous factory. But it was in the evening that the real show business took place.

The experience started out with champagne and music for the guests in a site on the factory grounds. Suddenly, aerial acrobats burst through the paper ceiling, whisked away the band, and then tore away the walls surrounding the audience—opening the room up into a new space for the audience, the world of Volkswagen's new customers. As they walked forth into the specially designed environment, the dealers found themselves immersed in the lifestyle of their target customer. The space was divided into four zones: Home, Calm, Work, and Play, and in each there was a connoisseur who guided the audience through a presentation about one aspect of the affluent target customer's lifestyle, including wine tastings, tai chi, sailing, aromatherapy (with freshly-rolled Cuban cigars), and watchmakers discussing the machinery of the most elite timepieces. Each area served food that reflected its environment—the sailing-themed zone featured oysters, shark, and crab—and live music.

Mazda, another car company, has also used a live show to educate channel sellers. The company created a training event that traveled the U.S. to dealers and their sales forces, helping them to understand and focus on the Generation X car customer. The traveling show featured an apartment decorated and filled with the possessions of an imaginary Gen X customer. The dealers were sent on a scavenger hunt to see what they could find in the space and what they could learn about the occupant from it. The audience also did role-playing, with actors playing Gen X buyers, to learn how to deal with

FIGURE 10-1   Light shows and aerial acrobats introduced the Volkswagen Phaeton to its new European dealers. Photo courtesy of Jack Morton Worldwide.

the customers, their interests, and feelings about buying cars. Like the Phaeton event, the Mazda show created an unforgettable experience that helped dealers step inside the world of the target customer and understand the type of purchasing experience that this customer requires.

INTERNAL SPACE SHOWS: COCA-COLA AND SERVICEMASTER

Show business for internal audiences can also take the form of immersionary spaces like the ones we've seen for customers. VW's *Gläserne Manufaktur* was the indispensable set for their internal show; other companies have taken experience right into the space of the daily working environment.

FIGURE 10-2   Experiential zones introduced car dealers to tai chi, sailing, and the experiential world of their new customers. Photo courtesy of Jack Morton Worldwide.

For the launch of Coca-Cola's Life Tastes Good ad campaign, the company created an internal experience for employees at their Atlanta headquarters that introduced the campaign to them and helped employees experience the key idea that Coca-Cola is "incidentally important" at key points in people's lives. Kiosks had already been used at the headquarters, and management was wary of broadcasting commercials indoors, which might feel like an invasion of employee space. Instead they decided to create what was called the Glass Quilt. The company collected stories from employees about the role of Coke in their own life, as consumers, not as employees. Two twins described how their grandmother would always give them 5 cents to go to the store to buy a Coke

FIGURE 10-3 Employees' stories and pictures become part of the show in Coca-Cola's Glass Quilt. Photo courtesy of Jack Morton Worldwide.

whenever they visited her; another employee described how he received a Coke as his father's gift at college graduation, and then came home to find 100 shares of Coca-Cola stock on his table.

The stories, and pictures of the employees, were woven together into a colorful glass tapestry of words and images that was installed in the Reception Building, delivering an emotional experience of the brand and what it means to people. Employee response was enthusiastic and emotional, and led the CEO to extend the installation by several weeks.

ServiceMaster decided to incorporate show business into its own headquarter renovations as part of an ongoing effort to develop closer ties between its 13 stand-alone brands in home cleaning and maintenance. In addition to looking at new strategies for cross-selling to customers, the company realized it needed to make employees more aware of the other brands within the company and to help employees experience a new identity as a closer brand family. They began by displaying a series of graphic and video experiences about each brand and their interrelationships. The visuals are installed in the rotunda where employees enter the headquarters. They are also extending experiential space into the heart of the work place. The next stage of development is the creation of a series of conferences rooms to be shared by all the divisions, with each room devoted to an immersionary experience of one of the company's brands. Merry Maids—an older brand with a consumer focus on cleaning homes—will be evoked in a room with chandeliers made out of vintage vacuum cleaners. TruGreen—a yard work and fertilizer brand—will have a room with walls covered with green grass that looks as if a lawn-mower has just passed through it.

Amusing and boundary-breaking, the ServiceMaster show wins extra points for imaginative design and just plain wacki-ness (especially with products and services that can be so... unexciting). With a show like this, it would be hard for employees to resist talking about, thinking about, even feeling familial about the other brands in their family.

INTERNAL WEB SHOWS: J.D. EDWARDS'S MOSAIC

Internal shows can also use interactive media like the Web or intranets, just like customer shows. These media can be important tools for creating experiences that not only provide information, but also contribute to a sense of brand identity and interactive community.

As part of its 25th anniversary and a worldwide relaunch of their brand, J.D. Edwards decided to create an experience on their intranet that would help to unify employees around the new branding campaign. Brand champions in each of 54 offices worldwide were sent a package with a digital camera and a copy of the company's new brand manifesto. The cham-pions shared the manifesto and other information learned from the company's new branding university with their colleagues and collected their personal thoughts on how they experienced the J.D. Edwards brand as employees. They also took pictures of as many colleagues as possible and sent everything back to the home office. There, these thousands of personal postings (from nearly three-quarters of all employees worldwide) were converted into a virtual company directory in the form of a graphic mosaic showing the thousands of faces of contributing employees. Now, rather than just looking each other up by telephone number or email, J.D. Edwards's staff can find each other online and put a face, and a personal story of the brand, to the coworkers they collaborate with across 22 countries. Employee feedback to the mosaic has been enthusiastic, and site tracking has found that users are returning on a regular basis to use it as an internal communications resource.

INTEGRATED INTERNAL SHOWS: THE MARY KAY MODEL

The best cases of internal show business come from organizations that use integrated show business throughout their company to vividly communicate the experience of their brand identity and core values to every employee at every opportunity. Our internal show biz answer to the integrated customer shows of Victoria's Secret is the integrated employee-focused model of Mary Kay Cosmetics.

The company's founder, Mary Kay Ash (who died in 2001), built this billion-dollar privately held company from an initial $5,000 investment through an incredibly dedicated independent sales force—most of them women. She used show business to communicate to them the distinctive spirit of her company and its corporate mission: to enrich women's lives.

Mary Kay strove to build her business around a culture of mutual support and praise and collaboration rather than competition. New sales consultants start out by receiving a ribbon when they make their first $100 sale. Weekly meetings of each sales unit are held to provide a built-in network of support, to share enthusiasm, and to foster learning. Handwritten notes of praise get the message across, too. But at Mary Kay, praise is not only given, it is elevated to show business, and is an experience for all employees to celebrate.

The biggest shows in honor of Mary Kay's employees are held at the company's annual training seminars. Held over three days in Las-Vegas-style convention settings, these multimillion dollar extravaganzas attract more than 35,000 sales reps and directors, as well as academics from Harvard Business School paying to attend the education sessions to write a case study. The show business peak of the event is Awards Night. There, the company's highest achievers are each lionized and given awards in a show to rival the best in Vegas. The winning sales consultants walk across the stage waving to their colleagues while wearing gowns, sashes, and crowns like pageant queens. These sales stars are awarded Cinderella gifts, lavish presents chosen not as prudent investments, but as indulgent luxuries that make a show of how valued they are. Prizes include signature jewelry such as the diamond Bumblebee Pin (to show they've "flown to the top"), the jewel-encrusted Ladder of Success pin, exotic dream vacations, and, most famously, the Mary Kay pink Cadillac, more than 10,000 of which have been bestowed on Mary Kay achievers.

"Recognition is the key," Ash said. "If you give somebody a 40-cent item in a $1 box with $100 worth of recognition, that's a thousand times more effective than giving a $100 gift in the same box but with 40 cents of recognition!"[11]

By making show business out of her company's mission to empower women, and by giving her own salespeople a starring role at every turn, Mary Kay transformed the company into a family. Her empire of pink and pageantry, glitzy as it seemed to some, built an amazing and successful sales force committed to her vision. Long recognized by *Forbes* magazine as one of the 100 Best Companies to Work for in America, Mary Kay Cosmetics has grown to include 850,000 independent agents in 37 countries (more employees than the U.S. Postal Service), and has produced billions of dollars in sales and 151 women millionaires.

Keeping On-Brand for
Internal Shows

Now that we've seen several examples of shows for internal audiences, let's return to the topics of Part II and see how some of our business lessons for show business play out for internal shows.

Keeping a show on-brand is just as important for internal audiences as for external ones. Unfortunately, it is even more likely to be neglected in practice. Too often, companies think that by hiring a band and adding light shows and good food to an internal event they will improve the experience and therefore create a more effective presentation. But internal shows need to be integrated with their brand and message throughout every stage of implementation.

"A good internal event should be a mirror of your external branding events," says David Laks of DSL Global Event Marketing. "The event needs to be about the company, and the company's culture, and how the employees can support that culture. You need to position your brand highly in their minds to keep them motivated." In great internal shows like Mary Kay Cosmetics's seminars or Volkswagen's launch of the Phaeton, the same care and creativity is taken to communicating the brand at every touch point as it is in a show or in advertising for customers.

Knowing Your Audience at
Internal Shows

One of the most difficult parts of show business for internal audiences is trying to determine who your audience will be among many internal constituents. For example, a campaign to introduce a new IT system and build buy-in for it throughout a global retail company would require targeted communications to: executive leadership, administrative and support offices, retail outlet managers, retail outlet employees, IT management, IT staff, and affected product manufacturers and suppliers.

In a branding campaign it is especially important that all internal audiences be reached, because if they are not all aligned around the new brand identity, discrepancies will occur in customer experiences. Too often, important internal audiences are left out, especially executive leadership, which is assumed to always know everything about the brand and to need no alignment with company initiatives.

After a company has identified all the internal audiences it needs to reach, it then needs to craft a message that will be relevant to each particular one. There may be overlap between these different communications, but each one should be thought of separately and tracked to measure its effectiveness.

With so many audiences, is it realistic for a company to try to put on a great show business experience for each one? Not always. A good way to prioritize internal audiences and target a show for internal brand building is to follow these four steps:

- Identify your key external audiences (most valued customers).
- Identify which internal audiences will have the biggest impact on the brand for these external audiences.
- Identify the internal brand touch points that convey the brand to these internal audiences.
- Create a show business experience at these touch points tailored to these internal audiences.

SBBRM FOR INTERNAL SHOWS

We can learn more about how internal show business works by returning to our Show Business Brand Relationship Model and seeing how it applies to internal shows. In these cases, a company's personnel help to build the brand by creating the show; they also relate to the brand by experiencing the show; and they help develop the brand by participating in the show (see Figure 10-4).

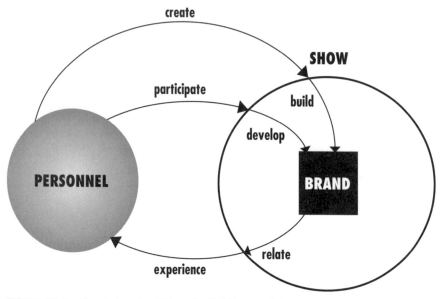

FIGURE 10-4   Show Business Brand Relationship Model for internal shows.

The SBBRM for internal shows reveals a parallel to the model of customer shows, where customers not only put on the show for each other, but they also experience and respond to it. In fact, internal show business is very much like customer shows in which the same audience is creating and experiencing the show, relating to each other, and creating a sense of community through the show.

EXTENDING YOUR INTERNAL SHOW

The most common way that companies extend their internal shows is through the technique known as *cascading*. Key personnel are given the opportunity to experience the company's show business itself, and then are given the responsibility to return to their work groups and convey their information, enthusiasm, or understanding of the brand to those who couldn't see the show directly. With larger companies, a well-planned cascade greatly enhances the natural diffusion of ideas throughout the organization. It also makes show business more feasible (it's not often that a company can afford to put on a great experience for every single employee) by delivering widespread impact when only a fraction of the total internal audience can experience the show directly.

Both the Lloyd's TSB brand alignment show and the creation of J.D. Edwards's intranet mosaic were based around the model of a cascade. A best practice used in the Lloyd's TSB cascade was to identify pathfinders: individuals who were nominated by their peers as the people most respected among their group.

METRICS FOR INTERNAL SHOWS

Securing funding for measurement of internal show business is sometimes even tougher than doing so for customer shows because the budgets tend to be smaller. For many internal shows, companies use only anecdotal responses (what the CEO hears back from people) to evaluate the project, relying on word of mouth within the organization to give feedback.

Planned measurement tools will always provide much better information on what succeeded and what didn't for any internal show. Fortunately, internal show measurements can also be cheaper because the audience is easily contacted for follow-up. For example, for very large meetings (a few thousand or more), online attitudinal surveys can be done for as little as $3 per person.

It is especially important for benchmarking measurements to be done before an internal show because of their help in identifying key target audiences, understanding their needs, and matching the creative content to their greatest needs. Some agencies include such premeasurement in their brand-alignment projects even if a client company is unwilling to pay for post-measurements of the project's effects.

An industry insider described to us the case of a retail company that was planning a four-day celebratory event for all its store managers that was timed to coincide with the company's 25th anniversary. Business partners (manufacturers and suppliers) were also being invited as a gesture of hospitality, but the company was focusing its attention on creating a show that would help to align the most recently hired managers with the company's brand identity. After some early attitudinal measurements of all participating groups, however, it was discovered that the retailer's managers were quite well aligned with the brand identity, but that its business partners were surprisingly disaffected with the brand and sour about what they felt was "revolving-door" treatment from the retailer. The result of the measurement was a dramatic shift in the planning of the celebration so that it could refocus on making business partners feel respected as a part of the company. Measurement after the fact showed a significant shift in their perception of the brand.

BUDGETING FOR INTERNAL SHOWS

Budgets for internal shows tend to be smaller than for customer shows. But small budgets can still yield compelling experiences if shows are produced creatively with close attention to objectives. The J.D. Edwards mosaic cost less than $150,000 to produce, and that included a digital camera sent to every office and a poster of the mosaic for all 5,000 employees at the end. Funding for internal shows varies depending on the nature of the project. Funds may come from Human Resources, the Sales department, Public Relations, or an internal marketing communications budget.

Show business for internal audiences typically receives funding priority on occasions such as:

- Annual sales meetings or channel sellers events
- Product launches for channel sellers
- Launch of a new ad campaign
- Brand relaunch
- Mergers and acquisitions

- New internal business initiatives or process changes
- Boosting morale after restructuring or lay-offs

Internal shows are also much more likely to be done entirely in-house than are shows for customers. Large companies that produce hundreds of trade shows, seminars, and other events will often reduce costs by keeping a permanent project management team of their own that produces events and is called upon to create show business with the right vision and creativity for internal audiences.

CONCLUSION

Opportunities for internal show business abound, from live events like annual sales meetings to the design of company workspace and virtual company intranets. In any internal show, the same show business rules apply: keep the show rigorously on-brand, identify your key audiences and create an experience that is relevant to them, find ways to extend the impact of your show, and use metrics to plan your show and to measure its effectiveness after the fact.

Internal shows often have to make do with less funding than shows for customers, but the importance of internal communications and the rising recognition of internal branding mean that more and more executives are coming to realize the value of a great show on the inside.

As we mentioned, these internal shows are much more likely to be produced on the inside by managers within the company. For that reason, in the next chapter we would like to offer a few practical guidelines on how to turn your own internal communication needs into a great show.

11 How to Run Your Own Show: The Three P's and the IBM Opera

When a company puts on a show for customers (as in the cases that we saw in Part I), it usually manages the project in conjunction with an outside creative agency. By contrast, show business for internal audiences is often produced by internal departments alone.

In this chapter, we provide guidelines for those readers who plan to develop a show business project on their own. We will begin with what we call the Three P's of Show Business. Managers need to address these three issues when they begin the process of creative implementation:

1. **The Players**—because every show needs people to fill specific roles
2. **The Plot**—because every show needs a story
3. **The Place**—because every show needs a stage

After some guidelines for handling the Three P's, we will present a detailed behind-the-scenes case of how the Three P's were used in the development of a creative show business production for an internal corporate audience at IBM.

THE PLAYERS

The first P of show business is the players. A manager needs a variety of players in order to mount a successful show business production. The main roles will include financiers (who handle the budget and expenses), organizers (project managers for a show), creative directors (scriptwriters, art directors, copywriters), performers (actors, stunt men, guides, and ring leaders), and roadies (logistical support).

If you are producing a show internally, you should try to fill these positions with your own managers and company employees as much as possible because they best understand your company's business strategy and how it relates to the production. Getting them involved in putting on a show can also be a great way to inspire and engage some of the best employees in your company.

You may need to look outside to fill some of your creative positions (musicians, actors, designers), although you should first make a thorough inventory of what hidden resources your company may possess. If it has a trade show production unit, set and lighting designers will be available internally. Show business also has a way of bringing the secret talents of company employees out into the light of day. Perhaps your finance officer is also a jazz singer. Maybe your IT department includes a scriptwriter.

Of course, job descriptions may need to go through some stretching if you are going to mount a show business production with your own staff. In-house show business requires a nontraditional view of employee roles. For the purpose of staging a show, a marketing manager may need to view their job as a producer, a finance officer may need to become a show financier, and performers will need to be chosen from all levels of management. Finally, your front-line employees may be recruited to handle the more mundane grunt work, but they should also feel that they are part of the show—viewing themselves as show business roadies who perform cool tasks. Gaffer, anyone?

THE PLOT

The second P of show business is the plot. Your plot is the concept that will bring your strategy to life by giving it a dramatic embodiment. It is central to any show business production because the plot's job is to deliver your corporate message and to do so in an unusual and memorable way.

There can be various levels of plot, depending on your type of show. Some shows have a narrative plot, with characters, story, climax, and conclusion. Think of the fictional scenario of the viral epidemic and its Costa Rican antidote that drives the drama of J.D. Edwards's Corridors of Chaos show. For other shows, the plot is more of a guiding concept or theme, such as the use of bondage and sado-masochism in the G-Shock launch party, or the world of fantasy, indulgence, and glamor evoked by Victoria's Secret's shows. In other cases, the plot may simply be the experience or impression in which the show immerses its audience, like the elegant hospitality and gracious consultation of the Shiseido Studio experience.

The plot for your show will come out of the first five steps in our framework for keeping a show on-brand (see Chapter 6). These steps will ensure that your plot is aligned with your brand, suits your audience, and focuses on the strategic communication objectives for your show.

But in addition to that, the plot needs a creative element to focus the experience. We see three stages that you should go through in developing a plot: picking a recognizable genre, finding your underlying dramatic themes, and developing possibilities for humor.

PICKING A GENRE

A genre should give you a framework that your audience will immediately recognize. We have seen shows that were built around the genres of song-and-dance musicals (think of The Story of Saturn with dance, music, and video telling its story), fashion shows (Victoria's Secret's events), and aerial acrobatics (the opening of VW's Phaeton launch). Other possible genres to exploit could include detective stories, late-night talk shows, pulp romances, action hero movies, Saturday-Night-Live-style sketch comedy, science fiction, epic histories, or even a night at the opera.

A genre will always bring with it lots of stock characters, themes, and story elements on which to draw. The talk show has its host, the sidekick, and the chatty bandleader. The fashion show has its models and the eccentric designer. A detective story always has to begin with a late night appearance at the detective's office by a distraught and good-looking client of the opposite sex.

A good show business plot always incorporates these genres to its advantage (as the saying goes, great writers don't borrow, they steal). If you're telling a story, don't reinvent the wheel. Using elements from pre-existing texts (but not copyrighted ones!) makes any show more familiar and readily digestible, even if the audience doesn't recognize your sources. Saturn's musical show borrowed elements from successful Broadway shows like *Tap Dogs* and *Stomp* in its use of percussion music created by playing on car parts, for example. The characters in your show business plot should likewise be familiar or recognizable faces (you aren't writing a literary novel here).

Likewise, your plot should include references or topics that your audience recognizes such as insider perspectives and current events from your own company, the industry, or your audience's lifestyle.

PLOT THEMES: SEX, MONEY, AND POWER

The next part of developing your plot will be identifying its themes. These themes are the simple dramatic ploys used to keep your audience's attention (as opposed to the specific strategic message you are trying to convey about your business or brand).

Literary theorists and high school English teachers have enumerated countless themes for art such as man against nature, individual versus society, or oedipal conflict. We suggest you consider the universal appeal of three great themes behind almost every great play, opera, or poem from the ages: sex, money, and power (and in that order of universal appeal). Briefly,

- **Sex.** The oldest theme in the book for marketing. Yes, sex sells, but it does best if you keep it fresh and find a new angle. The Victoria's Secret show is built around fantasies of beauty and desire. Pushing it further, Abercrombie & Fitch has made a successful show out of pictures of naked and strapping young men and women in its clothing catalogs (who ever thought a clothing catalog should show people with clothes on?). Look for a possible theme of sex in your show, of course.

- **Money.** Why do we love gambling? The lottery? The rags-to-riches-to-rags story? Because of the universal allure of wealth. Think of Mary Kay's fabulous diamond-studded pins, or the top-rated TV game shows about who wants to be a millionaire, or marry one, or knock one on the head and steal their identity.

- **Power.** For another great theme, think of *Julius Caesar*, *The Godfather*, or *The West Wing*. Some of the most attractive shows are dramas about power and who gets to have it. To see a great example of how American Express has made a show out of status and prestige, see *Centurion: The AmEx Snob Show* on page 182.

MAKE 'EM LAUGH

One last point on developing a good plot: don't forget a sense of humor. Good show business is often amusing and never takes itself too seriously, so humor is an essential part of your plot. Irony, parody, slapstick—each has a place in different shows for different audiences. Humor needs to grow out of an understanding of your audience; it must be in tune with them. Different audiences will have different senses of humor. If your show is for IT programmers, for young sales associates,

CENTURION: THE AMEX SNOB SHOW

An American Express card used to be a mark of distinction, before a green card was given to every kid who entered college and a gold to anyone who got a job. So much for exclusivity.

Of course, nowadays we all talk about the importance of offering competitive service for every customer, but in many quarters, old-style snobbishness and exclusivity still rule. In the late 1990s American Express entered the world of ultimate snob shows with its "black card," the Centurion. Available by invitation only, and only to AmEx's most elite customers, the black card is American Express's stylish move to snatch back some of the cachet that they cashed out on when they offered their original green and gold cards to the broad public.

With an annual fee of $1,000, the Centurion card needs to make you feel special, and it does. Sure, there's a list of member privileges that sound really great: personal shoppers to assist you at Neiman Marcus, complimentary consultation from Provident Financial Management, and a range of travel services for the pampered class (access to airport clubs, dedicated check-in, and upgrades to the Concorde). For some travelers, these benefits might all add up to value that exceeds the annual fee. The real point of the card's benefits, however, is their prestige. It doesn't really matter if you never have time to use the personal shopper—the Centurion card is something you want as a status symbol, first and foremost.

American Express puts on a real show to make you feel the Centurion's status. Not only can you not apply for the black card (as it boldly says on the web site), but those select few who are invited don't even have to lift a finger to place an order for one. It simply arrives at their door like a mystery present, in a sumptuously padded black box with the assurance that they are one of only a few thousand special people in the world to be given this magic charm.

Obviously, this won't work for many kinds of businesses that are built around a broad customer base. But, as American Express has shown by extending its brand between the democratic (green) and the aristocratic (black), sometimes you can have it both ways. Other brands like Victoria's Secret have taken similar tactics (think of their hyper-expensive Fantasy Gifts versus their affordable but seemingly upscale lingerie). Offering an exclusive product with a big show of its status power can shower a little aspirational glow on your other offerings.

or for senior finance managers, you ought to know what they find funny.

Don't think that humor can only work in shows selling frivolous products or whose message is light-hearted. It is often a serious message that most needs humor to win its audience.

One example is Polyp Man, who was invented for a public health show after serious communications had failed. Polyp Man is the villain and central character in a series of public service announcements created for TV by the American Cancer Society and the Advertising Council.

Polyp Man is a low-budget and tacky sort of villain, dressed in an enormous bulging red spandex body suit. In the ads, he runs from doctors in chase scenes that are parodies of reality police shows like *Cops.* The noble doctors inevitably catch him and bring him to justice. In one silly sequence Polyp Man is caught in a kitchen stuffing his face in front of an open refrigerator; in others he is apprehended at a school, or in a chase down an alleyway.

This silly piece of show business was created to meet a sobering public health challenge: half of all colon cancer deaths in the U.S. could be prevented by screening, but only 44 percent of Americans over 50 get screened. The point of the comical TV campaign is to raise the subject of polyp testing in a way that reduces embarrassment, gets people talking about it, brings it out of the realm of denial, and motivates people by letting them view doctors as able to help them tackle the problem.

Previous public service announcements about the issue had taken a serious tone (shots of graveyards and so on), but the American Cancer Society found that their somber message was ineffective at motivating people. By contrast, the new Polyp Man ads have tested well for motivating the audience while getting the message across.

Our message: don't be afraid to try to be funny, whatever your message! A sense of humor is often just the thing to get your audience engaged and motivated.

FIGURE 11-1   Humor in the unlikeliest of places: Polyp Man. Photo courtesy of Campbell-Ewald.

THE PLACE

Once you have the players for your show and you've started fashioning your plot (including its genre, theme, and humor), the last piece of your production is the place where your show will be held. This is the third P of show business.

As we've seen by now, an internal show can happen in all kinds of places: on the Internet, at a factory, a dealership, a headquarters rotunda, a conference room, or a giant sales conference.

In selecting the right place for your production, we advise that you look at three key considerations:

- **Available audience.** Where can you best reach your target audience—sales staff, middle managers, sales channel partners, or senior executives? Who will see your show if you stage it in a given location, or at a given event?

- **Image impact.** How will the location affect the impact of your message? Will it enhance it? Detract from it? Overshadow it? In some cases a well-chosen place may have scenery or an environment that actually plays up and reinforces the strategic message of your show.

- **Cost considerations.** How expensive is a location? Is it a good value for the audience you will be able to reach? What quality of production will be demanded by your location and what costs will this incur for your show to make the best of its location?

Once you have selected the place for your show, you need to be sure to tailor the production to the facility. This will involve several questions: What expectations does your stage create in an audience? Does it demand a particular caliber of production? (This requirement will differ between a board-room, a small amphitheater, or a huge convention space.) What special facilities or technologies are available in this place that you could incorporate in your show? What other associations will your audience have with the place that you might make use of in your plot? What other experience may your audience have just had (arriving on a train, hearing a previous speaker at an event, etc.)?

In planning your show, don't forget to scope out its place very carefully beforehand for any details that will affect your show (Where are the sources of electricity? What kinds of projections or technology are available? What kinds of lighting can be used or brought in? Where are the entrances and exits off stage?). With careful consideration, you will be able to make the best use of whatever place you have selected to maximize your own show.

Now that we've discussed some of the more practical issues involved in turning a show business strategy into an internal show, let's look at one case in detail to see how the Three P's may be applied. Here we will take a look behind the scenes of a project we did with IBM, where we created a show to help the company address a pressing internal communication need. The goals were typical of internal show business: to educate managers and motivate them to implement a change in business process.

THE CHALLENGE: BRAND CONFUSION AT IBM

In early 2001, IBM approached us to help them address the issue of brand confusion at their company.

IBM is one of the leading, most recognized brands in the world. Indeed, the IBM corporate brand had been well managed for many years. In the public perception, IBM was considered to be in a much stronger position than in the early 1990s when the company had a record loss of $5 billion in one year. Due to the focused and disciplined approach that Lou Gerstner, IBM's CEO, had taken throughout the 1990s, IBM had experienced an amazing turn-around. As Gerstner writes in *Who Says Elephants Can't Dance?*, the corporate brand played a key role in this turnaround.

The problem now was the more than 900 additional brands that existed within the organization—brands such as Lotus, Intellistation, Websphere, Workpad, Storewatch, and many others. Consumers often either had not heard of them, confused them with other IBM brands, or did not even associate them with IBM. These lesser-known brands had unclear and confusing identities in the marketplace. A corporate identity manager had been hired by IBM as a change agent to alter this situation, and she called us to help.

Up until now the company lacked a systematic process for evaluating new names. Whenever a strategic business unit or division decided to take a product to the market, it made up a new name and designed a new visual identity. There was little central control. Numerous acquisitions further contributed to the brand confusion. What IBM needed was a systematic approach to brand naming and to building a brand architecture that would organize all the brands into a coherent whole. The brand architecture would lay out which names would carry the IBM umbrella, which ones would be endorsed by IBM, and which ones (if any) should be presented to customers as stand-alone brands.

To help develop such an approach, IBM hired the naming and corporate identity agency Interbrand. The company was also interested in using a creative experience to convey the key issues to its own employees and get their buy-in for making changes to the branding process. That's where we came in—to put on a show.

IBM's Audience and Objectives

IBM identified their key audience as top management within the company across all product divisions; these were the personnel who would need to buy into the new naming process they were devising in order for it to succeed. The challenge of our show was to build support for a new branding system among this group by convincing them that change was necessary and in their own best interest.

Because these managers would be giving up some turf and authority as part of this new change, we wanted to counteract any possible tensions by using humor and a live show that would dramatize the issues in a funny and disarming manner.

Our objective was to use a story to convey three points to motivate leaders in the company to change the status quo:

- IBM's current approach to naming had spun out of control.
- The lack of a systematic process for branding within IBM was confusing to customers, and this had negative consequences for IBM products and services.
- Input, valuable contribution, and compliance to new processes are required from everybody within the company to create a more consistent approach to branding.

Because this was an internal issue that affected the audience's own work processes, we felt the show should take place at the company's headquarters as part of an overall educational event for upper middle and senior management so that in-depth discussion of the management issues involved could take place before and after the performance.

IBM'S CHOICE OF GENRE

We decided that the genre of opera would be most appropriate for addressing the naming issues. The opera that we produced was called *Der Turm von Babble, Inc. (The Tower of Babble, Incorporated): A tragic opera about brand strategy and naming.*

We chose opera as a genre because it provides a highly dramatic form in which we could address the issues in an engaging and entertaining format. Many people do not easily relate to opera (they think it is a strange and outdated art form), and we thought that this attitude would be ideal for getting the audience to step back a bit. They might then be more susceptible to a message that could be surprising and perhaps even threatening to them.

The many languages of opera made the genre a natural choice for addressing naming and language issues. Our opera was performed in German and Italian, which allowed us to rattle off names of IBM products in multiple languages and address the importance of language as one of the essential issues of branding. Of course, as is customary in modern opera houses, English supertitles (translations of the text that appear above the stage) were provided as well—which added to the joke: mock 19th-century opera lyrics about servers and software solutions.

IBM'S PLAYERS

In producing the opera, we had to make decisions about the Three P's of Show Business: players, plot, and place.

There were numerous players involved in bringing the show to life: the financier (the IBM corporate identity manager), the organizers (project manager and stage director), the creative directors (script writer, music director, lighting designer, and set designer), the various performers (a pianist, a mezzo-soprano, an African drum ensemble, and dancers), and the roadies (stage manager, driver, and video crew).

The main character in the opera was the customer—Brünn-nhilde, the CEO of a small business looking for software solutions provided by IBM. The other characters in the main part of the opera were all IBM employees and despite their excitement, they did not speak a word. Instead, they were represented by dancers who acted on stage in pantomime and stylized movements that expressed their inability to communicate with the customer.

In addition to these roles, there was also the unusual speaking role of "The Business Professor," a character who appeared between acts. This character served two functions: first, he provided an *outside* perspective and interpretation of the corporate spectacle, and, *by doing so*, The Business Professor, *in complicity with the audience*, represented the audience *on stage*. Being a one-man version of the Greek chorus, he brought the corporate audience into the production, allowing them to watch and participate in the operatic staging of themselves.

IBM's Plot

Our next step was to translate our strategic goals into an entertaining plot for the show. (An act-by-act narrative of the opera can be found in *Synopsis of the Plot of Der Turm von Babble, Inc.* on page 192.)

Our first decision was to use a familiar reference point for our story about name confusion. We chose the biblical tale of the Tower of Babel, the original skyscraper, built by a prideful people who were then struck down and cursed with a confusion of languages. To update this, we imagined a company called Babble, Inc., and decided that it, too, was building a tower and was pridefully ignorant of its customers' needs for clear language. (A corporate tower had resonance because it can be seen as a symbol of strength, but also of lack of external perspective.)

Since we were playing to an internal audience, we also wanted to use elements from IBM themselves. We used actual IBM product names under discussion at the management event that day, and we chose to integrate one of IBM's current television ads into the opera.

Before writing the script (libretto) for the opera and deciding what music to use or commission, we identified three key themes that the plot needed to dramatize:

- Internal and external aspects of branding
- Interactions in which the brand matters and comes to life
- Name proliferation and the danger of confusion

The theme of internal versus external aspects of branding was included in the opera's structure: Act 1 played within IBM, Act 2 played outside IBM in the world of the customer, and then in Act 3 the two worlds were juxtaposed. Each act was also associated with a particular attitude or feeling (joy and hubris, expectation and disappointment, despair and revengeful triumph)—illustrating the emotional, and not just the rational, side of branding.

Interactions focused around the brand occurred at critical points. In Act 1, the Tower of Babble, Inc. is erected upon the shaky foundation of brand proliferation. In Act 2, we witness the monolith's brand representatives in their chilling interactions with the customer. In Act 3, the brand experience has turned inward, with the customer contemplating suicide but ultimately turning aggression outward.

Name proliferation was visually displayed in Act 1 by having the "employees" stick the numerous names of IBM product divisions on the erected tower. In Act 2, the distraught customer is faced with a confusing profusion of product brochures. In Act 3, we encounter again the stark image of the name-encrusted tower, now in darker lighting.

IBM's PLACE

IBM wanted us to perform the opera at their headquarters in Armonk, New York, which is located in the middle of a forest. To allude to the venue, we wrote a plot that featured the erection of a massive tower by the different divisions of the company in the middle of a forest—a symbol of the energy and drive of a large organization and the positive outcomes that are likely to happen if these energies are channeled in the right direction.

To plan the staging for the production, we examined the space, opportunities for sets and lighting, amplification and places for musicians. It turned out that we were dealing with a small theater with only limited lighting resources. Moreover, the theater did not allow for extensive set designs. We turned this constraint to our advantage by using striking visual design and computer imagery on backdrops as well as colorful props that got the audience to focus on the key story elements. We felt, however, that we needed an impressive image at the end of the opera, and our lighting designer created it in the form of a rainbow—a powerful and memorable symbol for the transition point in IBM's branding strategy.

CONCLUSION

The IBM opera and the management conference of which it was a part were a success. Since then, IBM has made significant progress in branding issues and received the buy-in from employees. The project was especially well received by the key executives involved in the naming initiative. The corporate identity manager said that the naming opera was "absolutely fabulous" and the perfect way to get the point across that IBM wanted to do things more creatively and more strategically. The president of Interbrand called the production creative and innovative. Yet, the highest compliment to us came from one of the audience members who said, "This is the first opera I saw that didn't put me to sleep."

We've seen now how show business can play an important role within an organization for engaging and communicating with a wide variety of internal audiences. We have also looked at how a company that is focusing on show business can put on its own shows for internal audiences. But show business inside an organization can also be an important part of leadership. More than any other member of an organization, a corporate leader needs to communicate effectively in order to engage a wide variety of audiences: employees, business partners, investors, and customers of all kinds. In the next chapter we will learn how show business can be used to link leadership to the ethos of a company and communicate it to every audience.

Synopsis of the Plot of Der Turm von Babble, Inc.

Prelude

The opera begins with the voice of a narrator announcing the world premiere of *Der Turm von Babble, Inc.*, which is, according to the announcer, an unusual piece that melds 19th- and 20th-century traditions in a unique 21st-century business opera. The narrator explains that *Der Turm von Babble, Inc.* is in a mixed genre, calling for a Germanic libretto with Dionysian dancing, African drumming, and low-quality electric keyboard.

Act 1 Der Turm wird gebaut (Building the Tower)

After a drumming overture that bubbles with anticipation, Act 1 begins in a place somewhere in the forests of Armonk, NY, at the turn of a new century. Once again, Babble, Inc. is having a very strong year, with growth in its operations worldwide. Senior management has decided to invest in building a corporate tower for its headquarters. A site has been found in the forests of Armonk, and the managers from every division have come to participate. After sanctifying the location, construction is ready to begin on the tower. Each division of the corporation is brought in to help in the building of the tower, as part of a team-building initiative. Each division decides that it will use the occasion to select an excellent new name and to announce it on their own brick of the Tower. The managers of Babble, Inc. are overjoyed at the richness and diversity of their Tower and its many names. When it is finished, they open the Tower for business, presenting it to the public, ready to provide their business solutions.

SYNOPSIS OF THE PLOT OF DER TURM VON BABBLE, INC. (CONTINUED)

INTERMEZZO

The intermezzo after Act 1 introduces the unusual role of The Business Professor, who explains the relevance of Act 1 to the audience in business terms (*Managing Brands Strategically: Internal Perspectives*).

ACT 2 BRÜNNHILDES HOFFNUNG (A NEW HOPE FOR BRÜNNHILDE, THE CEO)

Act 2 starts with the IBM advertisement "Crash Site," which shows a CEO leading an emergency meeting after her company's web site has gone down. Onstage, enter Brünnhilde, the CEO of a medium-sized technology company. She is faced with a serious crisis of software integration and calls her deputies into an emergency meeting. Brünnhilde is distraught. She awaits news from her two middle managers whom she sent to hire Babble, Inc. They come back with good news: Babble, Inc. has taken on the job to solve their systems integration problem. Brünnhilde is overjoyed (*Oh teure Halle gruess ich Dich*—O mighty tower, I give thee greeting). Brünnhilde's business indeed recovers successfully from its systems crash. Brünnhilde decides to hire Babble to handle all her e-business needs. The scene changes to the boardroom in the Tower of Babble, Inc., where Brünnhilde has arrived to hear of their products. The offerings are overwhelming and confusing in their endless product names. Brünnhilde is increasingly perplexed and frustrated. She wonders how this company can help her with systems integration when they haven't integrated something as simple as their names (*"Ich weiss nicht, wo ich bin, was ich tue"*—"I don't think a company with a confusing brand strategy can help me"). In Table 11-1 you can read the lyrics and translation to this aria.

INTERMEZZO

The Business Professor appears again, explaining to the audience the meaning of Act 2 (*Managing Brands Strategically: Customer Perception*).

SYNOPSIS OF THE PLOT OF DER TURM VON BABBLE, INC. (CONTINUED)

ACT 3 BRÜNNHILDES VERKLÄRUNG (THE MADNESS OF BRÜNNHILDE)

The final act takes place outside the tower. Brünnhilde appears in a bloody sheet, waving the quarterly earnings report. She is in deep monetary and existential pain over the inconsistency and senselessness of naming at Babble, Inc. She thought they could transform her business, but she doesn't even understand whom she should talk to at their company or how. Having gone mad, she has decided to kill herself with a dagger and sings now in Italian (*A, Scostati*—Ah, Babble Inc.!). Yet, ultimately, she turns her aggression against the tower and runs it over, exiting the stage with a frantic, triumphant scream. After she has left, a mysterious rainbow appears, filling the entire stage.

POSTLUDE

The Business Professor appears and delivers his final remarks (*Managing Brands Strategically: Aligning the Organization*).

TABLE 11-1   Lyrics to *Ich weiss nicht, wo ich bin, was ich tue*[a]

SUNG IN GERMAN	ENGLISH TRANSLATION
Ich weiss nicht, wo ich bin, was ich tue,	I don't know what I need anymore, or what they are doing;
Bald in Netview, bald in Netvista ohne Ruhe!	now they speak of Netview, now of Netvista.
Jedes Mädchen, ach, macht mich erröten,	Every product makes me change color;
Jeder Dame erbebet mein Herz Jeder Dame erbebet mein Herz Jeder Dame erbebet mein Herz	every service makes me tremble.
Hör das Wörtlein Tivoli ich nur Thinkpad OS/X, Fühl in Glut ich die Wangen entbrennen,	My breast becomes nervous and upset, at merely the words "Tivoli," "Thinkpad OS/X,"

TABLE 11-1   Lyrics to *Ich weiss nicht, wo ich bin, was ich tue*[a] *(Continued)*

SUNG IN GERMAN	ENGLISH TRANSLATION
Ach, und doch treibt mich von Liebe zu reden	and a desire for simplicity,
Ein Verlangen, ein Verlangen,das ich nicht deuten kann Ein Verlangen, ein Verlangen,das ich nicht deuten kann	a desire that I can't explain— leaves me confused.
Ich weiss nicht, wo ich bin, was ich tue,	I don't know what I need anymore, or what they are doing;
Bald in Netview, bald in Netvista ohne Ruhe!	now they speak of Netview, now of Netvista.
Jedes Mädchen, ach, macht mich erröten,	Every product makes me change color;
Jeder Dame erbebet mein Herz Jeder Dame erbebet mein Herz Jeder Dame erbebet mein Herz	every service makes me tremble.
Rede von Lieb' im Wachen	They talk about solutions when awake;
Rede von Lieb' in Träumen	They talk about e-business when dreaming.
Mit Intellistation, Workpad mit InfoSpeed und WebSphere Mit StorWatch und mit Lotus	About Intellistation, about Work Pad, about InfoSpeed, about WebSphere, about StorWatch, about Lotus...
Und all' die süssen Klagen, tragen die Lüfte fort, tragen die Lüfte fort	...which carry away with them the sound of futile words.
Wachen red' ich von Liebe	They talk about solutions when awake;
Rede von Lieb' in Träumen	They talk about e-business when dreaming.

TABLE 11-1 Lyrics to *Ich weiss nicht, wo ich bin, was ich tue*[a] *(Continued)*

SUNG IN GERMAN	ENGLISH TRANSLATION
Mit Intellistation, Workpad mit InfoSpeed und WebSphere Mit StorWatch und mit Lotus	About Intellistation, about Work Pad, about InfoSpeed, about WebSphere, about StorWatch, about Lotus...
Und all' die süssen Klagen, tragen die Lüfte fort, tragen die Lüfte fort	...which carry away with them the sound of futile words.
Und mag nich neimand hören, Und mag nich neimand hören	And if I don't have someone to explain it to me,
Red' ich von Lieb' mit mir, Red' ich von Lieb' mit mir	I'm not going to love their business.

[a] Set to the music of Mozart's *Non so piu cosa son cosa faccio*, from *The Marriage of Figaro*.

12 PERSONA, MYTH, AND ETHOS IN LEADERSHIP

Show business is essential to business leadership. A public role—from leadership of a major company to deputy for one of its branch operations—requires the ability to communicate to a wide variety of audiences. Leaders need to inspire and motivate action within their organization, and they need to embody and project the ethos and spirit of their organizations to their various external customers. To be a leader, you must take the stage.

Show business leadership isn't just an act. It is a crucial part of communication and persuasion. If you are going to be a leader of thousands (or millions) of people, you need to be able to make the right choices in managing your organization and get your ideas accepted. In a modern corporation, leaders need to promote their agenda—everything from increasing productivity to instilling a culture of praise and recognition from peers; from emphasis on consistently innovative design to customer-friendly attitudes. They need to communicate effectively to large numbers of people both inside and outside the organization. To do so, as we will see, they need to link the three components of successful leadership: persona, myth, and ethos.

SHOW BUSINESS IN POLITICAL LEADERSHIP

The world of politics offers convincing evidence that captivating performance is the key to leadership. Any great leader must, first and foremost, be a great actor, says the great American playwright Arthur Miller in his book, *On Politics and the Art of Acting*. Acting is not just polish, it is a vital part of what we respond to in our leadership—whether in politics or business. "We are moved more by our glandular reactions to a leader's personality, his acting, than by his proposals or by his moral character," Miller writes. "We are ruled more by the arts of performance... than anybody wants to think about for very long."[12]

Like it or loathe it—as Miller himself does—show business politics is a fact of life. This is only natural, as Miller observes, because in the modern era we are surrounded by actors as never before—TV news anchors, movie stars, advocates and spin-masters—and immersed in a world of assumed performances. Our major sources of information are all packaged, designed, scripted, and performed, and this is how we have come to expect to learn and to be persuaded. This is how, in effect, we have learned to see the world and ourselves.

What used to be news media are increasingly entertainment-based today and concern themselves more and more with the entertainment value of our world's events. This can be seen clearly in the media's responses to political leadership; for example, in its coverage of presidential election campaigns and conventions.

Did you notice that the candidates and conventions of the 2000 U.S. presidential election were wholeheartedly received as show business by the press? The TV news and front page stories were more like theater reviews, detailing which "actor" stepped on his applause lines, debating whose style was more relaxed, wondering how Bush got all those minorities to practically outnumber the Republican leadership on camera, and gossiping about who wrote or revised the candidates' scripts. Gore's biggest score in his entire campaign was his "spontaneous" and passionate kiss of his wife onstage at his convention entrance. Meanwhile, coverage of the speeches' contents or proposals got brief mention, usually buried deep in the papers. This is true of most elections. Similarly, tough issues mostly appear in the business press when there is a flare-up of public interest (stock options, accounting scandals) or when tied to a captivating story.

To lead in this environment, to be effective in business, you must use show business. But don't misunderstand us: this does not mean that show business is *sufficient* for leadership. The leader who is a master only of his or her show, but does not otherwise know how to shrewdly manage and guide his or her company, is headed for a fall. Show business is part of an integrated approach to leadership.

PERSONA, MYTH, AND ETHOS IN THE SHOW BUSINESS LEADER

What is the show business leader? A role model, an aspirational hero, the champion of brand champions? A leader who is larger than life, whose charisma, integrity, or force of personality becomes part of the brand legend? Any of these could describe a show business leader.

However, the show business leader is not just a forceful personality. He or she is a leader whose personality, personal story, and sense of values, mission, and operational strategy are all integrated, so that the qualities of that leader are both easy to grasp on the surface and deeply connected to essential elements of the brand.

Is the show business leader acting? Not necessarily—except in the sense that he or she plays the central starring role in the drama of his or her business. Then he or she uses this starring role to focus everyone within reach on the essentials of the brand—on its goals, identity, and values—and to motivate them to believe in the brand and act for the brand.

Show business leadership is usually at least a little showy and is sometimes very deliberately staged.

Show business leadership makes for better business because it helps galvanize the motivation and energy of personnel and can help attract and keep the faith of customers and personnel even in hard times.

In all of the cases we will consider, show business leadership has three main ingredients: persona, myth, and ethos. These are, not surprisingly, a lot like the essential elements of drama identified by Aristotle in *The Poetics*, which is still the most widely read book on dramatic theory ever written. By our definition, *persona* is the larger-than-life personality of the leader, whose essential qualities are dramatized in the leader's and the company's story: the *myth*. *Ethos* is how persona and myth translate to the living spirit and action of the company—its visions, values, and quality of performance.

- **Persona** in simple terms means personality—a leader's public and social face. The most effective kind of leadership persona is not a false façade, and not a mere mirror, but a magnification of the leader's strengths and attractive personal qualities. These qualities should be central to the leader's role in the life of the company. Persona attracts the attention and allegiance of the audience (personnel, clients, customers, the media, anyone who comes into contact with the company). Persona can help endow a leader with distinction, attractiveness, and sometimes even charisma. Whether the leader is a titan of performance standards, an efficiency guru, or a golf-playing, luxury-loving playboy, persona should be relatively consistent. Of course, dramatic changes that occur through the leader's self-realization and self-reconstruction can enhance persona in a visible way. This is one way persona can gain added dimension through the ongoing use of myth. Persona is also integral to establishing a company's ethos, which reflects the personal qualities, values, and methods of the leader.

■ **Myth** is the plot, the leader's personal story. In the best cases, this personal story is linked to the story of the company. Let's clarify: myth is not a phony story; it must be based on truth. But it is also not just your unvarnished track record. Myth is a well-crafted, dramatic, and compelling story that has the power to fascinate. It crowns the persona with celebrity-hood, whether local or global. Myth inspires belief in the leader and the company, and provides an explanation for the leader's values and motivation, which support the corporate ethos. Myth also excites emotions—such as fear, envy, empathy, desire, affection, adoration, even love. It motivates and inspires emulation, hard work, respect, and loyalty. One typical myth plot is rags-to-riches, but there are many variations. Most importantly, myth is not just about the leader's and company's past, it is the dynamic plot of the present and of ambitions for the future. It is the unfolding drama in which the audience (again, everyone from your receptionist to big-name business journalists) participates. In this way, myth helps instill confidence in, and emotional connection with, the company. It shapes corporate ethos and keeps a corporate mission on track and exciting. In the best of cases, myth also immortalizes the leader and the company.

■ **Ethos** is the set of guiding beliefs, the mission and values, of the leader and of the company itself. It is not just those beliefs, but those beliefs put into action. If persona is the head and myth is the heart, then ethos is the soul—reflected in the actions of the corporate body. This is true whether the leader is a moral straight arrow or somewhat more provocative. Ethos is acted in living color by the persona and immortalized by myth. For example, look at the empowerment and customer service ethos of Mary Kay Ash. Here we can see that ethos is reflected in the leader's work and management style, but most importantly, ethos integrates the guiding spirit and action of the whole enterprise.

CONCLUSION

In our next chapter, we will look at cases of five extraordinary show business leaders, each with a very different persona they have put to use to help lead their company. We'll see in each case how a myth was built around the persona and how that persona matched, supported, and inspired a central ethos within the company, and thereby helped lead it to success.

These leadership shows vary greatly, but in each one there are lessons in how show business style and entertainment can be used to communicate and integrate that central defining leadership persona. We will see examples of highly ethical leaders and an example of one leader who saw he was heading down the wrong path and corrected himself in time.

After this hall of fame, we will explore the three pitfalls of show business leadership as well. We will see how to handle the challenges of succession and the risk of dishonor. We will look at the culture that surrounds business today and pose some advice on how show business leadership can navigate changing cultural terrain and find the right role to play for its audience.

Before you get to all that, you might enjoy reading a few more lessons for leadership from the masters of show business: the world's politicians. If so, see *Lessons from Show Business in Politics*:

LESSONS FROM SHOW BUSINESS IN POLITICS

Politics in the U.S. is big-time show business. Like the stars of Hollywood blockbusters, our presidents and candidates rely on an army of professional coaches, wardrobe and makeup artists, scriptwriters, ratings watchers (pollsters), and directors to help them create their performances. Political conventions are staged as giant extravaganzas with light shows, personal theme songs, warm and fuzzy home movies of the candidates hugging puppies or clowning in their jeeps, instant replay screens of "big moments" right after the speeches, and staged heartfelt moments with family.

LESSONS FROM SHOW BUSINESS
IN POLITICS (CONTINUED)

But this is no longer just an American phenomenon. Show business in politics is also catching on in the other democracies of the world.

LESSON 1: SHOW BUSINESS LEADERSHIP IS A GLOBAL PHENOMENON

Japan, the Asian powerhouse, has elected a cast of captivating characters at the level of mayor and governor, with a comedian and a former vaudevillian in charge of Osaka and Tokyo, respectively. In 2001, faced with economic stagnation and a great need for political reform, Japan's voters elected their first show business prime minister—Junichiro Koizumi. A media sensation, closely watched by millions of Japanese fascinated by his speaking skills and charisma, Koizumi won the voters' hearts with his rebel act and his oft-remarked hairdo—which has been described as more typical of a country-and-western singer than a Japanese prime minister.

Don't underestimate the hair issue. In Germany in 2002, the race between incumbent Chancellor Gerhard Schroeder and his challenger, Edmund Stoiber, became fixated on the issue of whether or not the Chancellor dyed his hair. The nonscandal erupted when a rumor of artificial color was floated in a popular German newspaper. Seizing on an opportunity to divert the electoral coverage from unemployment figures to something simply outrageous, Schroeder brought a major suit against the publication and refused to accept a settlement despite the paper's retraction and apology. Instead, the Chancellor's hairdresser became a major celebrity witness, and the German public engaged in a bizarre and amusing show.

Other examples of show business in world politics abound, from Italy's Prime Minister Silvio Berlusconi (a flashy and charismatic billionaire media tycoon whose glamorous personal history includes countless legal troubles and an early start as a lounge singer) to the porn-star-turned-parliamentarian Cicciolina, who, in the Italian hall of Parliament, exposed her left breast as a statement of her left-leaning politics. Cicciolina has since considered a bid to enter Hungarian politics as well.

LESSONS FROM SHOW BUSINESS IN POLITICS (CONTINUED)

LESSON 2: DON'T LET YOUR SHOW GO OVERBOARD

Ecuador has had a show business president, Abdulla Bucaram, who found time while ruling to release an album and give concerts, dancing onstage amidst light and smoke while singing a Spanish version of *Jailhouse Rock*. Perhaps Bucaram pushed the show business too far, though. He was eventually ousted by the congress as mentally incompetent. Heed the warning of Lesson 2.

The Gore Bush contest of the 2000 U.S. presidential election presents a good example of our last lesson:

LESSON 3: KEEP YOUR SHOW CONSISTENT

Yes, your leadership persona may evolve in response to the environment, but you can't let yourself become a puppet whose strings are jerked about by advisers and public opinion.

Al Gore's greatest failing was an inability to choose what role to play. His pollsters continually urged him to try different styles of speech and clothing to appeal to the voters. One of his worst moments came in a bizarre and highly visible about-face between the presidential debates. In the first debate he came on hard as an aggressive numbers-cruncher accusing his opponent's proposals of not adding up fiscally. In the second (overeager to be loved by the pundits who had called him too aggressive), he lounged back in his chair as he languorously drawled that he really did agree with Governor Bush on most of the issues.

Meanwhile, his opponent, a Texas millionaire and heir to two generations of Washington leadership, consistently played the "regular fella," a straight-talking, blue-collar gentleman who drove a pickup truck and drank the same beer as you—a pose that the voters found likeable enough—and he was smart enough to never stray from it. The result was that he was perceived as much more genuine. What show business!

13 THE SHOW BUSINESS LEADERSHIP HALL OF FAME

Look at any successful business leader and you will find a persona that inspires confidence, gives direction, and projects his or her vision. Scratch any business leader and you will find a myth. Analyze any successful business and you will discover an ethos at work. In show business leaders, persona, myth, and ethos are seamlessly integrated in both leader and business.

In this chapter, we look to five extraordinary leaders for show business lessons—our Show Business Leadership Hall of Fame. These five are all leaders on a grand scale. But it doesn't matter whether you appear nightly on national TV or only once a year at your local chamber of commerce, the same aspects of show business apply. Lesser known leaders would give examples just as good, but really, isn't it more fun to analyze Warren Buffett? That's the first lesson: talking about show business leaders is fun and engaging.

EMPOWERMENT PRIESTESS: MARY KAY ASH

Some day, when you're stuck in traffic, try to count all the famous millionaires who have become powerful celebrities by putting on a big show about empowering others. Empowerment is a great ethos and makes great show business. The most powerful empowerment celebrity in the world today is, of course, Oprah. Her elder sister in female empowerment was skin-care empress Mary Kay Ash, whose empowerment show is analyzed and taught in top American business schools.

The Mary Kay myth pulls all the cliché heartstrings (don't underestimate the power of cliché, though). She was 45 and a newly widowed mother of three in 1963 when she took her life savings of $5,000 and a patent for a skin care cream, and through what was roughly a pyramid scheme (but an honest one), grew a business with revenues well over $1 billion at the time of her death in 2001. Her personal story was synonymous with her business mission: to empower women. As she put it in the title of her second book, *Mary Kay: You Can Have it All.* Her persona made this boast seem unselfish, even homey: the original self-made woman, a family-values feminist, at once flamboyantly glamorous and familiarly down-home.

Mary Kay reigned over her employees and salespeople as if they were her personal brood to mother and motivate. Using a great show business performance style, she distinguished her business from business as usual. With a feisty yet lady like frankness and maternal zeal, she redefined traditional business terms to suit her ethos: "I say, 'P&L means people and love.' Of course I'm concerned about profits and losses. I just don't give them top priority."[13]

Here's where persona and myth translate into ethos. Ash advocated that you can become important by making other people feel important, and that you can engage others to replicate your success story with their own self-made versions. By selling Mary Kay products, women could raise a family and get rich on their own schedule of hours, with integrity and respect, providing a quality product and a model of inspiration to their customers.

As befits show business, Ash's corporate ethos was expressed clearly and succinctly: Do unto others as you would have them do unto you. This Golden Rule, she insisted, must guide every business decision. The thoroughness of her show depended on communicating this ethos throughout every level of her business, broadcasting it in her public performances and private consultations with employees, consultants (as she called her sales people), colleagues, and customers.

The moral language guiding her show is transparent. Success is more than just wealth; it includes integrity and love, or as she phrased it, achieving "balance in our lives with God, family, and career in harmony."[14] This message had power because the Ash act communicated passion and energy. Click on the Mary Kay web site to experience the show of her God-given drive. Notice how her image of tough determination is balanced by the appeal of a pink rose-petal softness.

Here are some pointers from Mary Kay Ash for developing your own show business:

- Understand your audience and relate to them. Ash's show business centered around a Christian and democratic ethos that had wide appeal among her target audience and that reflected the motivational strategy behind sales operations: "God didn't have time to create a nobody—just a somebody. I believe each of us has God-given talents within us waiting to be brought to fruition."[15]

- Have strong maxims (or soundbites). Ash wrote her own script and kept it simple, quotable, and consistent. If you can't write, find a professional speechwriter to work with you to condense your philosophy into succinct sayings that get the main points across. Use these when speaking to personnel, press, and clients. Let these become truths.

- Repetition is key. Many of Ash's phrases—like The Golden Rule—became company mantras.

- Reinvent the leadership role. Don't feel you have to resemble the top brass under whom you trained. With all her business acumen and success, Ash was never arrogant or dismissive. She recast the CEO as a gracious, cheerful hostess: "If I criticize, I sandwich it between layers of praise." "Nothing is more contagious than optimism."[16]

- Keep in mind that the successful leadership persona is not one-dimensional. It often involves contradictions held in suspense, like Kay's softness and toughness. As you shape your own leadership show, remember that it should be straightforward enough to be immediately recognizable and get attention, but it must be multidimensional in order to hold attention.

- Don't get defensive. Like many great acts, Mary Kay Ash was also a target of humor and criticism. She never seemed to mind—and this too was part of her persona (ladies don't stoop to acknowledge improper behavior). Other show business leaders have dealt with unflattering attention by joining in on the joke. Take Jack Welch, who has a chapter in his book called *Too Full of Myself,* in which he humorously takes himself to task for overreaching with his acquisitions efforts.

- Try to keep your ego to yourself. Take a lesson from the man who won over the American burger-eating public by presenting himself with consistent self-effacing humor—that was always dignified, by the way. This was Dave Thomas, our next subject.

THE FAIR AND SQUARE BURGER MAN: DAVE THOMAS

A Wendy's-sponsored survey found that 90 percent of Americans knew Thomas as Wendy's's founder and 70 percent recognized his name. His persona has practically universal appeal. Anyone familiar with it will immediately understand the show business advantage of not taking yourself too seriously. Laughing or smiling at your own persona can convey—without words—that you are honest and down-to-earth, that you are like your customers. According to psychological studies, we tend to trust people who can confidently find humor in themselves because we implicitly sense that they are not deceiving themselves with puffed-up notions of their own perfection.

Let's look at the myth and ethos cultivated in the Dave Thomas persona. A legend in advertising circles, Dave Thomas had the longest-running persona-based TV ad campaign in history. Droll and slightly self-effacing, with goofy floral shirts and corny ties, he had a smile that said, "Yeah, I know I'm corny; so are my values and that's why you can get a good meal for a fair price, at a friendly place, whenever you enter a Wendy's."

Like Mary Kay Ash, whom he admired, Dave Thomas embodied a promise of value and respect to customers and employees. His persona put him on that level—not above. His myth gave dimension to this: he, too, rose from humble beginnings. An orphan, Thomas was adopted as a baby, only to lose his adoptive mother when he was 5 and two stepmothers before he was 10. His father was a reticent man, a laborer who frequently moved to find work. At 16, Thomas chose to stay behind in Columbus rather than move again with his father. He worked in fast-food franchises and found good mentors before opening his first restaurant in 1969 and christening it with his daughter's nickname, Wendy.

The Wendy's myth starts out in the popular genre of the quest story: apparently, Thomas couldn't find a decent burger place in Columbus, so he had to build one. It is also a myth about respect for the wisdom of your elders. According to his oft-told story, Thomas's only close childhood relationship, and his main role model, was his grandmother. He distinguished his business by giving credit to her wise words, "Hard work is good for the soul," and "Don't cut corners." Symbolically, this is inscribed in the Wendy's burger, which is square. Terrific: every product is a visual reminder of his myth and ethos.

You won't find a business leadership persona more square than straight-talking "Dave." The Dave Thomas myth is also a source of the service and leadership ethos that he embodied. Dave didn't like impersonal, stratified business management. According to Thomas, as a young boy working in a burger-joint, he saw the boss of the business pull out a bucket and start mopping. Thomas coined the phrase "mop-bucket attitude" to describe leaders who are practical, unpretentious, and put their heart into bringing the customer back. When this founder of the world's third largest restaurant chain expressed an opinion, he was fond of prefacing his remarks with "I'm just a hamburger cook, but..." Thomas earned respect with this self-effacing style. It was a great way to communicate the Wendy's ethos.

Part of the Dave Thomas myth is that he seemed always to have been pushed into prominence. The way Thomas told it, he was ashamed of his childhood story for years and never made it public until the late 1980s. During a motivational speech he gave to a group of Wendy's managers, he mentioned his own story as a way to emphasize that humble origins are no bar to success. An employee urged him to go public. Thus began Thomas's involvement in adoption advocacy, which led to his being publicly honored by the U.S. Senate and the first President Bush.

When he died, thousands of employees, fans, and friends lined up outside the funeral home to pay tribute. Thousands also lined up at Wendy's franchises for the same reason, resulting in a huge sales day nationwide, and helping effect a 10 percent increase in revenue for Wendy's International, Inc. for that quarter.[17] A retrospective of his ads, spanning 13 years and 800 commercials, played to a sold-out audience at the Advertising Federation of Columbus, Wendy's's home town.

Some lessons from Dave are:

- Show your ethos to your customer. Thomas's leadership show business communicated the Wendy's mop-bucket ethos of unpretentious quality service to millions of customers as well as to his own employees.
- Understand your audience and relate to them. Thomas approached his employees as "a hamburger cook" and his customers as a man in search of a decent burger. If you don't share the same background as your audience, work hard, listen, and learn what you have in common.
- Put it all in a few words. Dave's quotable sayings, "mop-bucket attitude" and "don't cut corners," summed up his persona, myth, and ethos all in one. Keep it simple, memorable, and meaningful.

■ Don't be afraid to be a star. Do you have any natural on-camera charm? Test it out. Dave was a one-in-a-million match for the camera. But don't limit your imagination to the camera. Maybe you have a great voice. Cultivate it and use it—on the phone, on web audio, at meetings. What's remarkable about you? Discover your personal attributes and understand how they come across.

THE BADDEST BOY TO RULE THE RUNWAY: SEAN "PUFFY" COMBS

You don't have to be a do-gooder to have a solid gold ethos. And you don't have to be as unchanging or as solid as a rock, either. Look at Sean "Puffy" Combs, or P. Diddy, or whatever he is calling himself at the moment. The Combs persona is a work in progress. Combs, who is still under 40 and worth some $300 million, has a great show that blends ghetto and chic, party-boy and workaholic. Recently this triumphant bad boy pulled a persona switch and turned his own myth inside out—just when the press thought they had him pegged. His new act captured the public eye and the new spirit of the good-boy era that followed after Enron's failures and made respectable behavior fashionable again.

Combs's original persona was gangster sly and "ghetto fabulous" (his clothing styles actually gave rise to the fashion term). He began as a rap producer who made guest appearances on his artists' videos, then became a rap star in his own right while building a business empire that also includes publishing, restaurants, and the Sean Jean clothing line.

Posing as a born-and-bred hood, Combs was actually raised in a suburb where he was a Catholic School student and an altar boy who honed his performance skills in church theatricals. There are other facts behind his myth, though. Born in Harlem, he was just three years old when his mother moved the family to the suburbs of New York after the murder of his father. He started his first business at 12 years old, subcontracting his news delivery routes to other boys. He attended the prestigious black college, Howard University, becoming a big name on campus for his entrepreneurial and party-throwing talents. He landed an internship at Arista Records and was handed his own label there at age 24. He called the label Bad Boy and acted the part, drawing media attention and superstar status.

His persona was naughty and outrageous—just short of thuggish. He flaunted his wealth by wearing diamonds and furs, and cruising with babes in his Bentley. Combs integrated his managerial talent with a leadership show based on an outsider ethos: he chose challenging artists to record, became the defining prince of cutting-edge hipness, and staged way out-of-the-box entertainments.

His business talents gained him the respect of colleagues and artists. But while colleagues reported him to be a workaholic and perfectionist who labored long hours in the studio, the Combs creed seemed to be, "Party like there's no tomorrow," a fitting ethos for a gangster act. In the heyday of his bad-boy persona, Combs spent $60,000 on his own 29th birthday party at posh downtown restaurant Cipriani, where such celebrities as Sarah Fergusen and Muhammed Ali were willing to wait on line to get in. He appeared regularly in tabloids for rough-housing episodes and supposedly terrorized a fellow record producer who dared include an unflattering representation of Combs in a rap video. He sired two sons with two different women, while unmarried to either of them. His friend and star rap recording artist Notorious B.I.G. was gunned down. He was investigated by the Justice Department for suspected connections to gang activity (no evidence turned up). Critics griped that he was a disgrace to the race because he perpetuated the image of violent, reckless ghetto youth, but their complaints only brought him greater notoriety. All of this added to his myth. He dated superstar Jennifer Lopez. His clothing line became another extension of the whole bad-boy act. For the first time in a long while, men's fashion wasn't a bore. It was sexy and edgy.

Then his glamorous gangster act landed him in jail. In 1999, inside one of New York's hottest night clubs, someone—and Puffy was in the thick of the scuffle—pulled out a pistol and shot a man dead. Though not charged in the murder, Combs was arrested and tried for weapons possession and bribery.

For a while this just upped the ante on his outlaw myth. He flaunted it like never before. In the middle of his trial (which happened to coincide with New York City's Fashion Week), while he was out on $30,000 bail with the verdict still in doubt, he threw a million-dollar fashion show extravaganza. The show, called Revolution, took place just a few blocks from the scene of the crime. Combs orchestrated a production that managed to combine images of Martin Luther King, Jr. and race riots with full-screen blow-ups of Jennifer Lopez, all as a backdrop to a parade of buff male models strutting down the runway in minks, super-suedes, and diamond necklaces.

Though the judge had imposed an order of silence on Combs, he defied it in his own way, using a quotation from black poet Maya Angelou to proclaim his innocence: "You may write me down in history with your bitter, twisted lies…. You may trod me in the very dirt but still like dust I'll rise." These words filled the screen at the close of the show, as Combs bounded across the stage to embrace his sable-clad mother and one of his two sons before flashing victory signs with both hands and dashing off stage again.

Combs was acquitted. Then his show took a sudden new turn.

Within a year of his acquittal, Combs rematerialized as a self-professedly maturing adult, more urbane than urban. This budding persona helped clear the way for him to record a gospel album, while he became a film actor in critically-acclaimed movies. He talked to reporters about the follies of youth and how he was growing up, about wanting to use his power to promote positive change, about being a child of God and struggling to be a good father. Even his fashions became more gentlemanly, elegant and tailored—almost British.

But while his look and his message changed, and the myth became about Combs's new ethos, his persona still communicated the same crowd-pleasing, in-your-face brazenness. These days Combs captures media attention more for his self-comparisons to Christian apostles, saints, and prophets. As if that weren't shameless enough, he still parties on publicly and recently bought back half of Bad Boy entertainment from Arista so that he could really run his own show.

While sporting the party style necessary to keep hold of a hip young audience and maintain his allure with other celebrities who want to be on his A list, Combs built his business with real management skills as well. His close attention to business matters and artistic seriousness and innovation won him loyal artists and colleagues, and a respect in the music industry that spread into larger business realms as he pursued brand extensions. Combs has always been a double-persona man, with depths known only by those who work closely with him.

His lessons are:

- Let your lifestyle speak for you. Your life outside of the office should reflect the lifestyle you want your company to project. If it doesn't, you can't be authentic and your audience will remain unconvinced.

- Look like a threat, but don't be one to your own business. Though Combs styled himself a gangster and fed that fantasy with his clothing styles and high-profile antics, his business is strictly legitimate and his adherence to legal and financial standards is unchallenged. You can thrill your audience when you act like you're walking on the edge, but make sure you know where the line is and that your business is grounded on the right side of it.

- Be all that you can be. Don't confine yourself to one path, one image. Sure, show business leadership requires consistency (Combs's business capabilities were very consistent), but don't lock yourself into a persona that you may outgrow.

- Work your myth. Don't just put it out there and lie back. Add a new twist, some drama. When Combs claims that he has come around to religion, he's using the oldest dramatic element in the book: conversion. Conversion myths have a built-in power to seduce.

- Show business is essential to business, but it is not sufficient. Be more than your myth.

WALK SOFTLY AND CARRY A BIG SECRET: WARREN BUFFETT

Warren Buffett is widely considered the greatest investor of the 20th century and is synonymous with an investing ethos that he has made world-famous: pay a reasonable price for stock in comprehensible, fundamentally sound, and sustainably competitive companies, then hold onto that stock through market ups and downs. Perform with discipline and common sense, be rational not emotional, and be patient. We could also add, be a mystery.

Buffett is the antithesis of the high-risk, high-profile investor who helps drive stock prices perilously above value. This is not to say that his persona lacks excitement. Although his ethos seems down-to-earth, his persona is entirely enigmatic. Called the silver fox of investing, Buffett delights in a sly game of hiding his intentions and pulling global surprises, like his 1998 purchase of 16 percent of the world's silver market—a move that defied his own presumed philosophy of caution and sent silver prices into the stratosphere.

Buffett shuns the press like a reclusive guru. The so-called Sage of Omaha lives quietly in an ordinary house near his office. Though he hobnobs with the powerful, he prefers to do so in small private gatherings. Even the size of his office staff is startlingly small, numbering between eight and twelve. Aside from the company's annual meetings, Buffett doesn't make many public appearances.

And so, once a year, his public comes to him. Only Buffett could turn Omaha into a mecca for the 10,000–15,000 stockholders who flock to Berkshire Hathaway annually. He calls this Woodstock for Capitalists. A regular Wizard of Oz, he appears within his own headquarters, but he knows the whole world is listening. At the May 2002 stockholders meeting, he took the stage in Omaha to denounce fraudulent U.S. accounting practices. In closing, despite all his disgust with corporate America, he remarked that he could not remember a time when he had had more fun. Then he and his eternal sidekick, Berkshire partner Charlie Munger, took questions for a six-hour stretch.

Munger is another element of Buffett's show business. More accessible and life-sized, he is a perfect foil for Buffett's allure and can also be sent in as a Buffett surrogate, allowing the Silver Fox to minimize his own public appearances.

If you don't speak to the media, how do you broadcast your ethos? In writing. Buffett's chairman's reports to stockholders have been collected by a law school professor into a book of essays. In these quirky reports, Buffett quotes the likes of Ralph Waldo Emerson, the American transcendentalist philosopher who advocated independent thought and spirit. Mark Twain is another of his favorites, whom Buffett resembles in telling satirical tales and coining wry witticisms. Of the major corporations Berkshire Hathaway controls, Buffett says: "we delegate almost to the point of abdication."[18] To old age, he responds: "gray hair doesn't hurt much in this playing field: you don't need good eye-to-hand coordination or well-toned muscles to push money around (thank heavens)."[19]

Buffett's personal myth? He makes the media hunt for it. And they do, using it as an explanation for his reclusive ways and workaholic style. A recent (unauthorized, of course) biography tells of how Buffett's stockbroker father lost everything in 1931, and Buffett—to escape his mother's sudden fits of rage—retreated to the world of numbers and money. He made and sold a business before he was 17. He attended Wharton School of Business for two years as a teenager, and studied under the tutelage of investing guru Benjamin Graham at Columbia Business School. Even Buffett's charity is shrouded in reclusiveness. He has eschewed big philanthropy (and has been accused of stinginess for that) but says he will leave his wealth to a huge new foundation described in his will. Every time Berkshire's price drops, the media rush in to gossip about Buffett's fall from grace. But that fall just doesn't happen, in part perhaps because Berkshire is buoyed by investors' faith in Buffett.

As for Buffett's own decline, rumors of it in February 2000 sent Berkshire stock plummeting, so much so that it had the rare effect of forcing a public statement about Buffett's personal health. He has been quoted as saying that he will retire about 10 years after he dies. A statement more true than it looks on the surface, if Munger succeeds him for that decade, because of the uncanny closeness between them—which is part of Buffett's show business.

His lessons are:

- If your myth is famous and credible enough, it can help shelter your business from a stormy economy. Witness the way Berkshire, with large insurance company holdings, was buffered from the 9/11 blow that hit the insurance industry.
- You don't have to be loud to command an audience, but carrying a big wallet doesn't hurt. (By the way, it is rumored that Buffett once raised thousands of dollars for charity by auctioning off his wallet. More mystery: there were no reports of its contents.)
- Find a Munger. Especially if you want to be the kind of show business leader who shuns the media, choose someone to be your sidekick, your confidant, your right-hand woman or man. Choose carefully. In many cases, this is the person who "gets things done," and is your unofficial spokesperson. He or she should be relatively modest and utterly reliable. His or her stature and competence is essential not only to your business but to enhance your aura, as everyone knows that there is one trusted colleague, second only to you in genius or power, who has your ear and hears your thoughts. A Charlie Munger also helps assure stockholders that Berkshire will prevail even if something happens to Buffett.
- Once you have some fame, try underexposure: access is worth more to people if it's hard to get. A bit of reclusiveness makes your presence more valuable (though too much can put you out of sight and out of mind).

ACTION MAN, RENAISSANCE MAN: LARRY ELLISON

As the press ripped into corporate greed after the exposures of Enron and WorldCom, we were told that greed was dead. But we hope you didn't rush out and buy flowers for the funeral. Though many of the mighty have fallen, the fault lay not in their love of money, but in their overblown or underhanded business methods.

The high rollers won't go out of style. Narcissists—despite what the business moralists are saying—will come back. Because, as psychologists know, they're attractive even when their ego is repellent. Take Larry Ellison, a celebrity leader who doesn't care whom he offends. The ethos here is simple. Forget empowerment, forget about having people like you, forget even about values. Instead, be the biggest and the greatest, the most vulgar in your self-aggrandizement. This is the high-testosterone ethos: conquer, and the world must give in to your superiority.

Larry Ellison, the founder and CEO of Oracle (the relational database giant), has a larger-than-life show business persona and vaunts the superiority of himself and his business as if they were one. It wasn't just Ellison's mouth, of course, that made Oracle's profits. It was also technical expertise, industry savvy, brilliant timing, and boldness. But his persona and ethos boosted his team to success. As *Fortune* magazine put it, Ellison is a "master at rallying the troops."[20] Those who know the Ellison act point to his over-the-top style and his raw, dramatic force. When he speaks at a conference, people line up for hours outside the hall. His entrance is staged like a siege in a rock opera, with the sounds and flashing lights out of Spielberg, only more hip. The auditorium throbs, giant screens are blazing, sensory experience is charged to the max, and then he strides in, a six-foot colossus, flanked by his black-clad chiefs of staff. He's the commander of the shock troops of the IT revolution.

That's part of the myth of his show business leadership. Notorious for summary execution of executives who don't measure up, Ellison capitalizes on the power of anticipation, awe, and fear. Pitiless to adversaries, the Ellison ethos has a power beam of aggressive optimism. "His great strength," summed up Dave Roux, former head of corporate development at Oracle, "is to make exceptional employees do the impossible."[21] He does this by being larger than life. Especially in a sudden-death economy, Oracle's unabashed testosterone-driven ethos gets everyone's adrenaline going.

Each of our show business leaders has a distinctive costume and body type that spells out their persona. Ellison's much-photographed face (the intent gaze, the trim beard), the restrained athleticism of his strong, spare six-foot frame, and, of course, the Larry look: monochrome suit in a shade of gray or brown, worn over a dark mock-turtleneck or polo neck shirt. His trademark sartorial simplicity spells out more than individual taste, it expresses the Ellison ethos, embodying his winning business philosophy of simplicity. The message: Buy Oracle's integrated systems (rather than dole out millions to IBM to try and reconcile your hodge-podge, best-of-breed software), and let Simplicity transform your business. Ellison's clothes are like Oracle's systems: tailored to fit, integrated, trim, and spare to the point of severity. No extraneous frills, no fuss of coordinating colors or patterns. Not even a tie to complicate things. His sleekness spells readiness, the effortless flow of energy.

The myth behind this persona has an element of tragedy. A virtual orphan, Ellison never knew his biological father, and met his own mother only once. A self-made man, Ellison remains captivating by acts that verge on self-destruction. Before Ellison, most IT CEOs were tame geeks. Ellison brought swashbuckling to the relational database industry, creating new legends for himself in his adventures on the high seas.

The man-of-action myth that transformed him into a world-class celebrity began when he and his 80-foot yacht, the Sayonara, survived—and won—the lethal Sydney to Hobart Yacht Race of 1999. You may remember news of that perfect storm from hell. The hurricane ripped into 115 world-class yachts off the coast of Australia. Only 44 boats would complete the course. Five sank. Six top-notch sailors died. Worldwide news headlines gaped at the tragedy. Ellison walked away, with typically terse commentary: "This is not what racing is supposed to be."[22]

Weeks later, at San Francisco's St. Francis Yacht Club, he recounted his experience to a standing-room only crowd at an

American Red Cross benefit to raise money for the drowned sailors' families. The assembled yacht enthusiasts gasped, groaned, and marveled as he detailed the force of the gales, the precise angle and height of the killer waves, and the Homeric inventory of sails and yacht parts wrecked by the hurricane.

He described how the Sayonara emerged from the eye of the storm, tossing onto towering waves, dropping in seconds-long free falls; with crew members suspended in midair, then smashed back onto the deck. The entire crew survived, sustaining injuries including broken feet, ribs, and knees. Ellison had gone without food three days, and without even water on the last day.

Undaunted, Ellison sponsored a boat in the 2003 America's Cup and reportedly spent over $85 million on the new craft. Fans can read more at www.oracleracing.com.

That's the Ellison ethos—leap into the competition and outdo it. Here's the core of his myth, persona, and ethos: Ellison is the ultimate showman because his art seems artless. His artlessness personifies the ethos of simplicity in Oracle's integrated systems.

Ellison's lessons are:

- Don't sweat. At the height of the Italian Renaissance there was a kind of genius called *sprezzatura*, the most highly-valued quality of the courtier. *Sprezzatura* meant brilliance and daring, wrapped in an air of effortless mastery. *Sprezzatura* invoked something above mere respect, it invoked wonder. We live in a different era, with different values, but we still have our Renaissance men and women who achieve an air of effortless mastery.
- Be a magnet. It is said that power is the strongest aphrodisiac. We would add celebrity. In fact, celebrityhood confers power (though power is not sufficient to make you a celebrity). Celebrity comes from a show business style that can't be taught. It involves some kind of charisma that is inexplicable, which captivates and inspires wonder.
- Be inimitable.

PERILS AND CHALLENGES OF SHOW BUSINESS LEADERSHIP

Show business leadership is not without its challenges, of course. Having a corporate leader who takes on a significant role in the public imagination, both internally and externally, can have enormous benefits, but it also raises certain tough issues. If not properly handled, it can lead to peril. The three most important challenges raised by show business leadership are succession, changing cultural climate, and that beast within: the overblown ego.

SUCCESSION

If a business is dependent on its leader, what happens when that leader leaves, retires, or dies? Different shows have different answers to the succession pitfall.

If the ethos of your company is strengthened by the performance of your leader, it doesn't necessarily falter when he or she is gone. Mary Kay Ash is an example of someone who built an ethos to outlast herself, leaving so much empowerment in her wake that there was little commotion about succession.

Good show business leadership can prepare for succession if handled well. Wendy's is another example. Internally, Wendy's had suffered more than one shock around the time of Dave Thomas's death. The three leading CEOs who were his probable successors had all died within a six-year period, creating what could have been a devastating succession crisis. But the Dave ethos went so deep that there was yet another down-to-earth mop-bucket attitude guy to take over the company and run it "Dave's way." That's show business leadership used to create an immortal ethos.

What if the show is so identified with the persona that even the advertising campaign is captive to the leader's image? When Dave Thomas died in January 2002, ads and promotional material featuring Dave's image were immediately pulled. But his persona was so central that not only the customers, but the franchise employees and operators missed having their big life-sized Dave cutouts around. They were allowed, at their own discretion, to replace them. Seeking a tasteful solution, Wendy's's agency, Bates USA, resurrected Dave with a slogan proclaiming that the food is prepared "Dave's way." Given the lack of a suitable family member to replace him in the campaign, Bates picked his home town as "A place where things are better," and where they do things "Dave's way." The town represents the ethos. (Recently, Wendy's dropped Bates and went over to McCann-Erickson World Group, seemingly because of a big Bates media merger that threatened changes in media buying and planning. Did Wendy's have to look elsewhere for the mop-bucket ethos?)

But what if the show business leader is not such a clean-cut hero? What happens if your business leader is very high profile and then suddenly gets into hot water, disrepute, scandal—can you risk this? Show business leadership can sometimes put you at risk for tabloid-induced stock shocks, but communication, that key to show business leadership, must remain the rule. Silence will seem like self-incrimination. Lies are worse (as Martha Stewart and Bill Clinton learned). But if a show business leader in trouble appeals to his or her audience, the way Puffy Combs did, instead of hiding behind lawyers, there's a much higher chance of saving your face and your business.

CULTURAL SHIFTS

In every era there are celebrity leaders who lack scruples, morals, or even ability, who master more by power and personality than real know-how. The start of this century was marked by the unmasking of scores of such leaders. A retaliatory attitude thrived among suddenly righteous journalists who attacked companies that contributed to the escalation of rapid promotions and soaring stock packages. Clearly there was a lot wrong with the star system—as there was with plainly illegal accounting practices.

Bad or corrupt business practices are not good show business. But daring and risk-taking in leadership won't be washed away by the sins of the 1990s. The public loves the maverick, the rebel, the showman. These personas are too deep a part of

American culture to be banished. But they might have to go under cover at times.

Combs was ahead of the game on this, renovating himself before the roof fell in on his outlaw act. Certain types of personae are clearly better for certain corporate and cultural climates. Oddly enough, the personality type most attracted to show business (the narcissist) is also most likely to encounter some of the biggest problems in running certain kinds of shows.

WHEN EGOS GET BIGGER THAN BUSINESS

Narcissists, who love to put on a show, are—according to some business psychologists—good leaders mostly in times of rapid change. They have the ego to forge ahead in an uncertain environment. Their self-adoration inspires others to follow them. But they also tend to be expansionist and paranoid, unable to listen to criticism and too inclined to believe that their own bubble represents the real world.

In *Good to Great*, Jim Collins's book on America's corporate leaders, he argues that leaders who keep a low profile are more successful in turning companies around—basically because these leaders are not hotshot outsiders. They know their companies and they know how to listen. Certainly, this is a required formula for good show business leadership: stand by your business ethos, know your company, and learn from listening. But it doesn't have to be all somber and serious. Let's have a little fun while we're at it.

If you're a narcissist (and you probably are, if reading this has you all paranoid and defensive), get help. Find a good therapist, preferably one who specializes in business leaders, like Marshal Goldsmith, for example. Goldsmith gets CEOs to listen to their colleagues' and employees' criticisms of their behavior. Then he helps them change not who they are (leaving analysis of feelings to traditional therapists), but how they behave and how they are perceived.

Goldsmith is a good show-business therapist. Because his method involves continuous employee feedback, the therapy itself can become a show to rally everyone around the CEO's efforts to get better. The CEO's improvement becomes the subject of gossip, even of myth. It becomes a common cause and can transform you and your players into a great ensemble group and help spur that team-spirit ethos.

FROM THE ORGANIZATION TO THE CULTURE AT LARGE

Great show business leaders show us how persona, myth, and ethos can be used to deliver a show that communicates throughout an organization and to external audiences.

But show business and show business leadership are not only showing up in individual organizations. They are transforming entire industries and impacting our culture at large. In the final part of this book, we will focus on three examples that illustrate how show business is instrumental in creating an experience culture.

IV SHOW BUSINESS IN AN EXPERIENCE CULTURE

In the final part of this book, we explain how show business is transforming individual organizations, entire industries, and culture at large.

We start with the apotheosis of show business, Las Vegas, and see how the city has grown from a collection of individual show businesses into a mega-experience of its own (Chapter 14).

Next, we turn to the cooking industry, and the kinds of experiences that are emerging there in the shape of entertainers, TV shows, and destination restaurants and venues (Chapter 15).

Finally, we examine how show business is entering the business of the arts and transforming art exhibits, museums, and the role of architecture in society at large (Chapter 16).

We conclude that show business is erupting everywhere, breaking boundaries and overturning traditions, bringing vitality and vision to a wide range of industries. Regardless of what is being sold, audiences want to be entertained and enjoy participating in the show.

14 LAS VEGAS

No book on show business can be complete without a study of Las Vegas, the world capital of show business, a place where every square foot is devoted to entertainment and bedazzlement. Love it or hate it, you can learn a lot from its monumental glamour, glitz, and tackiness.

Las Vegas knows one of the key rules of show business: let the razzle-dazzle reign. But Las Vegas is also about extraordinarily high standards of professionalism in show business and its production—in service, operational efficiency, planning and execution, and production details.

FROM TACKY TO MAINSTREAM

Las Vegas teaches many lessons. The first is about the changing role of experience and entertainment in our culture—and how that cultural evolution has rehabilitated the city of vice and show girls from an illegal sideshow to a popular but tacky attraction and then to a celebrated jewel in the entertainment crown of America.

Prehistoric Las Vegas was a wet and fertile marshland. Later, the site was an oasis known only to Native Americans. On Christmas Day in 1829, it was discovered by Mexican traders

FIGURE 14-1   Old Las Vegas: the city of gambling, gangsters and glitz. Photo courtesy of Nick Peterson.

who veered off course while taking the Spanish trail to Los Angeles. It was named Las Vegas, "the fertile plains," a name that proved both ironic (Las Vegas is now a desert) and prophetic: it has given birth to a new world of entertainment. But in the meantime, Las Vegas became a crucial transit stronghold controlled by Mormons, then Native Americans, and finally, with the construction of the railroads, it was founded as a city: a tent town sprouting saloons, stores, and boarding houses beside the tracks.

Gambling flourished illegally in Las Vegas until 1931, when it was legalized to raise taxes for public schools. The seeds of future glory were planted in 1941, when hotelman Tommy Hull built El Rancho Vegas Hotel-Casino. In 1946, the Flamingo Hotel followed, built by mobster Benjamin "Bugsy" Siegel of the Meyer Lansky crime organization. Bugsy may be one of the few fathers of gambling who is remembered in the town he helped build; remembered because he was the first true Las Vegas showman, a fast living, risk-taking gangster who died in a burst of gunfire.

FIGURE 14-2 New Las Vegas: mega-resorts, the world on a Strip, America's entertainment capital. Photo courtesy of Nick Peterson.

Today, the city preens amidst a desert, a fantastical contradiction to her surroundings: a city full of moats, canals, and fountains, not one of which is natural. Las Vegas is a megaresort, an outrageous compression of the world's entertainment highlights, with New York City, Paris, Caesar's Rome, King Arthur's England, Hollywood, ancient Egypt, and the canals of Venice, all reconcocted to fit into a three-mile-long Strip. Gaudy, ridiculously tacky, festooned with phony architecture and pseudo-museums (Luxor's museum boasts an exhibit composed entirely of imitation Egyptian artifacts), Las Vegas is still an oasis for some and a burial ground—of alcoholism, prostitution, drug abuse, and financial ruin—for others.

But note this: lustful, wasteful, and false though it is, Las Vegas has become respectable. This is thanks to the seduction of show business and to a culture that increasingly prizes experience and entertainment in all things. The nonstop show and glitz of Las Vegas are no longer something that our culture associates just with sordid gamblers or tacky excursions from our daily life.

It has become the currency of our culture. Las Vegas is now mainstream. (Numbers of visitors grew from 21 million to 35 million a year through the 1990s, and revenues with them.)

Vegas has repositioned herself from a gambling enterprise to a comprehensive entertainment capital in which slot machines and roulette wheels take their place among top acts in music, comedy, art, and magic. The old Las Vegas was a show space for recycled vaudevillians; the new Las Vegas boasts today's biggest rock acts. Like the supermodels who disdained the first Victoria's Secret Fashion Show, then flocked to later shows for fame and fortune, legendary rock acts like Paul McCartney and The Rolling Stones now court Las Vegas and add to its appeal. Las Vegas, like no other city, is the America of today.

This unforgettable city provides a lesson for establishing showmanship as a priority within your own company. Show business can arise out of nothing. It breaks the rules. Showmanship flourishes in a hazardous environment. Don't worry if your company is a desert of creativity right now. That could be the ideal reason to start a show of your own.

THE IMMERSIONARY EXPERIENCE OF LAS VEGAS

Experience is said to be one of the crucial requirements for many service and entertainment industries, from restaurants and nightclubs to theme parks and clothing stores. Las Vegas creates an atmosphere, not as a decorative scene or event, but as a complete environment to be richly experienced. In this book, we have called this kind of environment immersionary because it immerses the audience in an imaginary, visionary world, and Las Vegas does this at its best. Caesar's Palace is a complete Roman world. The Luxor hotel places you in a wholly re-imagined ancient Egypt. Other hotels provide immersion in similar experiential worlds. But more importantly, the totality of Las Vegas itself is completely unique. It is not an experience that starts and ends when you walk out any hotel door. The entire city is a total immersionary experience for the visitor.

A shallow experience, perhaps, but it is completely focused on its one-dimensional essence: the razzle and the dazzle. This is what makes seeing a show in Las Vegas more mind-blowing than seeing one on Broadway or in Hollywood. There are other things to do in New York and L.A., so the show you see may be preceded or followed by experiences of completely different impacts and tones.

In Las Vegas, the razzle-dazzle fantasy tolerates no gaps, no stops. This is a great lesson to keep in mind for any show business: you want to immerse your audience in an experience that is all about the essence of the thing you are trying to say or offer. It should be all encompassing. Remember that while the Las Vegas experience is very one-dimensional, it is still very complex in its details. Its endless stunts, gags, and outrageous feats keep getting better as you go (strolling from casino to casino), like a progressively grander series of encores in a great show or a fireworks display.

An Immersionary Bavaria Show

A few other towns have succeeded in creating an immersionary experience for their customers. Branson, Missouri has become a leading domestic tourist destination by making itself the apex of a certain style of song-and-dance show business that caters to the over-50, country-music-listening, conservative, Christian, white America from the South. A less well-known, but charming success story can be found in the mountains of the Pacific Northwest, where the town of Leavenworth, Washington, has written its own rags-to-riches story by transforming itself into a Bavarian-themed tourist destination.

Nestled in the Wenatchee River Valley of the Cascade Mountains, Leavenworth was a small logging town facing a long slide towards extinction after the Great Northern Railway altered its course in the 1930s and the town's sawmill closed. For 30 years Leavenworth was almost a ghost town, until 1963, when the town leaders, in desperation, undertook a bold course to try to turn it into a tourist attraction.

Henceforth, Leavenworth was reshaped into a model Bavarian village. The town had no particularly strong German roots, but the Cascade Mountains could provide a suitably Alpine-looking backdrop. To render the transformation complete, zoning codes were passed requiring that all downtown buildings be redone in a traditional Bavarian style with wood shingle roofs and white plaster walls. A series of Bavarian festivals was instituted, including a Christmas Lighting Festival, Autumn Leaf Festival, Oktoberfest, Maifest, Fasching, and a Bavarian Ice Fest.

What could be tackier than fake Bavarian? Of course, the efforts of the town paid off. Today Leavenworth is a booming tourist destination attracting over a million visitors a year. Tourists can enjoy a variety of winter sports, mountain hiking, and Bavarian, Austrian, and Swiss merchandise and restaurants. It's just like being in Germany without the plane ride, they say. (Don't ask a German.)

The citizens of Leavenworth aren't content to go halfway. They are forever pushing for the next stage of authenticity. Currently, a new project, known as Projekt Bayern, sets 10 new objectives for the town: to form a town band, hold a used Bavarian clothing sale, introduce German in schools, create a sister-city relationship, erect a maypole (maibaum), hold a christkindmarkt (Christmas market), start a weekly column in the local paper on Bavarian customs and traditions, form a German dance group, build a beer wagon, and create a directory of where to purchase authentic items in Bavaria.

Lessons for your business in this? Don't be dismayed if there are no authentic roots to your show. Build it out of likenesses and dreams. Don't let it stagnate when it seems to have peaked. Tweak it ever up a notch to continue the excitement, the fun, and even the tackiness.

IMMORTALITY CAN BE YOURS: MYTHOLOGIZE

Another great lesson we can learn from Las Vegas is that show business thrives on legends and lore. You can create your own mythology and—if you're as successful a showman as Larry Ellison—immortalize yourself and your show in the process.

Las Vegas is immortalized in movies (*Ocean's Eleven*, *Leaving Las Vegas*), in literature (*Fear and Loathing in Las Vegas*), in pop music (*Viva Las Vegas*), and even in urban sociology and architectural theory (Robert Venturi's *Learning from Las Vegas*, a classic from the father of post-modern architecture).

As you develop your show business, don't forget to cultivate stories—funny, outrageous, sentimental, and bizarre. Lore is alluring and makes your show more intriguing and important. Let's take one example: the story of how Las Vegas's first casino hotel, El Rancho Vegas, caught fire in 1960 while Betty Grable was singing onstage in the cocktail lounge. The blaze was supposedly a gangster's revenge for being shown the door. If you check the Las Vegas lore web sites you can even find out the name of the bandleader whose saxophone melted in that blaze.

Even the darkest moments of Las Vegas's history have a mythic quality to them. On November 22, 1963, after the assassination of John F. Kennedy, the casinos on the strip were hushed for one hour. The fantastic lights of the casinos—which burn continually, day and night—went dark when Frank Sinatra and Dean Martin died, and after the terrorist attacks of September 11, 2001.

Trivia, you say. Yes, and trivia helps captivate and create community. Trivia tickles. Trivia keeps your audience at play in the discover-and-tell game. What is a community, after all, but a group forged by the desire to communicate about events, people, products—hopefully yours? Communities make good customer shows. Think of the film Vans made with the skateboarding community.

As your company puts on its own show, think of how your challenges, successes, characters, and exploits will be remembered in future years, and start spinning the yarn of legend right now. Your PR can only benefit from a grand myth in the public's imagination.

As part of an effort to bolster its public image after the Firestone tire catastrophe, Ford Motors chose to run ads that looked back to the heritage of the company's early days. The ads made much use of the company's new CEO, William Clay Ford, Jr., linking him to the American tradition of the Ford family and to tales of his great-grandfather, the original Henry Ford. Ads showed the founder on a camping trip with pal Thomas Edison and with Ford employees. Interestingly enough, Edison appeared in a heritage-based pitch by General Electric as well, in an effective 60-second spot run during the Salt Lake Olympics that focused on milestones of the company's history.

In troubled times, history can help restore consumer confidence—though acting with integrity is always better show business than pretending that you have integrity. Don't confuse mythmaking with business. This isn't an anything-goes world anymore.

Here's a look at the business side of Las Vegas—with lessons on the way you'll need to run your business if you want to have a show.

UNPARALLELED SERVICE

Las Vegas is like no place on earth for customer service.

Try this (we did): Walk into the Bellagio hotel, stand in the middle of the front lobby under its magnificent blown-glass chandeliers, and stop any bell-hop as he rushes past with a load of luggage: "Excuse me, can you tell me where to buy a t-shirt?" ("Right here, through the casino, turn left when you reach the Victoria's Secret store, and you can find t-shirts and sweatshirts; they're open 24 hours.") or "When does this waterfall thing happen?" ("The waterworks show is every 15 minutes until midnight, then every half hour; I'd advise the best view is either from the oyster bar's waterside seats, or out front from the viewpoint of the Strip.").

First lesson: From top to bottom of your business, make sure that everyone is informed and everyone is inclined to immerse the customer in service.

Is there a problem with a customer's reservation at the MGM Grand? The check-in person simply offers an upgrade, immediately, to a larger room. Of course, Las Vegas is famous for laying out the red carpet for high rollers. But they make the low rollers feel loved, too.

Second lesson: Any company that deals with its customers face-to-face needs to realize that making the customer feel important is one of most important shows. Shrewd retailers have found that going the extra mile to pamper a customer can distinguish their business from the competition's. Banana Republic has added some old-style touches to its premier stores in New York and L.A., including in-store concierges and coat and bag checking service. They've even creatively added some high-tech customer perks like cellphone recharging while you shop and uploads of store directories and city maps for your Palm Pilot. (Now that's a service show!)

Service in Las Vegas also tends to be 24 hours a day. At any time of day or night a visitor can do much more than just gamble—you can hire an attorney, have your carpet cleaned, you can get married or divorced. Marriage in Las Vegas has become such a tradition that it constitutes a long-running show of its own, starring such celebrities as Judy Garland, Zsa Zsa Gabor, Ann-Margret, Paul Newman, Rita Hayworth, Elvis Presley, Richard Gere and Cindy Crawford, Bruce Willis and Demi Moore, and Billy Bob Thornton and Angelina Jolie. Maybe it helps that there's never been a waiting period for wedding licenses in Las Vegas.

Remember this if your company is facing an M&A: if a merger is a marriage of show business companies, then it also deserves to be celebrated with Las Vegas-style showmanship!

EFFCIENCY AND SHOWMANSHIP

Another part of the Las Vegas miracle that we can learn from is its efficiency. Few shows in the world are consistently pulled off with such smoothness and meticulous planning and care of the city's convention halls, theater halls, and enormous dining halls. Everything operates like clockwork, but without any sense of rigidity or fussiness. The crowds come in and out, the shows go on (and on), and never is the fantasy disturbed by a delay, a long line, a technical error, a shortage of catering, or any of the little foibles and failures you run into daily in your work place and most other places you go for a show.

If you are in an efficiency-sensitive industry, this can be a great show to run. FedEx has come close to mastery here. The essence of their brand is "fast and easy." You call or drop it off, they put it on the truck, done. Of course, their whole operation is incredibly complicated but the best part of their customer interface is that they hide all this complexity from you. You should never be made aware of it. It's all prestidigitation, as old-fashioned magicians used to say.

THE IMPACT OF GRANDNESS

The 10 largest hotels in the US can all be found in Las Vegas. They include the MGM Grand Hotel & Casino, Luxor Vegas, Excalibur, Circus Circus, Flamingo Hilton, Mandalay Bay, Las Vegas Hilton, Mirage, The Venetian, and The Bellagio. The MGM alone has a 33-acre theme park as its centerpiece, over 5000 rooms, a 171,500 square-foot casino, 12 theme restaurants, a 1,700-seat production showroom, a 630-seat production theater, a 15,200-seat special events theater for concerts and sporting events, and a child care center. If you've stayed in the MGM, as we have, and tried to walk from your room to the convention hall, you probably wished you had brought your Razor Scooter along. Las Vegas knows about grandness.

McCarran International is the seventh busiest airport in the world. There are 2.1 million square feet of exhibition space for its convention business. Las Vegas boasts around 124,000 rooms, and the entire town is sold out for an average of 140–160 days every year.

Fifteen thousand miles of neon tubing delight the eye in Las Vegas. In fact, it is the brightest city in the world. Military satellites orbiting the earth 500 miles up have determined that it casts more light than Tokyo, Los Angeles, and even New York. The spotlight beacon that shines heavenward every night from the top of the pyramid of the Luxor Hotel is the brightest artificial light in the world.

The lesson that can be learned from all this grandness is that, if possible, through show business you want to "own" some category—such as intensity of brightness or number of burgers flipped. Let that category be yours and use it to define yourself to the world. McDonald's always touts its burger records; Microsoft is the one company that rates two or more executives in every listing of the ten richest people in the world (a nice bit of trivia to remind you of their power); and Italy holds the record for most changes of democratic government (though Japan is trying to catch up).

Las Vegas is a show of grandness about extravagant size and light, among other things. What is your show about?

SHOW BUSINESS JARGON

Any complete show has its own lingo or jargon. Las Vegas's lingo revolves around gambling: toke, comp, RFB comp, high roller, marker, shooter, stickman, boxman, shoe, and pit boss. If you scored low on this vocabulary quiz, you should get to Las Vegas more often.

The computer industry, of course, is full of incomprehensible jargon that is used to saddle companies with IT personnel (If you can't say what the problem is, how can you fire them?). Academics and truck drivers are famous for their codes and cryptic phrases, like, "discursive production of femininity" and "that's a 10-20, roger, over, over."

Having your own lingo helps make your show immersionary—like entering a foreign country. What kind of lingo can you come up with for your show? This kind of thing is a must for the live shows in the trading card business. Lingo isn't just for kids, of course; it helps create the sense of a vital, happening culture no matter what the age demographic.

THE DESTINATION EXPERIENCE

"Location, location, location," goes the mantra. In a lot of businesses, conventional wisdom says the most important thing to do is situate your business where the customers are.

Las Vegas operates on the opposite idea: don't follow the crowd. Become a mecca. Las Vegas is a destination experience. A destination experience is someplace that people go solely to experience the thing itself. The sole purpose of going to Las Vegas is to experience the Vegas show (okay, so maybe you have an excuse of a business meeting, but that will likely be a show too).

Making your show a destination experience is a very powerful idea. A great business application of it is the World Economic Forum, which is held annually in the tiny Swiss ski town of Davos (except for 2002, when they brought their show to New York). Political and business leaders from every major country and multinational corporation in the world, as well as leading artists and scholars, not only attend this conference each year, but travel to this quintessential remote location to get there. This gives the WEF a particular allure, transforming it from a mere gathering into a pilgrimage. The experience is unique and immersionary: there are not a million other tourists wandering around Davos to dilute the mighty significance of the WEF. Before long, Davos begins to exist in order to serve the show. The show's smooth orchestration becomes more than a business goal, it becomes a town's identity and way of life.

MAKE IT FREE

Las Vegas does not charge an admission for its show. Yes, to see Siegfried & Roy's act with the white tigers, or to catch Billy Joel singing at the MGM Grand, you need a ticket. But the show of Las Vegas itself, the Strip, does not require a ticket. Anyone staying anywhere in town can walk into The Venetian and stroll along its million-dollar fake canals beneath simulated puffy-cloud blue skies; across the street you can catch the hourly explosions of the enormous volcano outside The Mirage; and down at the New York, New York Hotel, you can take in all the tacky miniaturization of the sites and landmarks of The Big Apple. This whole show is free because that's what lures people to come here and spend.

And does it work? Well, the numbers have been pretty good for the Strip. Top quality convention space and lower costs for meals and rooms than all the competition (Orlando, New York, etc.), combined with the unmatchable show of The Strip have kept Las Vegas the top destination for business conventions ranging from the annual Comdex technology fete to the Western Shoe Association's annual meeting. Amidst the travel industry slowdown of 2001-2002, Las Vegas held steady in tourist volume and spending. So, if show business for free can turn a consistent profit with the biggest budgets in the world, imagine what you can do for your business if you learn how to implement free show business.

CONCLUSION

Now that we've revealed some of Las Vegas's secrets and shown how to use them to help shape your company show, we hope you have booked yourself a seat on the next flight out to the Grand City of Artificial Light. There is no substitute for being there. You must begin your journey by recognizing that you're headed for the real capital of the United States. The U.S., traditionally thought of as a model of modern democracy, is now quite clearly the worldwide source of entertainment ideas. Entertainment is, in fact, one of the great democratic experiences the U.S. has to offer.

In the next chapter, we turn to one of the most basic things in life, food, and look at the cooking industry, which no longer just fills our hungry stomachs, but also satisfies our needs for experience and entertainment.

15 THE COOKING BUSINESS

"**F**or the boomer generation, food has become sex, drugs and rock & roll," says Eroca Gruen, President and CEO of the Food Network.[23] And that makes a lot of sense. According to Miguel Sanchez Romera, a neurologist and star chef in Spain, food stimulates the same brain regions as sex, drugs, and music. Romera says that he selects the ingredients for his cuisine and food presentations accordingly—that is, to stimulate the appropriate brain regions.

Let's take a closer look at the cooking business and how something as elementary as the preparation of food has become outrageous show business. We will feature Emeril, the show business celebrity chef; *Iron Chef*, the world's most original cooking show; El Bulli, a restaurant in Spain where you can have the most outrageous dining experience; and Copia, where cooking businesses and cultural institutions have joined forces in a show.

EMERIL: THE SHOW BUSINESS CELEBRITY CHEF

One of the best performers in the business is Emeril Lagasse—typically just referred to by his first name. Emeril is a mediocre cook and a great showman. In fact, as the biography on his web site states, "the man really wanted to be in show biz," and originally his idea was "to be a rock star." In fact Emeril has been called "the gastronomic equivalent of Elvis Presley" because he really rocks the house.

Emeril's TV shows have included *How to Boil Water*, *Emeril*, *Essence of Emeril*, *Emeril Live*, and Friday appearances on *Good Morning America*. In these shows, Emeril has transformed cookery into show business largely by engaging the audience in lively and irreverent interplay, where the kitchen talk becomes the language of male bonding. His "Emerilisms" capture this let's-rock-and-roll style: "Bam!" "Oh, yeah, baby," "Pork fat rules," (this isn't diet food), "Kick it up a notch" (add some spice), and "We're not building rocket ships here," (cooking is easy).

Emeril invites the audience to take part in his celebrity, to roar and shout with him. Cooking with Emeril is like having 50-yard line seats at the Super Bowl.

Within a decade, Emeril has created an empire that includes six restaurants, his own line of cookware, a range of gourmet products (e.g., Emeril's Spices, Emeril's Pasta Sauces, Emeril's Hot Sauces, Emeril's Coffee and Chicory), and five best-selling books. At his book signings, lines start 12 hours in advance and uniformed security guards have been hired to provide crowd control (or at least, to make it look as if crowd control is needed). Between 2,000 and 4,000 people typically stop by. His web site, www.emerils.com, launched in 1998, reportedly draws more than 300,000 viewers a month.

Watching Emeril, we can see how any industry can profit from a show business personality. Celebrityhood has enabled Emeril to expand his product offers through line and brand extensions in many directions. Note that Emeril products have almost nothing to do with cooking well. They have to do with that 50-yard line experience, the thrill of show business.

IRON CHEF: THE MOST ORIGINAL COOKING SHOW

This prize goes to an award-winning Japanese show recently brought to the U.S. on the Food Channel network: *Iron Chef*. It takes cooking show business and really does kick it up a notch, turning cooking into an extreme sport, a gladiator event. The show has been a national obsession in Japan, followed like a soap opera and in the news every week.

Iron Chef is hosted by Takeshi Kaga—a show business personality characterized by flamboyant dress and behavior—and features warrior-style cooking competitions. At the beginning of the show, Kaga sinks his teeth into an enormous yellow pepper like a wild animal. He is portrayed as a wealthy and eccentric gourmet who lives in a castle surrounded by an army of Iron Chefs with fanciful names like the Delacroix of French Cooking, the Prince of Pasta, and the God of Japanese Cuisine, along with a Chinese Iron Chef whose philosophy is Cooking is Love, and a Japanese Iron Chef who proclaims that Cooking is Entertainment. (He, of course, is our favorite.) The plot of the show also includes other roles: a pair of sportscaster-style announcers, the weekly challenger cook, the celebrity judging team, the video crew, the culinary panel, and more.

The show is performed in the cooking arena. Like a sports stadium, this arena is a huge space surrounded by rows of stadium seating and outfitted with television crews and cameras to catch all the angles. Special stands are reserved for celebrity actors and TV personalities who also serve as judges along with members of the cooking academy and at least one silly and giggling actress. There are also special bleachers for Iron Chef groupies who support the contestants like cheerleaders—though in a Japanese way (by mumbling certain chants and snickering politely at the challenger). The competition is timed, the feats are dazzling, and the ingredients push the boundaries of taste—both in their unheard-of fusion of flavors and in their use of rare (and often revolting) delicacies. Unlike typical cooking shows that tend to minimize the more disgusting aspects of food preparation, the *Iron Chef* video crew follows the cooks as they stuff a sheep's bladder or chop off a live fish's head, capitalizing on the gore with slow-motion replays. *Iron Chef* is not really about food, it is about technique, daring, and prowess, like a samurai duel.

Iron Chef makes the kitchen a dramatic realm of exalted heroes. Making a sauce is theater. This is an important lesson for your business. Don't take the ordinary activities of your business for granted. Isolate them. Ritualize them. Celebrate them. Make drama out of the process. Make heroes of your players. Get some cameras and lights in there, some music, some cheering fans, and some celebrity judges. Find the action and let people see themselves as heroes.

EL BULLI RESTAURANT: THE MOST OUTRAGEOUS DINING EXPERIENCE

El Bulli (The Bulldog), a restaurant north of Barcelona run by Chef Ferran Adria, has been named Best Restaurant in the World by *Restaurant* magazine. Tucked away at the end of a remote beach and open only from April to September, the restaurant has a waiting list of up to one year!

El Bulli redefines dining—it is no longer for sustenance or sociability; all that has been subordinated to pure show business. As one critic writes, "This cooking... amazes and excites, but in no way does it nourish and satisfy. In no way is this real food."[24] This is exactly the point: outrageous and shocking, the food at El Bulli has been called fantastical, surreal. Adria himself uses words like magic, creativity, and freedom to describe what he does. El Bulli has become a pilgrimage for gourmets, including a large number of world-class chefs. Superstar Chef Paul Bocuse says Adria is "doing the most exciting things in our profession today."[25] Some food writers believe he will change the direction of gourmet dining.

A typical show business dinner at El Bulli lasts three hours and consists of a series of 25–30 courses, each a tiny gem of pure show business. Amounting to no more than an ounce or so each, these tidbits and tiny swallows are presented with child-sized cutlery and stemware, and each is served in a custom-designed manner: on a silver tasting spoon or delicate stick, in a tiny fluted glass, on a paper-thin, hand-made wafer. Adria's creations have included ice ravioli, deconstructed tiramisu, and foam of tea. They are served with precise suggestions about how they should be eaten. "Bite the shrimp, sniff the card, squirt the tube into your mouth, in that order," as one diner described it. And at a rate of one course roughly every six to seven minutes, they don't leave any time for conversation. The focus is entirely monopolized by each successive morsel; the experience is completely immersionary.

In his book *Gastronomia,* Chef Adria outlines his philosophy—or, rather, his approach to food show business. He explains his obsession with texture, taste combinations, and foams; his desire to surprise, intrigue, and provoke. He calls his cuisine ethereal, which could also describe the restaurant's web site. There is nothing about food to be found there. You will only experience show business words like "emocion" and "mysteria" and flashing images of clouds and the sky.

When Adria is not cooking at El Bulli, he goes on cooking-demonstration tours from Australia to Japan. The food writer Sheridan Rogers, who attended a cooking demonstration by the master in Australia, had the following impression of Adria:

> In many ways, he is to food what Salvador Dali was to painting—outrageous and at times shocking, a great self-promoter but certainly never dull. Some critics claim it's not food he serves at El Bulli but "constructs" of foam and rubber—and that he is more an alchemist than a chef.[26]

Adria's attitude demonstrates his belief that when you judge a creative chef, you have to judge their technique, not the taste of the finished dish—because everyone has different taste.

Adria's approach to cooking is not without its critics. "During this three and a half hour sensory onslaught, I never heard anyone use the word 'delicious,'" writes Anthony Dias Blue in *Wine Country Living*.[27]

That's just the way your critics are going to respond when you put on your ground-breaking show, so don't listen. Ed Razek created the Victoria's Secret Fashion Show against great odds: supermodels who wouldn't be bought and colleagues who wouldn't be sold on the idea. If you have something truly new, it is bound to be misunderstood by those who like the status quo—even though the status quo is going nowhere.

The reclusive location of El Bulli reminds us of another important lesson: Customers have to come to you. Don't chase after them. Make your flagship store, your headquarters, your factory, or your show business restaurant a destination spot.

COPIA: WHERE COOKING BUSINESS MEETS COOKING ART

Show business is transforming the cooking industry beyond television and star restaurants. Education and civic development through food are also becoming part of the plan as nonprofit organizations join forces with cooking businesses to find new ways to put on a great show.

The Napa Valley wine country has become one of the key tourist destinations for visitors to the San Fransisco area. The attractions of its vineyards and restaurants have been joined by a new show called Copia, the American Center for Wine—a $55 million dollar culture center situated on 12 gorgeous acres alongside the Napa River.

In the words of *San Francisco Chronicle* arts and culture critic Steven Winn, "Nothing signals the new glorified status of food culture more clearly than Copia, the modernist temple of wine, food, and the arts." Winn calls a day spent in the center "a comprehensive and slightly surreal experience,"[28] and it's easy to see why. Where else is cake artistry elevated to the status of a full-fledged immersionary experience?

Spearheaded with $20 million from vintner Robert Mondavi, with prestigious partners including the University of California at Davis, Cornell University's School of Restaurant and Hotel Administration, and the American Institute of Wine & Food, Copia is named for the goddess of plenty. A new genre in show space, the place is part culinary college and part funhouse for foodies, with exhibits like *The Birth of Coffee* and *Toasters! Pop UP Art!* Exhibits are extraordinarily professional, but the museum-quality character of the show is coupled with a witty, sophisticated approach, allowing humor to set the tone.

The center has garnered praise from the *LA Times, USA Today, National Public Radio*, and *The New York Times* by offering plenty: gardens, eclectic food and wine classes, an art-house film theater, music, dance, lectures, wine and food tastings, cooking demonstrations, and of course the Julia Child Kitchen. For nonmembers, admission is $12.50 and there are extra charges for some of the courses and tastings. Before it was a year old, the center had roughly 8,0000 memberships—at $60 to $1,000 apiece. Donations are mostly tax deductible.

A nonprofit institution with an educational mission, Copia has too much class to plug its contributors' wares. There's nary a brand name mentioned here—except for Mondavi's and those of other vintners. But foodies don't need banner ads: they can tell a brand of saucepan from 10 paces away. Like almost any museum, Copia can rent space to confer prestige—say, to Salton, which announced the relaunch of the Westinghouse brand at the Center.

What's being sold at Copia is, broadly, a whole lifestyle and the products that make that style possible, as well the city of Napa, which, with the addition of the center and a new opera house, is drawing new attention as a tourist destination.

CONCLUSION

As the case of cooking demonstrates, show business can transform an industry not just at its most commercial extremes (television shows and rock-star-like show business leaders), but also in the realms where commerce and culture, and business and community intersect.

In our final chapter we turn to the business of art, dominated by giant nonprofit museums and high-culture ideals. There we see how a cultural industry is being reshaped by show business from the inside out—from the art works exhibited, to the dramatic structures that contain them, to the very cities in which museums reside.

16 THE ART BUSINESS

In closing, we examine how show business is entering the business of the arts and transforming art exhibits, museums, and the role of architecture in society at large.

Some of the world's leading art museums are now on the cutting edge of popular entertainment—something that shocks old-school art lovers and pleasantly surprises new audiences. The first part of this chapter will show that museums are no longer shy about becoming brands, no longer afraid of fun and common popularity. Businesses are taking notice and creating museum-like spaces of their own with similar emphasis on experiential and interactive encounters with their brands.

This convergence of commerce and culture goes beyond museum interiors. The drive to transform art into entertainment is also transforming the physical structures of museums and of civic spaces as well. The second part of this chapter will focus on an international phenomenon: increasingly, public spaces are being planned as mass-entertainment destination sites that combine culture and retail. We don't mean the old-fashioned parade grounds, parks, and boardwalks of the turn of the last century or the quaint indoor/outdoor refurbished city markets of the 1980s. This is bigger, bolder, more dynamic, turning city planning into a carnival of civic spectacle. Show business architecture is transforming our urban and psychological landscapes with new and colossal structures and experiences.

THE SHOW BUSINESS MUSEUM AESTHETIC: FROM TUT TO ICE T

Motorcycles, a Star Wars space ship, Armani suits, Jimi Hendrix's electric flying-V guitar, disco lights, and Ice T's gold necklace: What do they all have in common?

They've all been on display in the world's top art museums in the past couple of years. Lately, when we enter an art museum, we often wonder if we have wandered onto a Hollywood set or theme park. None of this is coincidence. In recent years a new wave of show business has been rising in major art institutions.

The first wave of museum show business really began in 1976 with the traveling blockbuster *Treasures of Tutankhamen*. For six years, Tut's treasures toured seven American cities, bringing over 8 million people to museums. Pretty soon, museum managers rushed to imitate, staging Impressionist blockbusters, Picasso blockbusters, Matisse, Van Gogh—all the perennial crowd-pleasers. Suddenly there were long lines outside museums and new peaks in museum shop revenues.

But then it began to get boring: exhaustive shows with exhausted audiences, filing past masterpieces like cattle in a chute. The problem was that the audience wasn't really engaged. They were still mere spectators. The show design, the concepts, and the works themselves were still bound in tradition.

We are now witnessing a new era in museum show business. With the merging of art and technology, of commerce and culture, museums are facing an identity crisis. Like it or not, the definition of art itself has exploded into the drama of show business. Leading the way is Thomas Krens, Director of the Guggenheim Foundation, who, when not negotiating million-dollar deals with city governments and rich patrons, can be found roaring around on his trademark BMW motorcycle. Not a Harley, mind you. Krens, like his celebrity biker pals Lauren Hutton and Dennis Hopper, prefers the BMW for his upscale renegade act. Six feet, five inches tall and packing a Yale MBA, Krens has turned the Guggenheim New York museum into a living theater of popular culture. He has also built one of the architectural marvels of our time and spun a global franchise from the Guggenheim brand. He has made old-fashioned art lovers cringe, the media roar, donors take notice, and museum attendance soar.

MOTORCYCLES, HAUTE COUTURE, AND CARNIVAL

Krens's 1997 show, *The Art of the Motorcycle*, turned the hallowed white ramps of the Guggenheim into a parking lot for about a hundred gleaming, mint-condition motorcycles, with innovative styles that spanned more than a century. The art establishment was aghast. This was not art. Perhaps not, but the show pulled in a record attendance, bringing in a whole new audience to experience a new kind of museum show that reached out to embrace their tastes. The Guggenheim still sells motorcycle merchandise, including $1,000 celebrity-autographed helmets. The show traveled for three years, with financial support from BMW, drawing huge crowds at every stop. Was this product placement or public mission? Krens claimed the latter.

Again breaking the rules, Krens's next show, on the fashion of Giorgio Armani, raised art world hackles when it was revealed that Armani had pledged $15 million to the Guggenheim. While unabashedly sullying art with commerce, Krens and Armani also gave the audience a show worth the entrance fee. The combination of haute couture and show biz spectacle was a hit with fashion fans. Armani calls his styles costumes for the world stage and Krens gave him the chance to prove it by recruiting Robert Wilson, the world-renowned Pulitzer

Prize-winning theater and opera director, to design the set. Theatrical staging married high fashion, and anyone could attend the wedding. Again, art or not art, it was a unique and highly engaging experience, something like strolling into the world of a dramatic movie about fashion.

Brazil: Body and Soul was another popular triumph: a $6-million Brazilian carnival-style extravaganza with flame-colored projections, flamboyant costumes, stunning baroque religious art, and pulsating flat-screen videos of strange and fantastic religious rituals. That's Krens's show style: noisy, disorienting, chaotic, and riotous. Nothing like the previous Guggenheim, whose take on modernity had come to seem complacent and rather tame. Krens is a perfect example of a show business impresario, creating shows that have immediacy and turn audience members into participants, shows that draw from the excitement of popular culture and transform that culture by breaking the boundaries of what's acceptable.

PARTICIPATION AND CULTURE MALLS

In the two years before and the two years after the millennium, the museum world took a complete turn towards a show business aesthetic. For better or worse, the hottest new museum shows are now about participatory experience—dynamic interactions between audience and museum piece like the turntable at the Brooklyn Museum of Art's *Hip Hop Nation* show, where you could act out the fantasy of being a hot nightclub deejay. Museums have become multimedia producers, offering interactive entertainment, concerts, movies, and live performances. These shows are no longer about hands-off art; they invite touch, play, and interaction. Galleries have also caught on. One recent Manhattan gallery show included a gigantic wooden bowl for free use by visiting skateboarders. Crowds of young showoffs came spontaneously to perform.

Shopping and dining have also become central to the museum show business experience. Museums are now huge culture malls and visitors want to be a part of the show by buying part of it. Shopping is not restricted to one central gift shop. Enter most of the big museums and you will notice the proliferation of mini-boutiques. You can barely enter or exit a museum exhibition without passing through retail space, which is often crafted to blend into the exhibits. Boutiques are thematic and play music connected to the shows (also available on CD). Their merchandise looks a lot like the collection and is often even priced like real art. Among the items the Metropolitan Museum sells are $35,000 amethyst pendants and unique embroidered Indian shawls—from $2,000 to $6,000.

By the way, such sales bring tax-deductible income because they are inspired by the art in the exhibitions and thus are linked to the museum's educational mission. Though it is beginning to look like a lot of museums are adopting show business as their mission, most museums have nonprofit status. Dining, parking, attending a film series, and buying a luxurious silk tie decorated with some museum-related imagery all generate tax-free income for the museum. Meanwhile, sponsorship of a museum show is a tax-deductible donation. Not a bad way to get more for your money.

SPONSORS, PARTNERS, AND BRAND EXTENSIONS

Marketing has become more overtly connected to exhibition sponsorship as well. The Guggenheim is one of many museums that have defied the supposed boundary between educational and financial mission. The Armani show could be seen as a great example of superior product placement. The Brazil show was partially sponsored by BrasilConnects, a private not-for-profit foundation set up by Banco Santos to promote Brazilian culture around the world. (Brazil has also been touted as a prospective site for the next big international Guggenheim franchise.) Advertising executive Charles Saatchi—whose collection got such great exposure at the Brooklyn Museum's *Sensation* show in 2001—was the show's biggest financial backer. The Los Angeles County Museum of

Art's 2000 show, *Charles and Ray Eames: A Legacy of Invention*, was co-sponsored by the Vitra Museum in Germany, endowed by Vitra, a company that produces Eames Furniture. Another Eames furniture manufacturer, Herman Miller Inc., contributed money to LACMA and other American venues. There are other examples, large and small, too numerous to mention.

Talk about extending your show: Krens extended the Guggenheim show by bringing it to the world capital of show business. Two Las Vegas Guggenheims opened a month after 9/11, which could be seen as an act of faith in American culture. The faith was returned by new museum audiences and by a lot of press attention praising Krens for his imaginative leap into the so-called cultural void. But Vegas had already legitimized her act, as we've seen, so when Krens partnered with the most famous art museum in Russia, the Hermitage State Museum, and a Vegas Hotel owner, Sheldon G. Adelson, the marriage was not at all scandalous. Adelson, who owns the $1.5 billion, 3,036-room Venetian Resort-Hotel-Casino, anted up the space plus $50 million and the Hermitage contributed Picasso, Monet, Matisse, and Kandinsky for the opening show.

The other Guggenheim museum in Las Vegas opened with Krens's sure-fire hit *Motorcycle* show (backed by BMW). He hired Pritzker-winning architect Rem Koolhaas to design the big-box exhibition space: a 64,000 square foot cavern with a retractable steel skylight cover embellished with a replica of Michelangelo's Sistine Chapel ceiling, and a plaza that is a huge public forum. Celebrity architect Frank Gehry designed the exhibition, a dizzying funhouse with funky curves done in mirrors, where participants could observe themselves reflected like glittering celebrities and partnered by the sexy, magnificent motorcycles. Interactive and fun, the show got rave reviews.

A society that enjoys travel and novelty isn't much impressed with tradition for tradition's sake, but is voracious for opportunities to experience bona fide quality in exciting settings and locations. The 37 million people a year who visit Las Vegas offer a great challenge and a great opportunity for the Guggenheim. Taking the Guggenheim brand to a tourist destination was a logical move to follow the Guggenheim's greatest act: using the brand to create an international art destination, the Guggenheim Bilbao.

MUSEUM SHOW BUSINESS AND URBAN REBIRTH: THE BILBAO EFFECT

Show business is not just happening inside museums; it is also transforming the physical shape and architecture of museums.

The most significant and audacious show business achievement by an art museum in the past decade has to be the Guggenheim Bilbao, a Thomas Krens production designed by architect Frank Gehry. This museum, which opened in 1997, has outclassed (in sheer boldness and popularity) any other new art world attraction. It is also credited with reviving the once-moribund Spanish city of Bilbao.

In the 1990s, Bilbao was primarily identified with industrial decline, unemployment, Basque separatist terrorism, and pollution. Now it enjoys one of the highest standards of living in Spain and attracts world attention and emulation for the urban rebirth phenomenon called the Bilbao Effect. Meanwhile, Krens routinely receives calls from mayors and other heads of state applying to be the next Bilbao. (Los Angeles is scheduled to open its Gehry trophy, the $274 million Walt Disney Concert Hall, in fall 2003)[29].

The Guggenheim Bilbao is pure fantasy architecture. The art collection inside is only pretty good; the real attraction is the building itself. Glimmering titanium-coated curves swoop to embrace a rusty industrial bridge. A dramatic entrance staircase pours in from the city. The lobby atrium soars skyward in a spiral that erupts in erotic undulations. In the first five years, about 5 million tourists (double the expected number) have come to visit this masterpiece, helping to generate over $760 million in economic activity and spawning a tourist trade that is estimated to have

FIGURE 16-1 The "Bilbao Effect:" a museum which transformed a city. Photo by David Heald © The Solomon R. Guggenheim Foundation, New York.

brought in well over $100 million in taxes. The museum's construction cost, contributed by the city of Bilbao, was only about $100 million. The city also subsidized operating costs, agreed to create a $50 million acquisitions fund, and paid a one-time $20 million fee to the Guggenheim.[30] Not a bad investment.

FIGURE 16-2 Show business architecture outshines the artwork in new museums as it spirals, swoops, and shimmers. Photo by David Heald © The Solomon R. Guggenheim Foundation, New York.

Of course show business is about more than money. It's about transforming people's imaginations. The Bilbao effect enabled a whole city to reinvent itself with civic pride, spirit, and international renown.

This wasn't accomplished by a shot-in-the-arm kind of deal. The Bilbao show was integrated into a major urban revival. Krens didn't pick any city, but a particular city that was priming itself for greater tourist capacity with development of a state-of-the-art transportation infrastructure and access to traffic along the much-traveled geographic arc of the European Economic Community. He was looking for a place where daring architecture would be further magnified by contrasting urban decay and the drama of urban renewal. This was a city with nowhere to go but the future. Something to remember when thinking about the right place for your show.

The Guggenheim Bilbao opened simultaneously with Richard Meier's fabulous Getty Center ($1.2 billion) in Los Angeles. Together, they established museum architecture as a central entertainment attraction. Since then, museums and cities across the globe have rushed to plan and launch ambitious construction projects to boost their status and their economies. The age of international competition in entertainment architecture has begun.

Krens's Comeuppance

Are we really advocating Krens as a show business model? Krens, the notorious over-spender, criticized for de-accessioning works, for dipping into an endowment (untouchable in traditional museum management, except to enhance art collections), and for bringing the Guggenheim into financial disarray?

We agree he was riding for a fall—as were so many other expansionists of the pre-9/11 world. Drastic declines in tourism forced Krens to scale back his Manhattan operations, lay off workers, close the New York SoHo branch of the Guggenheim and the larger of the two Las Vegas outposts, and cancel his $20 million web site and a proposed Gehry-designed Guggenheim for lower Manhattan's waterfront. In 2002, Krens's board took him to task for expansionary spending, and Chairman Peter B. Lewis insisted on massive spending cuts before he bestowed a gift of $12 million, largely to pay debts. (Not bad compensation for a slap on the wrist.)

Krens's critics have a point: When art gives way to architectural entertainment, it's a big investment, a high-risk strategy that veers from the traditional museum mission. Other expanding museums have suffered in the post-9/11 environment and no doubt feel the crunch of post-Enron declines in the stock market. Like so many early 21st-century shows, the whopping new museum may have to tighten its belt in hard times, but never fear, the show goes on.

Despite the economy, museum construction continues to be an expanding business. Our count lists at least 15 multi-million-dollar museum projects planned for completion in 2003 and 2004, all with celebrity architects. In fact, in most cases the architecture surpasses the quality of the collection within and often relegates that art to secondary status—just like the Bilbao. Will these succeed as quality entertainment? A lot of cities, corporate donors, and foundations are betting they will—and they're counting on show business architecture to make it all happen.

SHOW BUSINESS ARCHITECTURE IN ART AND BUSINESS

Show business architecture has become a dominant force in our culture, affecting not just museum budgets, but corporate aspirations for brand building and even city planning.

Let's look first at the show business architecture aesthetic. Most of the new multimillion-dollar showcases don't have walls, they have show fronts: glass for transparency between the world outside and the world within, titanium and shiny metals to create dazzling reflections, huge projection screens, giant doorways, sexy and dynamic forms that jut, spiral, and swoop. In these spaces, the experience of the building becomes the entertainment. It's all about the drama of action and interaction. The new architecture brings the outside in and makes the participants part of the show inside and outside.

For example, French architect Jean Nouvel's plan for the $90 million Carnegie Science Center expansion includes cantilevered floors projecting 80 feet out over a river. The sides are planned to have fabric screens between layers of glass so that, at night, projections can be seen from inside and outside. The building will be an ever-changing spectacle, dissolving the problem of permanence in a show business culture where you must constantly reinvent yourself.

Ridiculous or sublime? Imagine the $620-million glassy Esplanade/Theatres on the Bay complex in Singapore that is covered with pointy reflecting sunshields and resembles a giant durian—that's a spiky Malaysian fruit. A new addition to the Milwaukee Art Museum looks like an enormous white, aluminum, glass-winged dragonfly. It's really a giant art space with sunscreens that open like wings. This $100 million architectural spectacle designed by Spanish super-architect Santiago Calatrava won *Time* magazine's best new design award for 2001 and more than doubled the Milwaukee museum's attendance (to 420,000 visitors) that year.

Show business architecture is reflected in some of the newest ventures in business show spaces, from hotels to factories, which also claim be cultural monuments. The new designs embody the same show business attitude we saw in the last chapter: Don't take the ordinary production or functional activities of your business for granted. Ritualize them. Celebrate them. Exalt them. Make drama, art, even philosophy out of them.

Volkswagen's *Gläeserne Manufaktur* (Transparent Factory) in Dresden is a perfect example. German industrial pride and aesthetics are celebrated in the building itself and on the *Gläeserne Manufaktur*'s web site (www.glaeserne-manufaktur.de), which has a page detailing VW's philosophy: "Only those who take new paths can create new values: a philosophy of an automotive culture." The factory (really an automobile assembly plant that emits no unsightly smoke or waste), symbolizes VW's focus on the essential "openness, cleanliness, clarity" of its products.

A stunning feat of glass and steel, the factory looks and functions like an art gallery on the inside, where airy loft spaces allow purchasers to watch their new VW Phaetons being built. The factory, a curving glass and steel structure with a racetrack on the roof, is a match for the famous Baroque extravagance of Dresden's buildings. Its most stunning feature, towering above the local parks, is a 15-story cylindrical glass tower that houses the finished cars as if they were works of art on display for the whole city. The factory boasts a museum, a film series, and live performances to complete its range of cultural attractions for visitors. It also has been used as a great show business site for Volkswagen's internal audiences (as we saw in Chapter 10).

Sprouting up around the globe are business museums that make the humorous World of Coca-Cola museum look like child's play, such as the Intel Museum in Santa Clara, California, and the Corning Museum of Glass in Corning, New York. Both of these are designed by Ralph Appelbaum Associates (RAA, who also did the Steuben flagship store), the groundbreaking experience-focused design firm that has created more than 100 spaces in more than 50 cities in the past two decades.

Appelbaum specializes in interactive, immersionary spaces that use storytelling as a way to sequence the audience's experience. He uses film, technology, architecture, and designed spaces for live performance, in order to make the experience moving, dramatic, and interactive. RAA is the brain behind the American Museum of Natural History's Biodiversity Hall, which uses lifelike, life-sized replicas and "soundtracks" of extinct species to create an eerie, sensorial virtual-reality. The Corning and Intel Museums blend boundary-breaking architectural design with breathtakingly beautiful exhibitions to allow audiences to experience the thrill of technological innovation. The mission behind all this, according to Appelbaum, is social relevance and shared social experience. Two values that mesh well with building brand relationships with customers.

Are show business museums too ambitious for tough times? Well, as New York Senator Hilary Rodham Clinton put it, responding to plans for two new Manhattan museums that have a combined construction cost of nearly $100 million, "If you go back and look at the great public works in our nation's history, they often happened in very difficult times." "You've got to have more of a vision," she said to *The New York Times*.[31] In fact, visions of a public or civic mission are cropping up in a lot of the show business cases we present in this book: from Leavenworth, Washington, the town that recreated itself as a Bavarian-style destination for tourists; to The World of Coca-Cola's contributions to revitalizing its neighborhood; to Crayola Works, with its goal of sustaining art education in public schools threatened by budget cutbacks; to the Dallas Cowboys's Legend Square, which will create a must-see tourist destination and spur economic development.

Show business has become part of this civic and economic vision and can work at many levels to promote economic value. Not only can well-conceived cultural attractions revitalize cities, but the cross-fertilization that takes place when a city welcomes culture and creativity can have far reaching consequences. Richard Florida's book *The Creative Class* shows that cities that can attract the creative class (people who think and create for a living) are most likely to become centers of innovation and thrive economically.

We don't want to leave you thinking that show business architecture is only about big architectural marvels. It's much bigger than that. It is a trend in urban planning, where it is becoming a central experience in politics and community participation.

Remember: show business is not just about showiness, it's also about creating real value. Think back to our UPDR vector, which offers a model for *understanding*, and *providing*, then using *dialogue* and *relating* to build community while enhancing innovation. The ultimate indispensable goal of show business is to create value for the customer and the company. Think of it as democracy that really works, and you'll begin to see why UPDR can be witnessed in action at the cutting edge of urban planning in the most momentous civic undertaking of our time.

DIALOGUE AND RELATE: REBUILDING LOWER MANHATTAN

An authentic drama of community participation began in New York City when the urge to "do something constructive," after the devastation of 9/11 was taken literally by dozens of civic groups and millions of New Yorkers who became engaged in the process of selecting plans for rebuilding lower Manhattan. The Lower Manhattan Development Corporation (LMDC), a state entity instituted to shepherd the public process, proclaimed that design priorities for rebuilding would be determined by "conducting the most comprehensive public outreach campaign ever undertaken."[32] Meanwhile, unprecedented community organizing and coalition building gave rise to the Civic Alliance to Rebuild Downtown New York, a coalition of more than 120 business, community, environmental, and transportation groups.

The campaign waged for over a year, with the involvement of countless organizations ranging from the Real Estate Board of New York to the influential Municipal Art Society to local community groups, city and state agencies, and the grieving families of victims. From the beginning, it was an intensely participatory experience, driven by virtual and face-to-face communications and forums: dozens of interactive websites, live and virtual town meetings, hearings, discussion groups, and a wide range of performance events that were held to dramatize the effects of 9/11 and stimulate ideas for rebuilding.

The strength of public engagement came to the fore in July 2002 when the city previewed architects' plans for rebuilding. They were roundly rejected by civic groups and city officers.

Ugly! Unimaginative! Boring! stakeholders cried, making front-page news in *The New York Times* and generating an avalanche of major media publicity. What did the public want? Something first-rate: an architectural design that would commemorate the lives tragically lost and add value to the lives of future generations.

Facing an outraged public, the LMDC launched a design competition that quickly attracted many of the world's leading architects. Five months of secrecy, suspense, and speculation later, the seven architectural teams who had been chosen for the competition unveiled their designs before a standing-room-only crowd.

This was public participation on a scale never before imagined for any city planning project. The unveiling was televised live for three hours, as architects presented their designs and argued for their value. The full-blown public process included six weeks of continuous public viewing of the nine stunningly dramatic architectural models in the grand glass atrium of Manhattan's Winter Garden. There were multiple channels for live and virtual public dialogue and response, some integrated and some spontaneous, and media-run web polls where the public could cast votes for their favorite design.

LMDC's website alone received over eight million hits. Over 100,000 people visited the Winter Garden display, boosting business for downtown merchants. *The New York Times* ran a lead editorial celebrating the show: "New York has been given what its citizens have asked for all along, plans that are proud, bold, and capable of helping us reimagine who we are in the wake of 9/11," and urged the public, politicians, and corporate interests alike to "grasp this rare possibility for civic and architectural triumph."[33]

A constellation of live public events orbited the main show, but instead of the usual stuffy architectural forums, these were dramatic, with high-pitched emotions and exclamations of civic fervor. At one forum, according to the *The New York Times*, top-name architect Peter Eisenman (a member of one of the New York teams) jumped up and cried out "It doesn't matter a damn, Frank Gehry, that we were paid only $40,000,"[34] (the modest amount the development corporation allotted to each team to cover costs).

The new designs were exciting, like the quintessential architecture of our era, with structures that were dramatic, even epic. They twisted and spiraled, bent and soared. Nearly all were glass or "crystalline" towers, with glittering reflecting surfaces or transparent walls that revealed the supporting structural grids. Some sported glass canopies, cantilevered elements, aerial bridges, reflecting pools, even a moat.

All of the designs attempted to address the gravity of 9/11 and to memorialize the painful losses; all of the designs also lavished some of their most desirable space on public entertainment areas, cafes, and cultural facilities including huge concert and opera halls, museums, and theaters. Four of the designs included a structure that would be the tallest building in the world. All of the designs were visionary and largely uninhibited by cost factors—sheer imaginative glory.

The competition reached its dramatic peak when two finalists were chosen: the New York-based THINK team, led by Raphael Viñoly, and Studio Daniel Libeskind, renowned designers of innovative, interactive museums. The final days of the competition were astounding—and, to some, painful—to witness. The finalists campaigned like politicians, appearing on the Oprah Winfrey show, hosting gatherings for journalists, and seeking the favor of the innumerable groups that had gained influence in the process. Like Hollywood celebrities, they even submitted to frivolous interviews about their signature styles of eyewear and clothing. For a while, the hoopla threatened to outshine the public process.

Finally the Governor of New York and the Mayor of New York City cast the deciding votes. The exuberant winner was Libeskind. Libeskind is the son of Holocaust survivors, a Polish immigrant to the U.S., who recalled entering New York Harbor at the age of 13 and passing by the Statue of Liberty. Libeskind, who was educated at the famed Bronx High School of Science and New York City's Cooper Union and went on to win international fame for designing the Jewish Museum in Berlin. This interactive marvel, with slanted walls and a foreboding tower, enables museum goers to experience Jewish history. The journey through the museum (which over 650,000 visitors have taken in the first year of its opening) evokes a difficult journey through medieval times, through the Holocaust, and into the present day.

Above all, it was Libeskind who, many groups claimed, understood the value of dialogue and relating. In the days before the final selection, each finalist had met with engineers and development specialists, with community groups and victims' families groups, to review and revise their designs. In this process, Libeskind lived up to his reputation of combining creative vision with the ability to improve his design to respond to the needs and perspectives of stakeholders.

At this stage, according to *New York Times* architecture critic Herbert Muschamp, the real winners are the public: "[W]eary of being condescended to," he writes, "New York has been awakened to more enlightened concepts of urbanism," learning through collaboration, "that public building is itself an educational process." He also notes that developers have been educated in their quest to provide "cultural value" through architecture: "Even business publications report on the value that developers hope to gain from architecture.... This is likely to continue as more cities turn to culture as an economic tool."[35]

New Yorkers are a decade away from knowing what will really unfold in downtown Manhattan as the rebuilding proceeds. Will culture and experiential architecture help bring back the economy? Will Libeskind be forced to compromise his design? Will he be able to respond to public needs and desires? Is it possible to satisfy so many thousands of stakeholders, now that they are engaged?

CONCLUSION

We opened this book with the observation that customers want experiences, and we close it with a brief synopsis of a massive public drama in which an engaged audience demanded an architectural experience that would honor, amaze, and add real value. Millions took part in the public process and the bar was raised for quality and responsiveness in urban development.

In business, the bar is also being raised for what customers expect from companies. Informed and independent customers of every stripe now expect more for their enthusiasm and loyalty.

They want experiences that engage them, delight them, invite their participation, and genuinely respond to their own perspectives and desires.

In response, show business is erupting everywhere—bringing these kinds of experiences to customers and bringing vitality and vision to companies in a wide range of industries. As it engages, entertains, and breaks boundaries, show business must also meet the challenge of a new era of consumer demand. Now that the audience is engaged and expecting, show business has to deliver.

In this book, we have provided the key concepts and tools that will make your show business initiatives deliver the right experience for your customers and the right strategic objectives for your business. By keeping your show on-brand, integrating it with your marketing, extending its impact, and measuring its performance, you will engage your customers and grow your business.

May your business thrive—through show business!

NOTES

1. "Trends in Event Marketing," George P. Johnson Company.

2. "Coca-Cola Goes Back to Its 'Real' Past," *The New York Times*, Jan. 10, 2003.

3. "Referral to the United States House of Representatives pursuant to Title 28, United States Code, § 595(c); Submitted by The Office of the Independent Counsel September 9, 1998," Narrative, Section X-c, lines 699–702.

4. *The Experience Begins*, www.eventmarketermag.com.

5. CEIR estimate, Jeff Tanner, Baylor University.

6. *1998 Tradeshow Week Data Book* (1998), p. VII.

7. *Trends in Event Marketing*, The George P. Johnson Company, 2002.

8. *Success Matrix*, MRA International Proprietary Research.

9. "BMW Films: The Ultimate Marketing Scheme," Imedia Spotlight, July 10, 2002, www.imediaconnection.com.

10. "Amore: Will NY Love Italian Scooters?" *The Economist*, November 14, 2002.

11. www.marykay.com.

12. *On Politics and the Art of Acting*, Arthur Miller, Viking, 2001, pp. 1–2.

13. "She Sure Was No Powder Puff Synonym for Success," *Investor's Business Daily*, May 24, 2002.

14. Ibid.

15. Ibid.

16. Ibid.

17. "In What May Be A Risky Move, Wendy's Will Bring Dave Thomas Back To Its Campaign," *The New York Times*, May 5, 2002.

18. "The Silver Fox Warren Buffett is a Clinically Shrewd Investor," *Sunday Telegraph*, February 8, 1998.

19. "Buffett Imparts Market Wisdom with Humour," *Australian Financial Review*, October 16, 1999.

20. "The Next Richest Man in the World," *Fortune*, November 13, 2000.

21. Ibid.

22. "Eye of the Storm: How a Yacht Race Tested Larry Ellison," *The Wall Street Journal Europe*, May 5, 2001.

23. www.theminx.com/bam/bam.html.

24. "The Future Is Now," Anne Willan, *Bulletin*, Fall 2000, www.lavarenne.com.

25. "Innovators," time.com, 2000.

26. "A Postcard from Sheridan," www.sheridanrogers.com.

27. "One Restaurant's Trivial Pursuit," *Wine Country Living Magazine*, Nov./Dec. 2001, Vol. 9, No. 6.

28. "Culture moves from the bedroom to the kitchen; Sweet and savory moments are turn-ons in today's films, plays, books, art." *The San Francisco Chronicle*. October 5, 2002.

29. "LA Awaits Opening of $274m Concert Hall." *The Boston Globe*, Nov. 22, 2002.

30. "The Basques Get Modern; A Gleaming New Guggenheim for Grimy Bilbao." *The New York Times*, June 24, 1997.

31. "More Museums for New York Despite Poor Economy." *The New York Times*, Dec. 11, 2002.

32. "Architects Criticize Ground Zero Publicity." *The New York Times*, Jan, 2, 2003.

33. "Visions for Ground Zero." *The New York Times*, Dec. 19, 2002.

34. "Appraisals of Ground Zero Designs." *The New York Times*, Jan 9, 2003.

35. "Not Solely Blueprints, But Cultural Insights, Too." *The New York Times*, Feb. 28, 2003.

INDEX

FINANCIAL TIMES PRENTICE HALL BOOKS

For more information, please go to www.ft-ph.com

Business and Technology

Sarv Devaraj and Rajiv Kohli
  The IT Payoff: Measuring the Business Value of Information Technology Investments

Nicholas D. Evans
  Business Agility: Strategies for Gaining Competitive Advantage through Mobile Business Solutions

Nicholas D. Evans
  Business Innovation and Disruptive Technology: Harnessing the Power of Breakthrough Technology...for Competitive Advantage

Nicholas D. Evans
  Consumer Gadgets: 50 Ways to Have Fun and Simplify Your Life with Today's Technology...and Tomorrow's

Faisal Hoque
  The Alignment Effect: How to Get Real Business Value Out of Technology

Thomas Kern, Mary Cecelia Lacity, and Leslie P. Willcocks
  Netsourcing: Renting Business Applications and Services Over a Network

Ecommerce

Dale Neef
  E-procurement: From Strategy to Implementation

Economics

David Dranove
  What's Your Life Worth? Health Care Rationing...Who Lives? Who Dies? Who Decides?

John C. Edmunds
  Brave New Wealthy World: Winning the Struggle for World Prosperity

David R. Henderson
  The Joy of Freedom: An Economist's Odyssey

Jonathan Wight
  Saving Adam Smith: A Tale of Wealth, Transformation, and Virtue

Entrepreneurship

Oren Fuerst and Uri Geiger
  From Concept to Wall Street: A Complete Guide to Entrepreneurship and Venture Capital

David Gladstone and Laura Gladstone
  Venture Capital Handbook: An Entrepreneur's Guide to Raising Venture Capital, Revised and Updated

Erica Orloff and Kathy Levinson, Ph.D.
  The 60-Second Commute: A Guide to Your 24/7 Home Office Life

Jeff Saperstein and Daniel Rouach
  Creating Regional Wealth in the Innovation Economy: Models, Perspectives, and Best Practices

Finance

Aswath Damodaran
The Dark Side of Valuation: Valuing Old Tech, New Tech, and New Economy Companies

Kenneth R. Ferris and Barbara S. Pécherot Petitt
Valuation: Avoiding the Winner's Curse

International Business

Peter Marber
Money Changes Everything: How Global Prosperity Is Reshaping Our Needs, Values, and Lifestyles

Fernando Robles, Françoise Simon, and Jerry Haar
Winning Strategies for the New Latin Markets

Investments

Zvi Bodie and Michael J. Clowes
Worry-Free Investing: A Safe Approach to Achieving Your Lifetime Goals

Harry Domash
Fire Your Stock Analyst! Analyzing Stocks on Your Own

Philip Jenks and Stephen Eckett, Editors
The Global-Investor Book of Investing Rules: Invaluable Advice from 150 Master Investors

Charles P. Jones
Mutual Funds: Your Money, Your Choice. Take Control Now and Build Wealth Wisely

D. Quinn Mills
Buy, Lie, and Sell High: How Investors Lost Out on Enron and the Internet Bubble

D. Quinn Mills
Wheel, Deal, and Steal: Deceptive Accounting, Deceitful CEOs, and Ineffective Reforms

John Nofsinger and Kenneth Kim
Infectious Greed: Restoring Confidence in America's Companies

John R. Nofsinger
Investment Blunders (of the Rich and Famous)…And What You Can Learn from Them

John R. Nofsinger
Investment Madness: How Psychology Affects Your Investing…And What to Do About It

Leadership

Jim Despain and Jane Bodman Converse
And Dignity for All: Unlocking Greatness through Values-Based Leadership

Marshall Goldsmith, Vijay Govindarajan, Beverly Kaye, and Albert A. Vicere
The Many Facets of Leadership

Marshall Goldsmith, Cathy Greenberg, Alastair Robertson, and Maya Hu-Chan
Global Leadership: The Next Generation

Frederick C. Militello, Jr., and Michael D. Schwalberg
Leverage Competencies: What Financial Executives Need to Lead
Eric G. Stephan and Wayne R. Pace
Powerful Leadership: How to Unleash the Potential in Others and Simplify Your Own Life

Management
Rob Austin and Lee Devin
Artful Making: What Managers Need to Know About How Artists Work
Dr. Judith M. Bardwick
Seeking the Calm in the Storm: Managing Chaos in Your Business Life
J. Stewart Black and Hal B. Gregersen
Leading Strategic Change: Breaking Through the Brain Barrier
William C. Byham, Audrey B. Smith, and Matthew J. Paese
Grow Your Own Leaders: How to Identify, Develop, and Retain Leadership Talent
David M. Carter and Darren Rovell
On the Ball: What You Can Learn About Business from Sports Leaders
Subir Chowdhury
Organization 21C: Someday All Organizations Will Lead this Way
Subir Chowdhury
The Talent Era: Achieving a High Return on Talent
James W. Cortada
Making the Information Society: Experience, Consequences, and Possibilities
Ross Dawson
Living Networks: Leading Your Company, Customers, and Partners in the Hyper-connected Economy
Charles J. Fombrun and Cees B.M. Van Riel
Fame and Fortune: How Successful Companies Build Winning Reputations
Robert B. Handfield, Ph.d, and Ernest L. Nichols
Supply Chain Redesign: Transforming Supply Chains into Integrated Value Systems
Harvey A. Hornstein
The Haves and the Have Nots: The Abuse of Power and Privilege in the Workplace... and How to Control It
Kevin Kennedy and Mary Moore
Going the Distance: Why Some Companies Dominate and Others Fail
Robin Miller
The Online Rules of Successful Companies: The Fool-Proof Guide to Building Profits
Fergus O'Connell
The Competitive Advantage of Common Sense: Using the Power You Already Have
Richard W. Paul and Linda Elder
Critical Thinking: Tools for Taking Charge of Your Professional and Personal Life
Matthew Serbin Pittinsky, Editor
The Wired Tower: Perspectives on the Impact of the Internet on Higher Education
W. Alan Randolph and Barry Z. Posner
Checkered Flag Projects: 10 Rules for Creating and Managing Projects that Win, Second Edition

8 reasons why you should read the Financial Times for 4 weeks RISK-FREE!

To help you stay current with significant
developments in the world economy ...
and to assist you to make informed business
decisions — the Financial Times brings you:

❶ Fast, meaningful overviews of international affairs ... plus daily
briefings on major world news.

❷ Perceptive coverage of economic, business, financial and political
developments with special focus on emerging markets.

❸ More international business news than any other publication.

❹ Sophisticated financial analysis and commentary on world market
activity plus stock quotes from over 30 countries.

❺ Reports on international companies and a section on global investing.

❻ Specialized pages on management, marketing, advertising and
technological innovations from all parts of the world.

❼ Highly valued single-topic special reports (over 200 annually)
on countries, industries, investment opportunities, technology and more.

❽ The Saturday Weekend FT section — a globetrotter's guide to
leisure-time activities around the world: the arts, fine dining, travel,
sports and more.

FT FINANCIAL TIMES
World business newspaper

The *Financial Times* delivers
a world of business news.

Use the Risk-Free Trial Voucher below!

To stay ahead in today's business world you need to be well-informed on a daily basis. And not just on the national level. You need a news source that closely monitors the entire world of business, and then delivers it in a concise, quick-read format.

With the *Financial Times* you get the major stories from every region of the world. Reports found nowhere else. You get business, management, politics, economics, technology and more.

Now you can try the *Financial Times* for 4 weeks, absolutely risk free. And better yet, if you wish to continue receiving the *Financial Times* you'll get great savings off the regular subscription rate. Just use the voucher below.

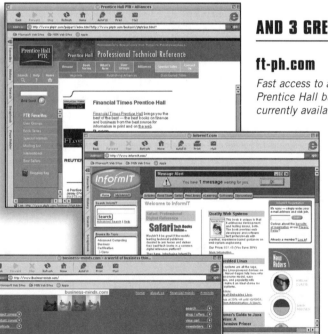